I N T E R S I G H T

published by:

UB SCHOOL OF ARCHITECTURE & PLANNING

a component of

Hayes Hall
3435 Main Street
Buffalo, NY 14214-3087

Printed and bound in the United States by Thorner Press.

2 3 4 5 6 7 8 9 | First Edition

Additional copies and back issues are available at the above address or by visiting the intersight web site: http://www.ap.buffalo.edu/~intersight.

Cataloging-in-Publication Data

intersight v2n1/ Alex Bitterman, Editor
p. cm.

ISBN 0-7907863-6-0
ISSN 1049-6564

I N T E R S I G H T

N U M B E R 6

LETTER FROM THE DEAN

intersight is the focus of publishing efforts in the School of Architecture and Planning and, as such, this journal is the result of great individual effort by students and faculty and, of course, the Fred Wallace Brunkow Fellow, Alex Bitterman.

Inaugurated in 1990, the journal is one window for students and faculty to view themselves, their work, the discipline, and the vital discourse of the pedagogy of design. The school celebrates its experimental and critical design research in the events and papers chronicled herein. Design pedagogy, while diverse and plural, remains a challenging journey of great uncertainty. The School accepts this challenge and *intersight* is that synoptic view into our searches.

The production of *intersight* is a herculean task, and one which deserves recognition. The editor and Brunkow Fellow, Alex Bitterman, as well as the many others in the community of the school, are to be commended for their contribution toward the realization of this sixth issue through their wisdom, persistence, stewardship, and dedication.

The School of Architecture and Planning is the recipient of two endowments which together have enabled us to produce *intersight*. We wish to acknowledge with deep appreciation Kathryn Brunkow Sample and Steven B. Sample (former President of the University at Buffalo) for the creation of the Fred Wallace Brunkow Fellowship, and the Cannon Corporation endowment for the publishing of *intersight*.

The School remains dedicated to the production of *intersight*. Therefore, the School of Architecture and Planning shares its thoughts, concepts, work, and all that is said and unsaid in the work of the school through this publication.

EDITOR'S ACKNOWLEDGEMENTS

intersight is made possible through the Fred Wallace Brunkow Fellowship, an endowment by Kathryn Brunkow Sample and Steven B. Sample, former President of the University at Buffalo, State University of New York. *intersight* would not be a reality without their continued support and generosity.

The generosity of the Cannon Design Corporation has made the production of *intersight* possible. Thank you to former Dean Bruno Freschi for his initial direction and foresight. Also thank you to former Architecture and Planning Library Director Ms. Deborah Husted Koshinsky for her early support and for her efforts in planning this issue of *intersight.*

intersight gratefully acknowledges the support of the Center for Integrative Studies and its director, Professor Emeritus Magda Cordell McHale.

Thanks to Barbara Pattoli, Cheryl O'Donnell, and to Assistant Dean Ruth D. Bryant for their constant managerial support and assistance. Thank you to Douglas McCallum, Samantha Stricklin, and Assistant Dean Bruce Majowski for their technical support and expertise.

Also thanks to Christian Aldrup, Joseph Sevene, Bonnie Ott, Bradshaw Hovey, Mark Ferrari and Annegret Richards for their editorial assistance and to Charlie Melonic and Kent Kleinman for their meticulous proofreading. Thank you to k629 design. Special thanks to Frank Gitro, Vice President of Graphic Design Services, Solomon Smith Barney, Inc. for his frequent graphic counsel, and to Morris Titanic for his assistance with pre-press and printing concerns.

Sincere thanks to all of the contributing authors, but especially to Bruce Jackson, Nan Ellin and Lynda Schneekloth for their outstanding guidance, careful and meticulous proofreading, and overall encouragement and support.

A special note of thanks to Dr. Jean La Marche and M. Beth Tauke for their unwavering encouragement, support, expertise and guidance.

A friend recently recanted a story about Jackie Kennedy Onassis. According to the story, Ms. Onassis always carried with her a small black book. Throughout the course of the day she would jot the names of those people she encountered who made a particularly favorable impression or provided some sort of assistance to her.

According to the story, upon her death, many boxes of these books were found. Each of the books was filled, cover to cover. with the names of people who had lent even seemingly, the most insignificant assistance.

Indeed, if the space provided, many books could be filled with the names of those who made this issue of intersight possible. For those whose names do not appear to the left, either by unintentional oversight or by request to remain anonymous, the deepest thanks.

C O N T E N T S

C O N T E N T S

G E O

boundaries on the map

N A T U R A L

breaking through boundaries in landscape

jagged grooves

hercules superior
p 215/75 r15 m+s

cooper cobra radial g/t
p 205 60 / r 15 m+s

kelly explorer
p235 75/r15

straight grooves

straight grooves

jagged grooves
kelly springfield voyager 1000
touring edition p205 65/r15 92s

straight grooves

kelly navigator 8000s
p205 / 70 r 14 93s

straight grooves

jagged grooves

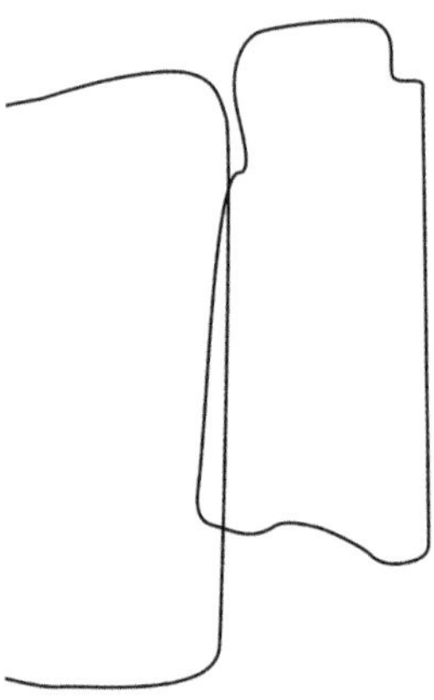

EDITOR'S PREFACE

Comments may be addressed to:
Alex Bitterman, editor
intersight
283 Hayes Hall
3435 Main Street
Buffalo, NY 14214-3087
U.S.A
or via e-mail:
alexbitterman@yahoo.com

At the beginning of my term as Fred Wallace Brunkow Fellow, Former Dean Bruno Freschi set forth my two-fold charge — to publish a journal that would highlight the diverse activity, scholarship and research conducted by the school, but one that would serve, what he referred to as "our community".

It became clear as this issue of *intersight* developed that "our community" is not only diverse, but also far-reaching. The 34-year-old School of Architecture and Planning has alumni in 40 states and 37 foreign countries and a present population composed of students, faculty and staff from every continent. Equally diverse in its multi-disciplinary approach to academics, research and scholarship the School is a unique resource which serves both its local community — the Buffalo – Niagara Region, as well its far-reaching worldwide community.

This universal perspective provides the thematic foundation for this issue of *intersight*. The book is separated into four sections. Each section explores a range of inquiry and/or examination while remaining allegiant to the common notion of boundary.

Boundary in the broadest sense connotes notions of demarcation, of limit, of extent, of separation, and of division. Planners and architects have begun to articulate the significance of exploring the concept of boundary in relation to the urban condition as well as to the constructed artifact. In some cases, this exploration is seemingly literal — "breaking through," or manipulating geographic or political boundaries. In other cases, the exploration is metaphorical — a sense of "pushing the limits," as is the case of material or philosophical inquiry.

The passion inherent to these investigations articulates the intention of this issue of *intersight*: to underscore the exploration of boundary with an overall aspiration to serve "our" richly diverse and global "community". I hope you will find the following contributions stimulating and interesting, but more so, that you find the work to truly transcend boundary — demonstrating its potential as borderless and limitless.

|Alex Bitterman, Buffalo, NY, April 2001|

opposite:
Completed by Christian Aldrup in the upper level graduate studio of Visiting Professor Shayne O'Neil. The image shown analyses and interprets tire marks on a wall, fragmentizing the event and uncommon context.

Mr. Aldrup is a 2000/2001 visiting Fulbright Scholar. He holds a diploma (Dipl.-Ing. Arch (FH)) form the University of Applied Sciences in Muenster, Germany. Originally from Germany he plans to return there to pursue the practice of architecture.

prints at left:

Completed by Vladimir Levin in the upper level graduate studio of Hugo Dworzak. The images shown are mixed digital media.

Mr. Levin holds a B.A. in Philosophy from the University at Buffalo, State University of New York. He will receive his M.Arch. in 2001 from the University at Buffalo, State University of New York; after which he plans to continue his journies toward architecture on the "other side of perception."

grosz

jansen

richards

EMBODY

INTRODUCED BY JEAN LA MARCHE

The body has played a significant role in Western culture from the body/mind duality in classical Greek and Cartesian philosophy to the body/geometry dyad of da Vinci's "Vitruvian Man." These frameworks have organized Western concepts of the body and the politics and practices associated with it for centuries. Recently, however, new concepts have challenged the earlier frameworks. While Freud focused on certain parts of the body as the sites of psychoanalysis and cubists fragmented it into spatio-temporal shards at the beginning of the twentieth century, at the century's end many argued that it was already fragmented or "morsellated" through language. Others proposed haptic, kinesthetic, empathetic, projected, moving, making, sexed, gendered, and virtual bodies.

This multiplicity is reconfiguring the Western concept of corporeality while also undermining the paradigms that were constructed around it. Because the spaces and movements of bodies are shaped by material, social, and cultural arrangements, the reconceptualization of the body suggests that the architecture which is necessary for its management, regulation, and care be reconfigured as well. The bodies of alternative perspectives suggest new forms of embodiment, new social and political organizations of space and power, and new architectures, disrupting centuries of cultural assumptions. Often emerging from the former occluded boundaries between feeling and form, inside and outside, making and viewing, language and being, new bodies have introduced a new free play of life and, in the wake of their emergence and the vacuum generated by the deconstruction of historical assumptions, have invited us to reconceptualize architecture as well.

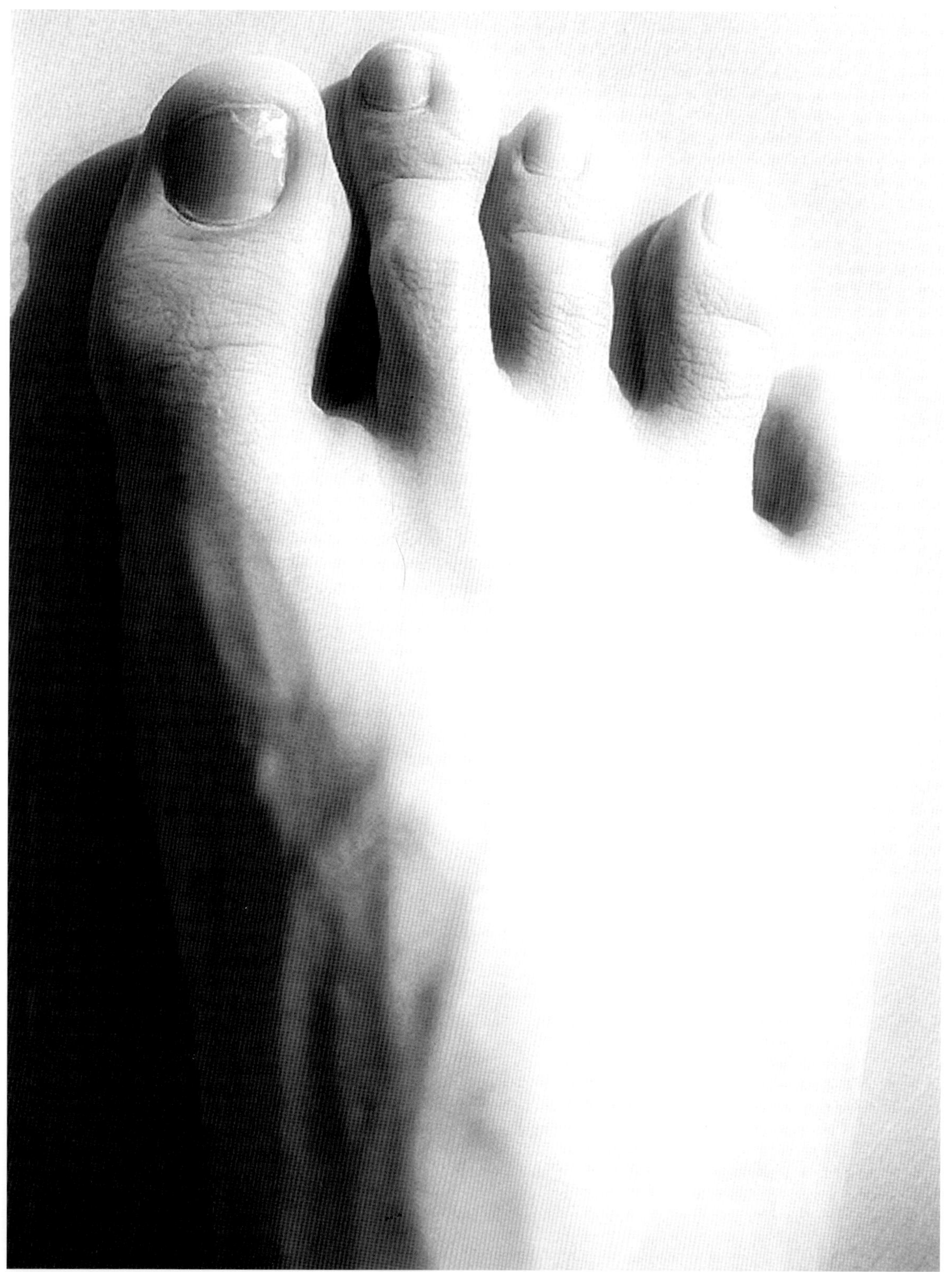

What is realized in my history is not the past definite of what was, since it is no more, or even the present perfect of what has been in what I am, but the future anterior of what I shall have been for what I am in the process of becoming.

(Jacques Lacan, *Écrits. A Selection*, p. 86.)

image at left:
foot 1 by Vladimir Levin.

ELIZABETH GROSZ

THE TIME OF ARCHITECTURE

the utopic

Elizabeth Grosz teaches critical theory in the Departments of English and Comparative Literature at the University at Buffalo, State University of New York. She is the author and editor of several books on feminist theory, contemporary continental philosophy and architecture.

Her book, *Architecture from the Outside. Essays on Virtual and Real Space,* is forthcoming from MIT Press.

Discourses of utopia have been with us since the advent of Western philosophy. Plato's *Republic* and *The Laws*, which foreshadow and anticipate Aristotle's *Politics*, provides the basis or ground for the more modern forms that utopic discourses, those structured around ideal forms of political organization, will take in the West. What is significant, and bitterly ironic, about Plato's formulation of the ideal social and political organization is his understanding that the polis, a city-state, should be governed by philosopher-kings, should function under the domination of an order imposed by reason. Like the orderly body, the city-state too functions most ably under the rule of reason, the regime of wisdom, for the well-ordered polis, like the well-ordered body, operates most harmoniously only in accordance with the dictates of pure reason, and the contemplation of the eternal. This is the basis of Plato's claim that the guardians, rulers of the Republic, need to be those most skilled in reason and the love of truth, yet also tested in the world for their moral character. Their theoretical or abstract reason must be put to the test of worthy concrete practices:

> [N]o perfect city or constitution, and equally no perfect individual, would ever come to be until these philosophers, a few who are not wicked but are now said to be useless, are compelled by chance, whether they wish it or not, to take charge of the city and that city is compelled to obey them.
>
> (Plato, *The Republic*, 499b, p. 155)

More recognizable as a 'modern' template of the utopic than the philosophical oligarchy Plato theorized should rule over the ideal republic is Thomas More's 1516 text, *Utopia*, which is, among other things, as More himself describes it, a complex and ambivalent sixteenth century 'treatise on the best constitution of a republic'. Utopia is the name of an island, which comprises an insulated and relatively self-contained community, space and economy, surrounded by a calm sea; and the people who inhabit this island. Access to foreigners and especially invaders is difficult, for the Utopians are protected by a perilous and rocky harbor, which requires their navigational aid for ships to be safe, guaranteeing the island against the dangers of uninvited entry. The sea which surrounds the island forms an inlet, an interior lake or harbor, a calm and windless space, surrounded and thus protected by dangerous rocks. The harbor inside the island reflects an internalized version of the sea surrounding it, almost like an interiorized mirror representation of its exterior. This calm, harmonious integration is exhibited not only in the climate and location, the geography, of Utopia, but also in its political organization, its devotion to solemn self-regulation, to the egalitarian distribution of goods, and to modesty, diligence and virtue. Its geography complements, and perhaps enables, its political organization. If the calm harbor reflects the serenity of the sea, the sea functions as emblem of political harmony, for the Utopians live in the best form of commonwealth, though one with its own terrible costs, the intense constraints on personal freedom that seem characteristic of all social contract theorists.

How [can] a city engage in philosophy without being destroyed?

(Plato, *The Republic*, Book VI, 497. p. 153)

Long recognized as a perplexing and paradoxical enterprise, More's text, like Plato's, involves the postulate of a rationally organized society, which is fundamentally egalitarian in organization, being founded on the notion of communal rather than private property, and collective rather than individual self-interest. This ideal commonwealth, which many claim anticipated the modern welfare state, is also, perhaps by necessity, rigidly authoritarian, hierarchical and intensely personally restrictive. While no-one is homeless, hungry, or unemployed, while gold, silver, gems and other material goods hold no greater value than their use in everyday life (gold, for example, is made into chamber pots!), where all individuals are free to meet all their needs, nevertheless they are rigidly constrained in what they are able or encouraged to do. Personal freedom is highly restricted. They are not free to satisfy their desires: debating politics outside the popular assembly is a capital offence; one must get police permission to travel, and even the permission of one's father or spouse in order to take a walk in the country-side. While extolling the virtues of this idealized culture, 'More', the fictional narrator of the two books comprising *Utopia*, (who is surprisingly close to More, the author of *Utopia*,) enigmatically ends Book 2 by dissociating himself from many of its customs and laws, claiming them absurd and ridiculous, even though he also claims that many others would be worth importing to Europe.

What is significant for our purposes here, though, is the question that intrigued so many of More's commentators: why did More invent a recognizably flawed ideal? The other, more obvious, alternatives – an idealized representation of a perfect commonwealth; or the satire of a bad one – seem more straightforward options. Why invent a non-ideal, or rather, an equivocal ideal? Why compromise and endanger the idealized dimension of the literary and imaginative project with a realism that explains the necessary conditions and consequences of the production of political ideals?

This dilemma is compressed into the very name of that ideal — Utopia. In More's neologism, the term is linguistically ambiguous, the result of two different fusions from Greek roots: the adverb <u>ou</u> — 'not' — and the noun <u>topos</u> — 'place': no-place. But More is also punning on another Greek composite, <u>eutopia</u>, 'happy', 'fortunate' or 'good' place. Many commentators have suggested that this pun signals the ideal, or fictional status of accounts of the perfect society: the happy or fortunate place, the good place, is no place, no place, that is, except in imagination. I would like to suggest a different reading of this pun – not: the good place is no place, but rather, no place is the good place. The utopic is beyond a conception of space or place because the utopic, ironically, cannot be regarded as topological at all. It does not conform to a logic of spatiality. It is thus conceivable, and perhaps even arguable, that the utopic is beyond the architectural. (Insofar as architecture is the domain for the regulation and manipulation of made-spaces and places, insofar as its domain or purview has remained geographical, geological, site-specific, location-oriented – that is, insofar as its milieu is spatialized, in the sense of both localized, as well as conceptualized only in spatial terms.) Architecture remains out of touch with the fundamental movement of the utopic, the movement to perfection or to the ideal, which is adequately conceivable only in the temporal dimension, and above all in the temporal modality of the future.

What Plato, More, and virtually every other thinker of utopia, shares, though the picture each presents of an ideal society fluctuates and varies immensely according to political ideologies, is this: the utopic is always conceived as a space, usually an enclosed and commonly isolated space - the walled city, the isolated island, a political and agrarian self-contained organization, and thus a commonwealth. A self-regulating space, autonomous from, though it may function alongside of and in exchange with, other states and regions. The utopic is definitionally conceived in the topological mode, as a place, a space, a locus with definite contours and features. As Margaret Whitford points out, the utopic perpetually verges on the dystopic, the dysfunctional utopia, the more modern these utopic visions become. The atopic, the inverted other of the utopic and its ghostly dystopic accompaniment, is not a place, but rather, a non-place (in its own way, it too is always ou-topic), an indeterminate place, but place and space nevertheless.

This is no doubt why the utopic has been a locus of imagination and invention for architects, as well as for political theorists, activists and fiction writers. But this may also help explain why the architectural imaginary that peoples such utopic visions (descriptions of buildings and municipal arrangements figure quite prominently in Plato's, Aristotle's and More's accounts of ideal political regulation) almost invariably produces an architecture of direct control (architecture as that which directly or neutrally facilitates the subject's control over its political and natural environment), an architecture of immense political inflexibility. Until the dimension of time or duration has an impact in the ways in which architecture is theorized and practiced, the utopic, with its dual impossibility and necessity, will remain outside architectural reach, and beyond its effect. The utopic is not that which can be planned and built, for that is to imply that it is already an abstract possibility that merely requires a mode or realization. It mistakes a possibility for a virtuality, a preformed structure for a dynamically and organically developing one. This failure to conceive of utopia as a mode of temporality and thus as a mode of becoming is clearly witnessed in the two large-scale 'artificial' cities planned, designed and built according to an abstract plan — Canberra and Brasilia, neither barely representative of utopic design but both planned as communities supporting a civic and political center, and thus as cities whose architectural conception would facilitate their functioning as the seat of government. Cities, in other words, that have come as close as possible, in their realization, to the abstract and rational plan that governs philosophical utopias. Ironically, of course, both cities have been long recognized, almost since their inception, as both supremely 'practical', as well as largely unlivable, cities, restricted in their capacity for organic growth and for surprise.

Can architecture construct a better future? How can it do so without access to another notion of time than that of projection and planned development (a time in which the future is fundamentally the same as the past, or increases in some formulaic version of the past)? What could a utopic architecture be, if architecture remains grounded in the spatial alone? How, in other words, is architecture, as theory and as practice, able to find its own place in politics, and, above all, its own place in the unpredictable becoming of the movement of time and duration? How can architecture, as the art or science of spatial organization, open itself up to the temporal movements which are somehow still beyond its domain?

the future

If Utopia is the good place that is no place, if utopias, by their very nature, involve the fragile negotiation between an ideal mode of social and political regulation and the cost of this that must be borne by the individuals thus regulated, then it is clear that they involve not only the political and social organization of space and power — which Plato and More have recognized and specifically addressed — but also two elements that remain marked, if unremarked upon, in their works: the notion of time as becoming (the utopic as a dimension of the virtual, an admixture of the latency of the past and the indeterminacy of the future, the mode of linkage between an inert past, conceived as potential, and a future not yet in existence); and a conception of the bodies that are the object of utopic, political and temporal speculations. In short, the utopic cradles in the force field composed of several vectors: its 'strange attractors' are triangulated through three processes or systems: a. the forces and energies of bodies, bodies which require certain material, social and cultural arrangements to function in specific or required ways, and which in turn, through their structuring, and habitual modes, engender and sustain certain modes of political regulation; b. the pull or impetus of time, which grants a precedence of the future over the past and the present, and which threatens to compromise or undo whatever fixity and guarantees of progress, whatever planning and organization we seek in the present; and c. the regulation and organization, whether literary or fantasmatic, or pragmatic, of urban and rural spaces of inhabitation.

This triangulation has been rendered less complicated by the common move of dropping out or eliding one of these three terms – usually that represented by time and becoming. It is significant that the question of the future in and of the Republic, the future of the Utopians, remains unaddressed; utopia, like the dialectic itself, is commonly fantasized as the end of time, the end of history, the moment of resolution of past problems. The utopic organization is conceived as a machine capable of solving foreseeable problems through the perfection of its present techniques. This is the image of an ideal society in which time stops, and, as Plato recognized, the timeless sets it. If we explore the plethora of other utopic visions, from Francis Bacon's *New Atlantis*, to the general project of the social contract theorists in the eighteenth century, to Voltaire, Rousseau's *The New Héloïse*, and *The Social Contract*, through to Hegel's *Phenomenology of Mind*, the ideal society, society in its perfection, is represented as the cessation of becoming, the overcoming of problems, a calm and ongoing resolution. While a picture of the future, the utopic is fundamentally that which has no future, that place whose organization is so controlled that the future ceases to be the most pressing concern. These utopias function as the exercise of fantasies of control over what Foucault has called 'the event', that which is unprepared for, unforeseeable, singular, unique and transformative, the advent of something new. Indeed it is precisely this idea of newness, creation or advent that the fantasy of utopia, of a perfect and controlled society, is developed to reassure us against. Utopias can be understood as further mechanisms or procedures whose function is precisely to provide reassurances of a better future, of the necessity for planning and preparedness, and rational reflection, in the face of an unknowable future.

What utopic visions, both those developed in the past, and those various visions developed today in science fiction and cinema, share – for very few share contents and specific arrangements, though there are common patterns – is the desire to freeze time, to convert the movement of time into the arrangements of space, to produce the future on the model of the (limited and usually self-serving) ideals of the present. Michele Le Doeuff argues that this may explain why so many utopian texts are actually double texts, texts which are composites, amalgams, with a self-contained utopic, fictional account, which is explained and justified through a theoretical addendum, commonly a text written after the more speculative and fanciful account. If we look at the history of utopic discourses, we can see that from the beginning, there seems a coupling of the fictional with the theoretical, without any adequate attempt to modify or transform the fictional or to incorporate the theoretical and justificatory elements into it. To the theoretical disposition of Plato's *Republic*, she counterposes his *Laws*; to Book 2 of *Utopia* must be counterposed the long analysis of private property and theft in contemporary England that comprises Book 1, to Rousseau's *Social Contract* there is *Project de constitution pour la Corse*, to Kepler's science fictional *Somnium* is his theoretical treatise, *Astronomia Nova*. Le Doeuff's explanation of this awkward but prevalent coupling of theory and vision, in brief, is that the theoretical or analytical doublet is written in part to contain the ambiguity, or as she calls it, the polysemic quality, of the visionary text in an attempt to fix its meaning, to provide it a guaranteed reading:

> The point is, in short, that if Utopia had consisted only in its second part, a de facto plurality of readings would be possible. But Book I establishes the canonical reading and privileges the political meaning of Book II at the expense of others: as Book I is essentially a critique of the social and political organization of England, a denunciation of private property and the English penal system, Book II is taken as being essentially a description of the best possible Republic. By writing Book I, More himself provides a principle for decoding his initial text.
>
> (Le Doeuff, p. 48-49.)

In other words, the function of theoretical doubling of the utopic texts is to contain ambiguity, to control how the text is read, to control the very future that the ideal is designed to protect or ensure. At the very moment when the impulse to project a better future takes form, it attempts to contain that which it invokes, the untidy, unsettling singularity of time, the precedence that temporal flow has over any given image or process, utopic or otherwise. What every utopic model both establishes and paradoxically undermines – why it commonly requires a duplicated theoretical justification, is that the idealized vision puts an end to political problems of the present and projects for itself no role as problem-solving in its future: Utopia has no future, the future has already come as its present (which is why it has no place, but also, even more ironically, no time: the utopic is that which is out of time).

While I do not have the time (or space) here to elaborate in much detail what such a conception of time involves, I have written elsewhere on the notion of duration, virtuality and the architectural field. What I can do here is outline some of its most salient elements:

1. Time, or more precisely, duration, is always singular, unique and unrepeatable. Henri Bergson, the great theorist of duration, has suggested that duration is simultaneously both singular and a multiplicity. Each duration forms a continuity, a single, indivisible movement; and yet, there are many simultaneous durations, which implies that all durations participate in a generalized or cosmological duration, which allows them to be described as simultaneous. Duration is the very condition of simultaneity, as well as succession. An event occurs only once: it has its own characteristics, which will never occur again, even in repetition. But it occurs alongside of, simultaneous with, many other events, whose rhythms are also specific and unique. Duration is thus the milieu of qualitative difference;

2. The division of duration — which occurs whenever time is conceptualized as a line, counted, divided into before and after, made the object of the numerical, rendering its analogue continuity into digital or discrete units

— transforms its nature, that is to say, reduces it to modes of spatiality. If, as Bergson suggests, space is the field of quantitative differences, of differences of degree, then the counting of time, its linear representation, reduces and extinguishes its differences of kind to replace them with differences of degree (the source of many philosophical illusions and paradoxes – most notably Zeno's paradox);

3. One of the most significant differences of kind within duration (which is commonly misunderstood as a difference of degree) is the distinction between past and present. The past and the present are not two modalities of the present, the past a receded or former present, a present that has moved out of the limelight. Rather, the past and the present fundamentally co-exist; they function in simultaneity. Bergson suggests that the whole of the past is contained, in contracted form, in each moment of the present. The past is the virtuality that the present, the actual carries along with it. The past lives in time. The past could never exist if it did not coexist with the present of which it is the past, and thus of every present. The past would be inaccessible to us altogether if we can gain access to it only through the present and its passing. The only access we have to the past is through a leap into virtuality, through a move into the past itself, given that, for Bergson, the past is outside us and that we are in it rather than it is located in us. The past exists, but it is in a state of latency or virtuality. We must place ourselves in it if we are to have recollections, memory images;

4. If the present is the actuality whose existence is engendered by the virtual past, then the future remains that dimension or modality of time that has no actuality either. The future too remains virtual, uncontained by the present but prefigured, rendered potential, through and by the past. The future is that over which the past and present have no control: the future is that openness of becoming that enables divergence from what exists. This means that, rather than the past exerting a deterministic force over the future (determinism reduces the future to the present!), the future is that which over-writes or restructures the virtual that is the past: the past is the condition of every future: the future that emerges is only one of the lines of virtuality from the past. The past is the condition for infinite futures, and duration is that flow that connects the future to the past which gave it impetus.

What does this mean for the concept of the utopian and for embodied utopias? That the utopian is not the projection of a future at all, although this is how it is usually understood; rather, it is the projection of a past or present as if it were the future. It is in fact a freezing of the indeterminable movement from the past through the future which the present is unable to directly control. Utopian discourses are those texts which attempt to compensate for this indetermination between past and future, and the failure of the present to represent a site of control for this movement to and of the future. The utopian mode seeks a future which itself has no future, a future in which time will cease to be a relevant factor, and movement, change and becoming remain impossible.

bodies

How do bodies fit into the utopic? In what sense can the utopic be understood as embodied? Here, I want to suggest two contradictory movements: on the one hand, every conception of the utopic, from Plato, through More, to present-day utopians, conceptualizes the ideal commonwealth in terms of the management, regulation, care and ordering of bodies. Each pictures a thoroughly embodied social organization. But on the other hand, there is no space or future, in utopic visions, for the production of a position that acknowledges the sexual, racial etc specificity and differential values of its subjects. No utopia has been framed to take account of not only the diversity of subjects, but the diversity of their utopic visions, that is, to the way in which visions of the ideal are themselves reflections of the specific positions occupied in the present.

All philosophical utopias have dealt with the question of bodies. While they idealize the potential relations between individual and collective bodies, none of them advocates a decorporeal or disembodied state. After all, what a social organization consists in, above all, is the production, regulation and management of bodies through the production of practices, habits, rituals and institutions. The problem is not that the various visions of the utopic promulgated over the last three millennia lack a concern for or interest in the corporeal. Moreover, it is significant that even the question of relations between the sexes seems to play a major role in historical representations of the ideal commonwealth.

In well-known passages of Book V of the *Republic*, for example, Plato expounds on the ideal arrangements between the sexes to ensure the maximal functioning of the polis. His argument is that, just as there are individual differences distinguishing men's capacities and abilities from each other, so there are individual differences distinguishing women's. There is no reason why the best of women, like the best of men, should not be educated to the guardian class, and be rulers of the Republic:

> With a view to having women guardians, we should not have one kind of education to fashion the men, and another for the women, especially as they have the same nature to begin with
>
> (Plato, 456e)

Furthermore, Plato suggests that marriage and sexual monogamy should be eliminated, and instead, a controlled, self-constrained sexual and child-raising collective be instituted in their place:

> All these women shall be wives in common to all the men, and not one of them shall live privately with any man; the children too should be held in common so that no parent shall know which is his offspring, and no child shall know his parent. (Plato, 456d)

This same concern for the place of women and children, and the status of sexual relations preoccupies a good part of the work of More. Because women work equally alongside of men, there is prosperity. Because twice as many people work in Utopia as in Europe, the work day is only 6 hours long. On the other hand, the rules governing marriage, divorce and sexual relations are strict and govern a narrow, life-long personal and non-deceptive monogamy. More explains that the Utopian marital customs may strike Europeans as strange, but they are more direct and honest:

> In choosing marriage partners they solemnly and seriously follow a custom which seemed to us foolish and absurd in the extreme. Whether she be a widow or virgin, the bride-to-be is shown naked to the groom by a responsible and respectable matron; and similarly, some respectable man presents the groom naked to his prospective bride. We laughed at this custom, and called it absurd; but they were just as amazed at the folly of all other people. When men go to buy a colt, where they are risking only a little money, they are so cautious that, though the animal is almost bare, they won't close the deal until the saddle and blanket have been taken off, lest there be a hidden sore underneath. Yet in the choice of a mate, which may

> cause either delight or disgust for the rest of their lives, men are so careless that they leave tho rest of the woman's body covered up with clothes...
>
> There is extra reason for them to be careful, because in that part of the world they are the only people who practise monogamy, and because their marriages are seldom terminated except by death – though they do allow divorce for adultery or for intolerable offensive behaviour...
>
> (More, Book II, p. 82-83.)

There is considerable detail in the texts of all the major thinkers of utopias of various arrangements, some apparently egalitarian, others clearly hierarchized, regarding marital rights and duties, and the sexual and social responsibilities and rights of men, women and children. There is an underlying assumption in them all regarding the fundamental unity and singularity, the neutrality and quasi-universality of the state (excluding slaves/ bondsmen). The commonwealth, though it may differentiate them in their roles, nevertheless equalizes them in the protection it appears to offer for their socially validated positions. So, although the question of embodiment, the relations between the sexes and the adjudication of their proper roles are discussed in considerable detail, nevertheless the question of sexual difference has not been adequately raised. Instead of this question, the question of women's place within an apparently neutral but visibly patriarchal and fraternal social order, takes its place – the question of accommodating women within frameworks that have been devised according to what men think is sexually neutral. This may explain the apparent strangeness of More's decree regarding the right of betrothed couples to view each other naked before marriage, as a man would view a horse he was purchasing! Egalitarianism consists in extending to women, or to other cultural minorities, the rights accorded to the dominant group; it does <u>not</u> consist in rethinking the very nature of those rights in relation to those groups whom it was originally designed to exclude or constrain. Plato extends to women the same rights he has already deduced for men. The same is true, and even more visibly, in More's text: women remain the same as men insofar as the law, the economy and the judiciary require it; yet they remain men's complements where it suits men! In Irigaray's terminology, relations between the sexes have only ever been subjected to a relation of sexual <u>indifference</u>, there has been no conceptualization of a <u>dual sexual symmetry</u>, or, in other words, any understanding that perhaps women's conceptions of the universal good may differ from men's has yet to be adequately articulated.

It is Irigaray's claim, that sexual difference is that which has yet to take place, it is that which has staked a place in the future. Sexual difference does not yet exist, and it is possible that it has never existed. In the history of the West, since at least the time of Plato, the ideals of culture, knowledge and civilization have practiced a resolute sexual <u>indifference,</u> in which the interests of women were seen as parallel or complementary to those of men. The sexes as we know them today, and even the sexes as posed in many feminist visions of a post-patriarchal utopia, have only one model, a singular and universal neutrality. At best, equal participation is formulated. But the idea of sexual difference entails the existence of <u>at least two</u> points of view, sets of interests, perspectives, two types of ideal, two modes of knowledge, has yet to be considered. It is, in a sense, beyond the utopian, insofar as the utopian has always been the present's projection of a singular and universal ideal, the projection of the present's failure to see its own modes of neutralization. Sexual difference, like the utopic, is a category of the <u>future anterior</u>, Irigaray's preferred tense for writing, the only tense that openly addresses the question of the future without, like the utopian vision, pre-empting it. Which is not to say, as I have already intimated, that sexual difference is a utopian ideal (this is Margaret Whitford's claim in her reading of Irigaray). On the contrary, because sexual difference is one of the present's ways of conceptualizing its current problems, all the work of sexual difference, its labor of producing alternative knowledges, methods and criteria has yet to begin. It is beyond the utopian insofar as no vision, narrative or plan of the ideal society, or idealized relations between the sexes can perform this work of making difference: it is entirely of the order of the surprise, the encounter with the new. This is why Irigaray saves herself from the tiresome charges of essentialism and utopianism by refusing to speculate on what this sexual difference might consist or how it might manifest itself, in seeing that the future for feminism is that which is to be made rather than foreseen or predicted: "To concern oneself in the present about the future certainly does not consist in programming it in advance but in trying to bring it into existence..."

(Irigaray, quoted in Whitford, 14)

How, then, can we understand the idea of embodied utopias? What would utopias that consider embodiment be like? And how might they be relevant to the concerns of architecture?

Here I have only some suggestions:

1. That architecture itself not be so much concerned with seeking to build perform or enact ideals, or ideal solutions to contemporary or future problems; indeed, it is a goal-directedness which utopic visions orient us towards, in neglecting the notion of process, precisely because they do not understand the role of time. The solution to the political and social problems of the present, while clearly a good thing for architects to keep in mind in their labors of planning and building, should not be the goal or purpose of either architecture, or politics. Rather, the radical role of the architect is best developed in architectural exploration and invention, in the recognition of the ongoing need for exploration and invention, in recognition of architecture's, and knowledge's roles as experimental practices. Philosophy, architecture, science, are not disciplines which produce answers or solutions, but fields which pose questions, and whose questions never yield the solutions they seek but which lead to the production of ever more inventive questions. Architecture, along with life itself, moves alongside of, is the ongoing process of negotiating, habitable spaces. Architecture is a set of provisional, highly provisional, 'solutions' to the question of how to live and inhabit space with others. It is a negotiation with one of the problems life poses to bodies, a spatial question-raising that subjects itself, as all questions and solutions do, to the movements of time and becoming;

2. Too much of politics is devoted to the question of blueprints, plans, preparation for the unexpected. While it is one of the functions of architecture to devise plans, to make blueprints, to prepare in every detail for the future building it is anticipating, this precision and determinacy of planning must not be confused with the kinds of planning that are required for political organization and reorganization, where, as concrete as they may be in conception, they always prove to be indeterminable in their application. An adequate acknowledgement of the vicissitudes of futurity would ensure that we abandon the fantasy of control of the future while not abdicating the responsibility of preparing for a better future than the present;

3. For architecture to have a future in which embodiment plays a self-conscious and positive role, it is crucial that sexual difference have its effects there, as well as in other spheres of life. This is not to be confused with the call for 'gender parity' in the profession. Rather, it is to suggest that in architecture's self-examination and self-reflection, it is crucial to acknowledge that the history of architecture is only one among many possible histories, and the debt that the dominant discourses and practices of architecture owe to the practices and discourses that were either discarded or ignored, or never invented or explored. This is the place that embodiment

plays in the history of architecture – the labor of architectural invention, the collective efforts of millennia of architects, builders, engineers, including those whose efforts are not preserved by history and those who were actively excluded from participation. This is to acknowledge that architecture as a discipline is always already a mode of embodiment <u>and</u> a mode of the disavowal of a debt to embodiment. This is, for want of a better phase, the critique of its own phallocentrism that architecture must undertake. Such a critique is not to be mistaken for the charges of gender imbalance, which are certainly relevant, but not enough. Architecture, like all other disciplines, needs to come to grips with its own <u>phallocentrism</u> (to use Irigaray's phrase), which is to say, its own structures of disavowed debt and obligation, to a recognition that its 'identity', as fluctuating and fragile as it might be, is contingent upon that which it 'others' or excludes. This other is its 'feminine', the virtualities not actualized in the present, the impetus for the future anterior. And finally,

4. The relation between bodies, social structures and built living and work environments and their ideal interactions is not a question that can be settled: the very acknowledgement of the multiplicity of bodies and their varying political interests and ideals implies that there are a multiplicity of idealized solutions to living arrangements, arrangements about collective co-existence, but it is no longer clear that a single set of relations, a single goal or ideal will ever adequately serve as the neutral ground for any consensual utopic form. Utopias are precisely not about consensus but about the enactment of ideals of the privileged, ideals of the government by the few of the many, ideals not derived from consensus but designed to produce or enforce it. In short, ideals need to be produced over and over again, and their proliferation and multiplication is an ongoing process, always a measure of dissatisfaction with the past and present, always the representation of ever-receding futures. The task for architecture, as for philosophy, is not to settle on utopias, models, concrete ideals, but instead to embark on the process of endless questioning.

images at left:
by Milenko Ivanovic.

Mr. Ivanovic was born in Belgrade and began his study of architecture at the University of Belgrade School of Architecture. He joined the University at Buffalo, State University of New York, School of Architecture and Planning in 1999 and plans to receive his B.S. in Architecture in the Spring of 2002, after which, he plans to begin study toward an M.Arch degree.

N O T E S

Deleuze, Gilles. *Bergsonism.* transl. Hugh Tomlinson and Barbara Habberjam. (New York: Zone Books, 1988).

Foucault, Michel. "The Discourse on Language." in *The Archaelogy of Knowledge.* (New York: Harper Colophon ,1972).

Grosz, Elizabeth. " Cyberspace, Virtuality and the Real: Some Architectural Reflections." in *ANYbody*, ed. Cynthia Davidson. (Cambridge, MIT Press, 1997). p. 108-117.

Grosz, Elizabeth. "The Future of Space. Toward an Architecture of Invention" ['The Virtual House' issue.] *Any* (19): p. 12-16, (1997).

Lacan, Jacques. *Écrits. A Selection,* trans. Alan Sheridan. (London: Tavistock, 1977).

Le Doeuff, Michele. "Daydream in Utopia." in *The Philosophical Imaginary,* trans. Colin Gordon. (Stanford: Stanford University Press, 1989). p. 21-28.

Le Doeuff, Michele. "The Polysemy of Atopian Discourse." in *The Philosophical Imaginary,* trans. Colin Gordon. (Stanford: Stanford University Press, 1989). p. 45-56.

More, Thomas. *Utopia.* (Cambridge: Cambridge University Press, 1975).

Plato. *The Republic*, trans. G.M. Gude. (Indianapolis: Hackett Publishing Co, 1974).

Rajchman, John. *Constructions.* (Cambridge: MIT Press, 1998).

Whitford, Margaret. *Luce Irigaray. Philosophy in the Feminine.* (London and New York: Routledge, 1991).

The Time of Architecture was delivered as a lecture to the School of Architecture & Planning on 14 November 1999.

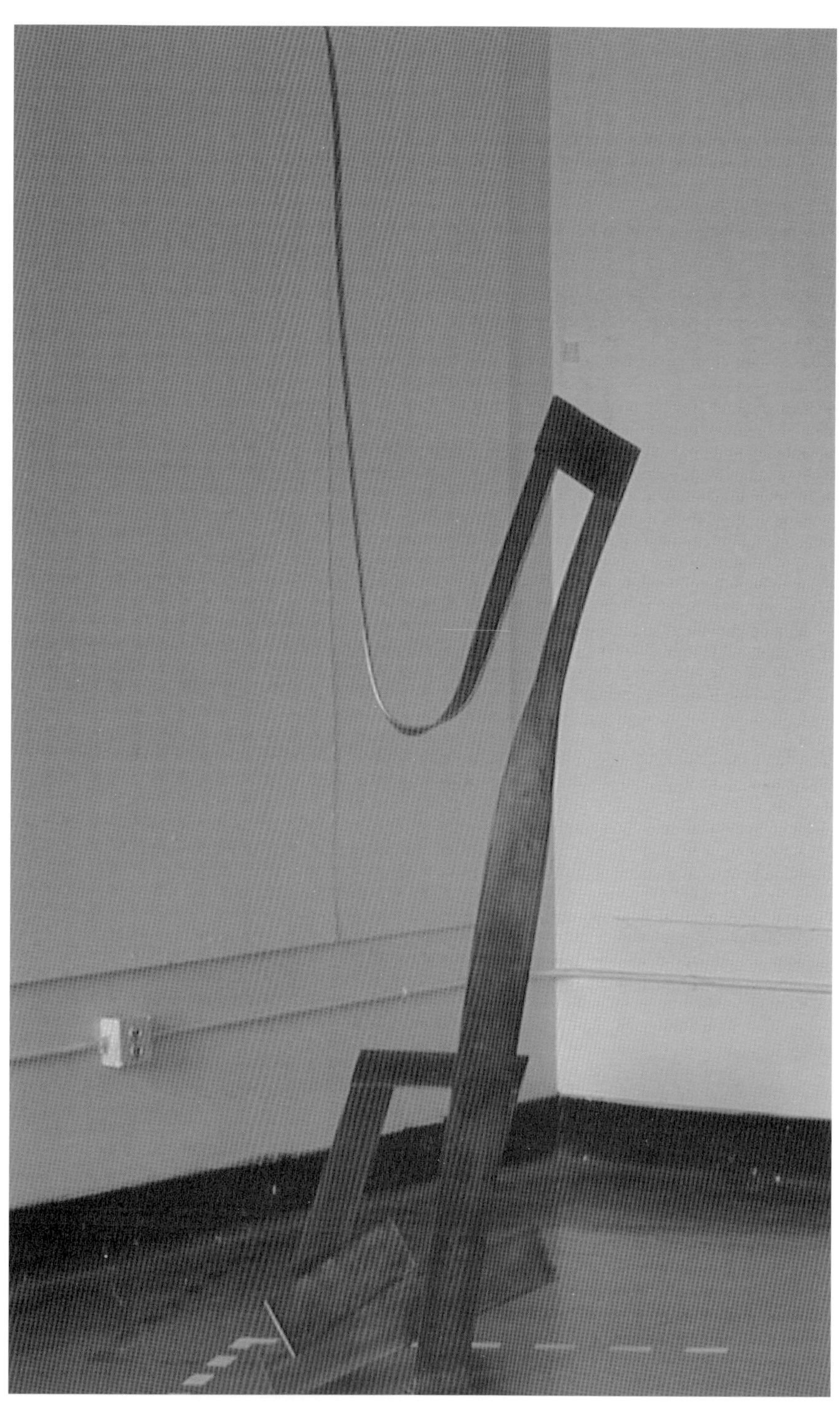

left:
as installed
pair 2. elevation.

BARRIE JANSEN

THESIS: ARCHITECTURE AS A PERFORMING ART

Architecture and choreography are at their essence structure, from the details of their individual elements to the composition of their complete works. Each employ or disregard compositional issues such as introduction, climax, and resolution, and their designers discuss rhythm, articulation, line, and mass. Usually intended to be three-dimensional objects in space, they are each reduced into two-dimensional images through architectural representation and dance notation. Although in different ways, both are affected by how the limitations of the body define the space being created.

This thesis project was one attempt to bring the shared concerns of choreography and architecture into built form. A construction of five pairs of figures placed within a notational system, it was based on a segment of the *pas de deux* for Apollo and Terpsichore in *Apollo*, one of George Balanchine's early choreographic works. The installation explored the inverse relationship of performer and audience in dance and architecture. In dance, the audience is stationary, while the choreographic composition unfolds in time and space. In architecture, as the building audience, we realize a composition as it unfolds as we move though time and space.

The steel constructions shown here were bent "cold" using human strength coupled with the leverage provided by a vise and long pipe clamps. This method required physicality not unlike a dancer's training; the more complex forms were made through a type of choreography in which contrasting pressures were placed on the steel in very specific and interrelated ways.

This project evolved as a negotiation between choreography and architecture, between the body and steel. At times, the properties of steel dictated the architectural expression of the choreography. In others, the choreography determined the relationship of the steel forms to their architectural environment. Comprised of movement, composition, notation, and structure, dance has a great potential to inform the understanding, design, construction, and communication of architecture. This project was one attempt to encourage architects to see choreography as a type of architecture, and to view architecture as a performing art.

Barrie Jansen received her M. Arch. from the University at Buffalo, State University of New York, in June 2000. After graduating, she joined the Western New York office of Cannon Design. Ms. Jansen currently is living in The Netherlands.

Committee Chair:
Frank Fantauzzi
Committee Member:
Tom Breen

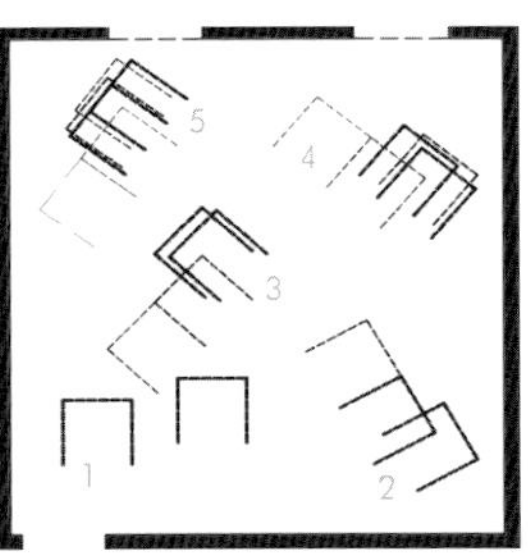

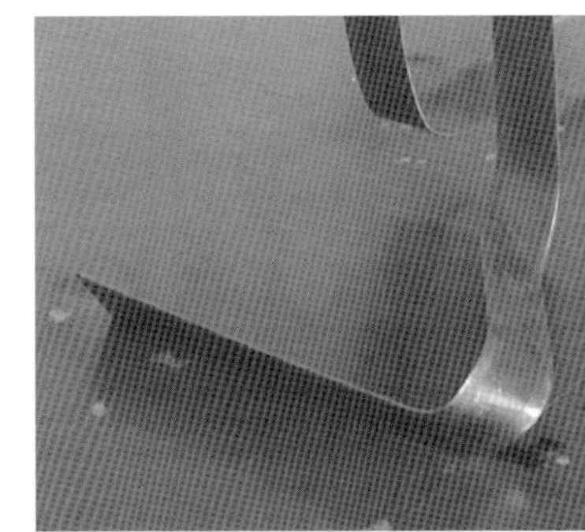

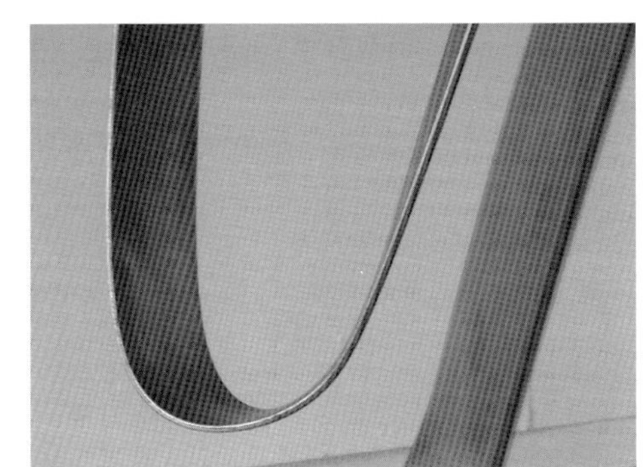

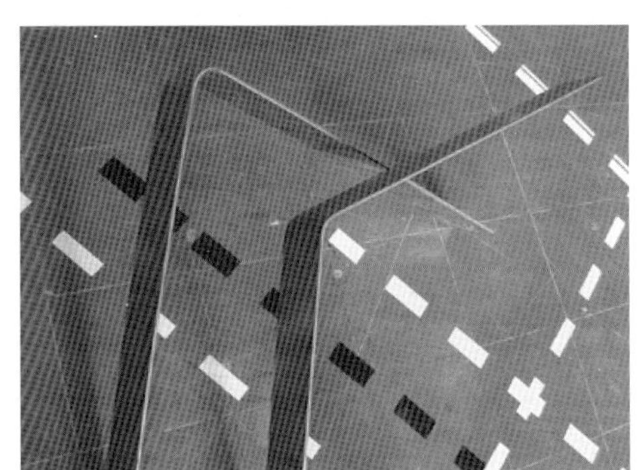

above:
diagram showing the configuration of steel sculptures installed.

at right:
as installed:
pair 1. *left:* elevation, *right:* detail.
pair 2. *left:* elevation, *right:* detail.
pair 3. *left:* elevation, *right:* detail.
pair 4. *left:* elevation, *right:* detail.

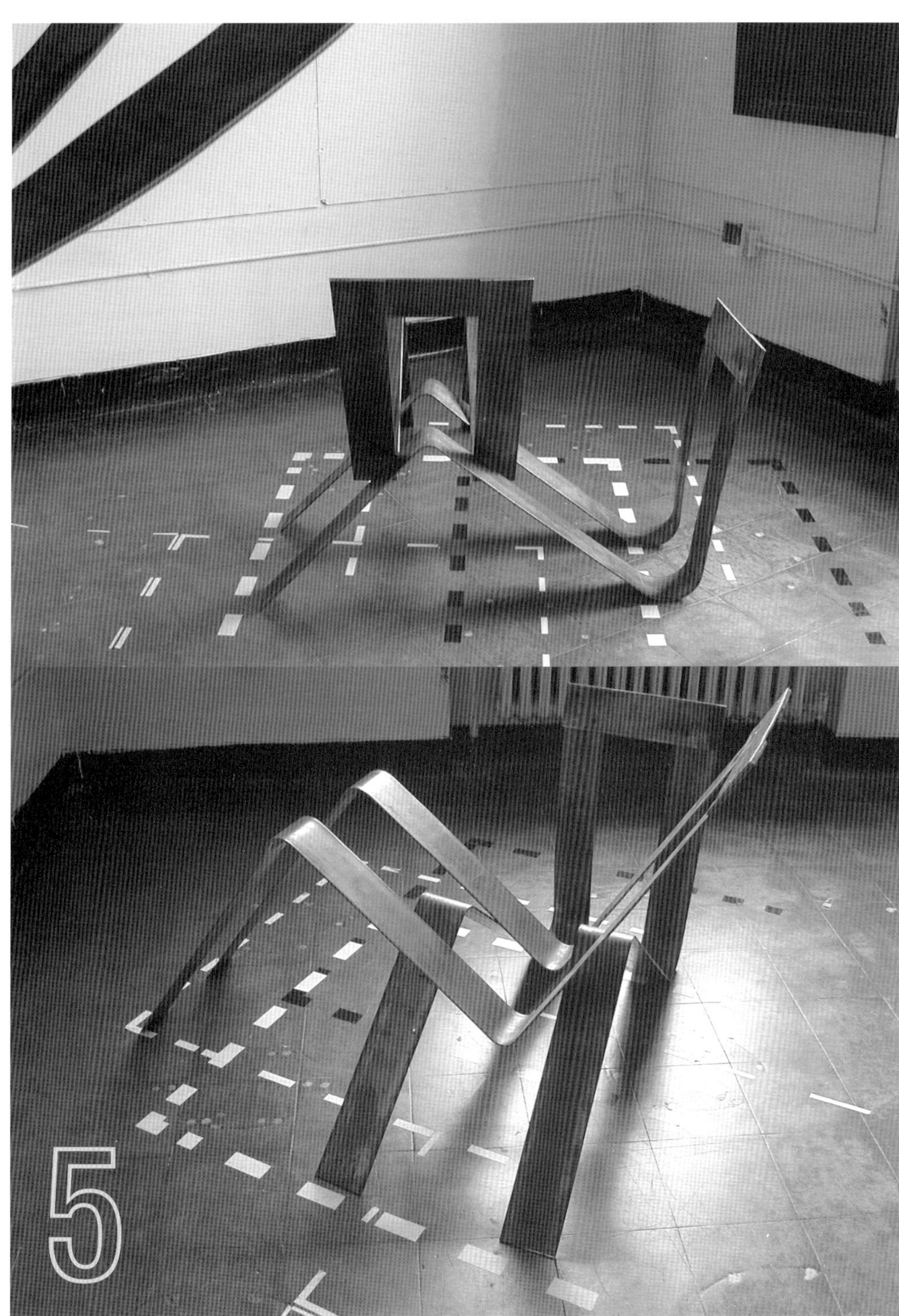

left:
as installed:
pair 5. elevations.

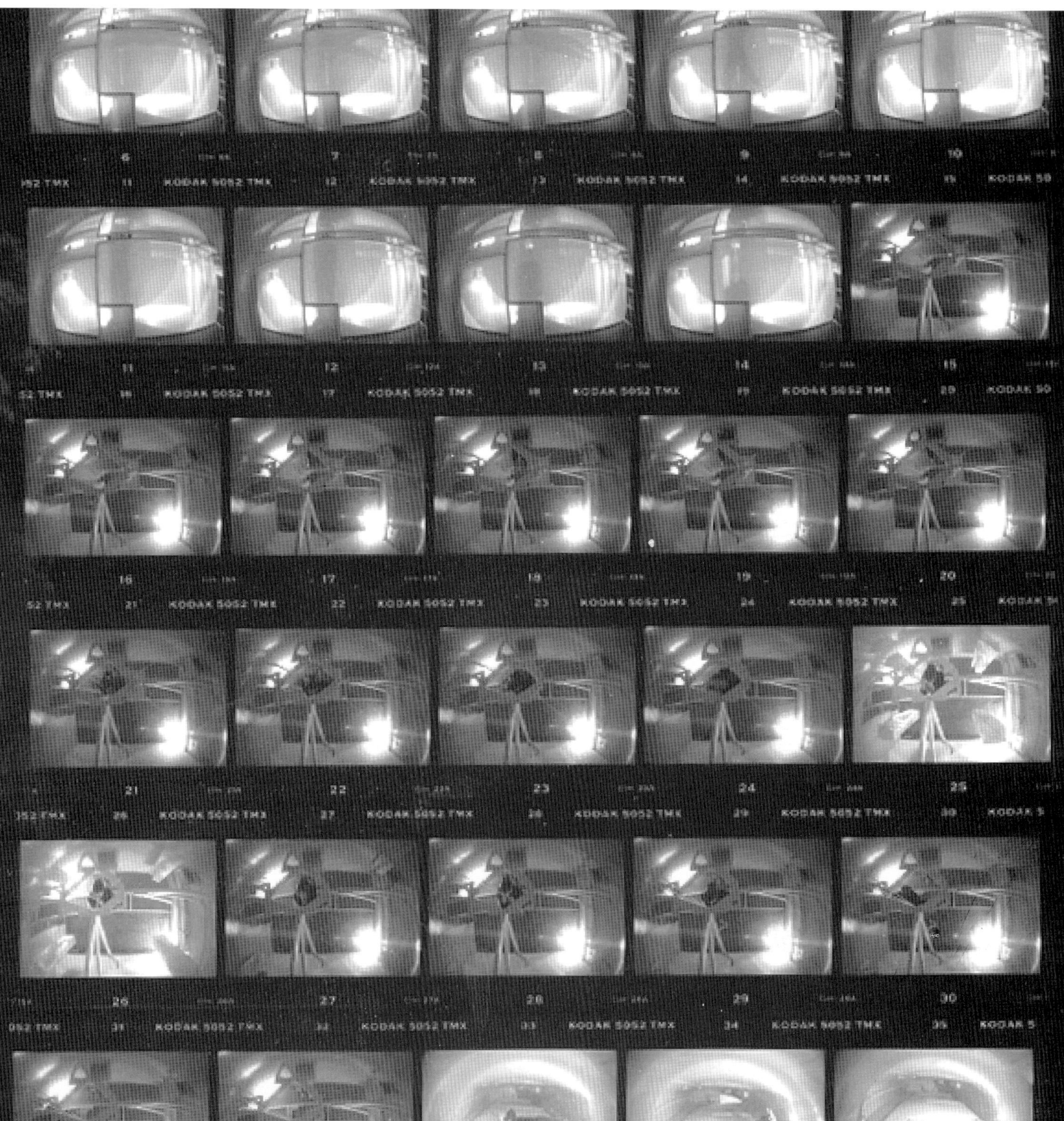

SHEILA RICHARDS

THESIS: 1 7 1 8 1 9

The human body significantly influences both architectural and clothing design. The fundamental principle behind these disciplines is to create an enclosure for the human body to occupy out of necessity. Yet despite this fact, what we as humans have found comfort in becomes more than an enclosure for the human body. Through design applications, the enclosure, whether it is architecture or clothing, expresses the intimate relationship of the interaction between human body and cloth and human body and wall based on how we inhabit each space.

Sheila Richards received her M.Arch. in May 2000 from the University at Buffalo, State University of New York.

Architectural design entails working through the same spatial and distance issues in relation to the human body as clothing design, but at a different scale. Realizing this connection and exploring the opportunity to merge the two disciplines will result in a mode of making in response to the human body.

Oftentimes it is through this exploration of other disciplines that we discover new design possibilities within our own discipline. This deviation to another discipline will expose similar design engagements and principles. This exploration of how clothing design encloses, accentuates and decorates the human body will indicate an architectural agenda more reflective of how a human body intimately inhabits space. And, since architecture designs for some of the same issues as clothing design, it should respond spatially to the intimate relationships between human body and wall.

opposite:
contact sheet showing overhead views of installation.

right:
initial explorations of clothing/body relationship.

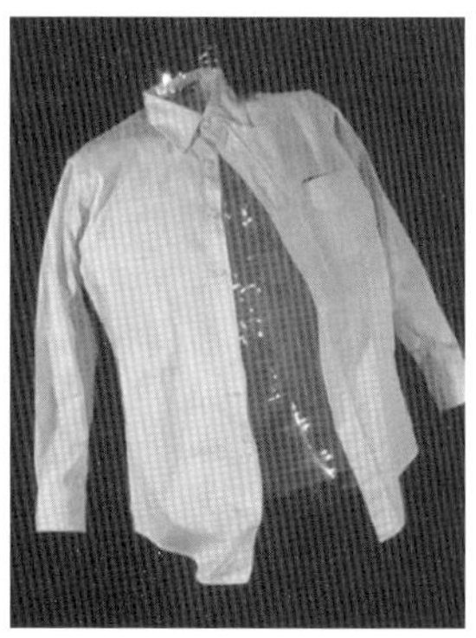

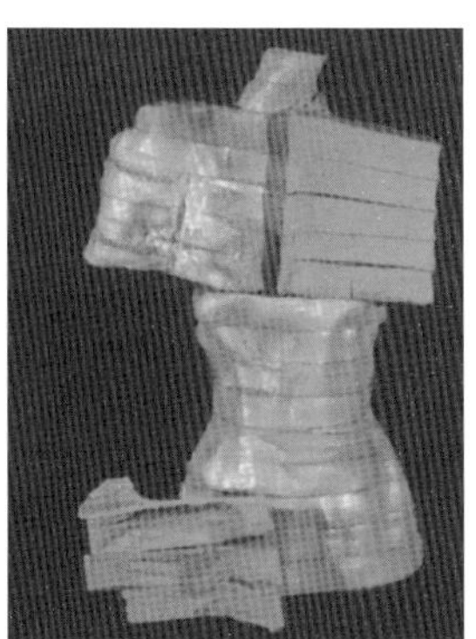

17 18 19 was installed over the course of the Spring 2000 semester in Crosby Hall at the University at Buffalo, State University of New York.

aro

hadighi

steiner

turturro

P U S H

INTRODUCED BY ALEX BITTERMAN

Oftentimes, in design, reference is made to testing limits, "thinking out of the box", "pushing the envelope," — in short, breaking through the boundary of material use, or of conventional or accepted thought. Inherent to and throughout the processes of design, analysis, and construction, nests curiosity — a spirit of exploration. The contributions in this section showcase material explorations toward this end.

opposite:
Buffalo Double project completed by Rachel Martin in third year undergraduate studio of Jean La Marche.

Ms. Martin is presently a Junior at the University of Buffalo, State University of New York. After completion of her undergraduate degree, she plans to pursue graduate studies in Architecture.

Ms. Martin is originally from Buffalo, New York.

The contribution of Manhattan-based aro explores the use of computer-aided design and computer-aided manufacture (CAD/CAM) and the possibilities of using such systems in the production of architecture. Hadas Steiner revisits the work of Archigram extending those original ideas toward the construction of the built artifact of the present. Mehrdad Hadighi's contribution features the incredibly intricate process of slip casting concrete, while Tom Turturro's piece researches the *techne* of the New York Stock Exchange.

Each contribution examines a simple material tested in a different way as a mode of definition — "pushing the envelope," in a sense — along a new path, toward breaking material boundaries, toward discovery.

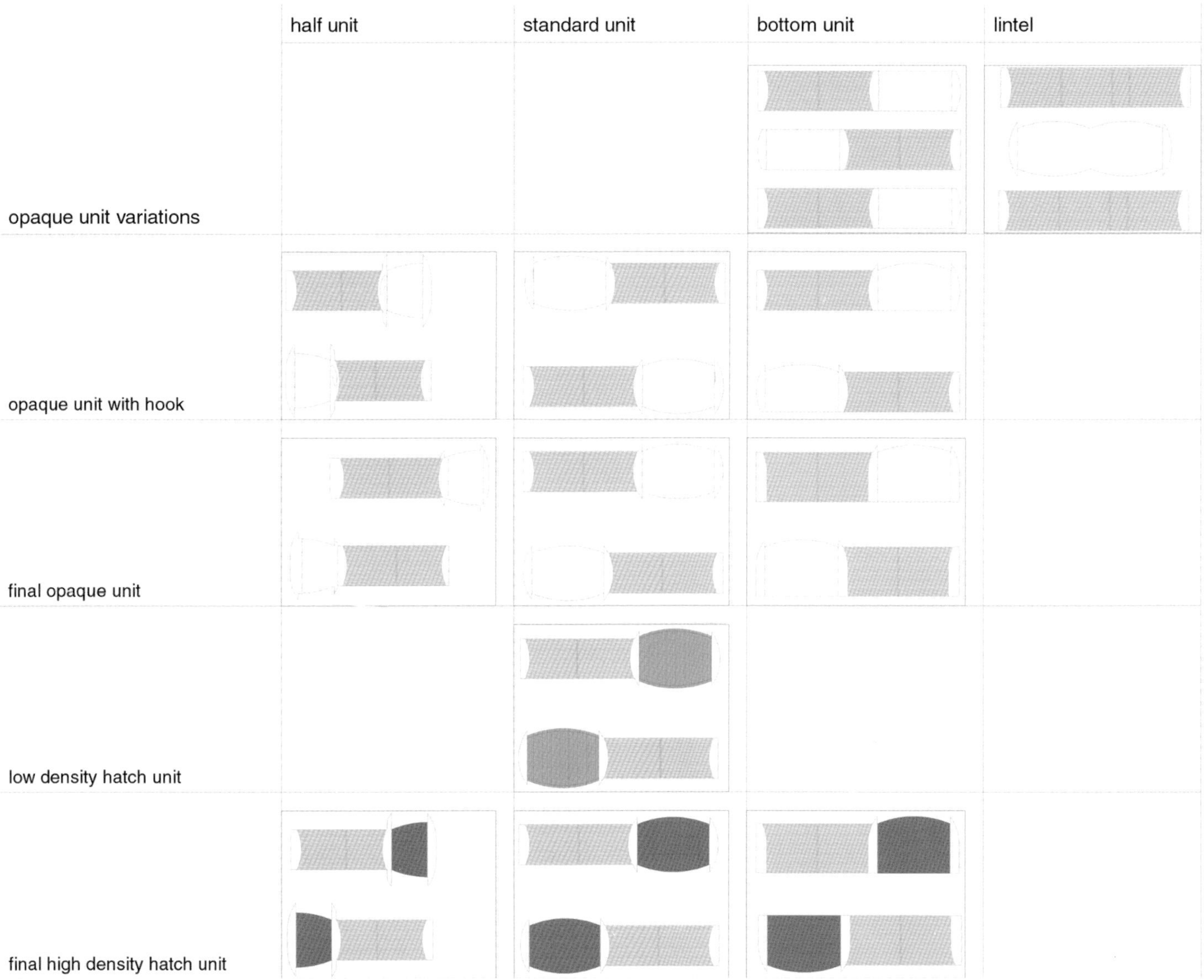

	half unit	standard unit	bottom unit	lintel
opaque unit variations				
opaque unit with hook				
final opaque unit				
low density hatch unit				
final high density hatch unit				

P A P E R W A L L

introduction

Architecture and design, which moved far from their craft roots in the age of mechanization, are undergoing a paradoxical return to those roots in a computer-age revolution driven by applications of Computer Aided Design/Computer Aided Manufacture (CAD/CAM). The integration of computer representation and the fabrication capabilities of computer-controlled equipment allow for a direct connection between the architect/designer and the finished product. This is changing the relationship between thinking and making. Few architects have ventured into this field pioneered by automobile and aviation engineers, the apparel industry, and the makers of prosthetic devices. The production and fabrication of architecture will change in the next ten or fifteen years as CAD/CAM technology becomes more available to architects and designers. CAD/CAM has the potential to transform the making of architecture in ways that are both fundamental and beautiful. It creates new material possibilities and allows the designer an unprecedented participation in the construction process.

Architecture Research Office, an eighteen person firm, creates designs of various scales and differing complexities, from furniture to free-standing structures. Each project begins with an assessment of its physical, social and economic conditions, as well as with an involved client. Every undertaking is a process of inquiry: research and analysis frame experiments in material and construction.

Current projects include a residential loft in Manhattan, the New York offices of Razorfish, and a War Remembrance Memorial at Columbia University.

phase 1 [research]

ARO, with a grant to Stephen Cassell from the New York State Council on the Arts (NYSCA), embarked on its research into the relationship between CAD/CAM and craft in November 1999.

The research began as an exploration into two separate but related interests. First, to learn how a computer-controlled laser cutter could be used as a design tool, and second, to explore how the capabilities and limits of the laser-cutter and the properties of a specific medium, paper, could inform an installation at Artists Space gallery in SoHo, New York City.

For ARO every undertaking is a process of inquiry; research and analysis frame experiments in material and construction from which an intuitive sense about design

above, left to right:
Reid Lase Cutter;
laser cut test patterns.

develops. Using the particular qualities of a project (program, site, client) as a catalyst, this intuition, that comes from experience, work and sheer repetition, evolves during the design process.

We generally work within specific material and programmatic limits. To exhibit our work in the gallery context, the physical constraints of the laser cutter and the characteristics of paper were the conditions with which we worked. The NYSCA grant allowed us to explore and implement our methodology.

Rather than starting with three-dimensional applications, we learned about CAD/CAM technology at a basic level by considering the laser cutter's simplest possible two-dimensional uses (the laser cutter operates on flat materials). Initial studies with 3 x 5" pieces of different materials familiarized us with the capabilities of the laser cutter. We developed a test pattern that we applied to the materials, methodically changing one of the laser's variables: speed, power and pulses per inch (ppi).

As we developed an intuitive familiarity with the laser cutter, we realized that there were many more variables to consider, aside from the speed and strength of the laser, such as the chronology of the laser cuts and the force of the air over the material that ventilates the machine. The better we understood how CAD/CAM technology worked with a specific material, the more it informed the process of designing and making.

Simultaneously, we developed an intuitive sense about the medium. With 3 x 5" index cards, we investigated how a single paper unit could be manually fabricated, tiled (to create a continuous surface) and formed into a three-dimensional shape. These early studies provided an understanding of the basic limits of paper: how much weight a paper connection could hold before it would tear, at what point a fold

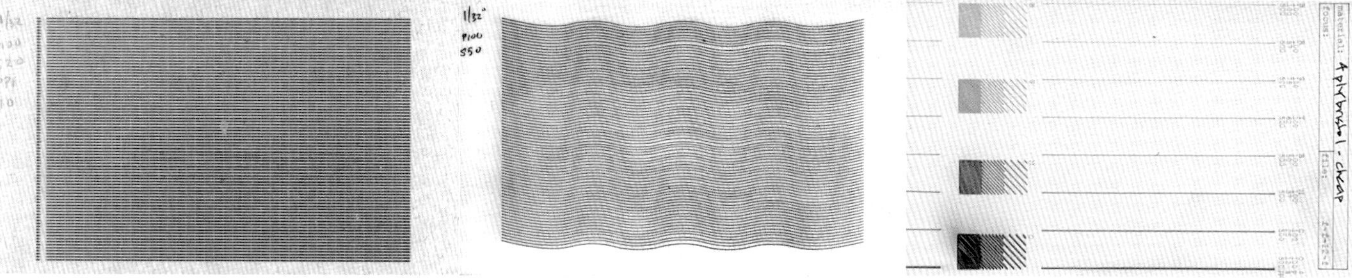

above, left to right:
laser cut test patterns.

would unfold if it was loaded, and how a flat piece of paper could be formed into a structural unit.

We then merged the two separate bodies of research and began drafting our ideas for paper tiles using a CAD drafting program, *MiniCad,* and cutting the pieces with the laser cutter. The laser cutter eliminated the time and difficulty required to fabricate each tile precisely by hand. It was suddenly possible to mass-produce a tile in order to execute an idea about creating a surface or a volume.

We began a series of studies and applications that examined the physical characteristics of paper. Paper's material properties, including its ability to bend, fold, twist, crumple, tear and be cut, acquired a new dimension with the laser cutter. We explored its tensile and compressive properties, connective abilities and volumetric potential. We learned to cut and score in ways that can not be done by hand and to achieve settings that would cut rather than burn the paper. Working directly with the laser cutter instead of outside fabricators, we were able to determine quickly what worked and what did not.

In order to maximize efficiency, we began to develop units from 18 x 24" sheets (the maximum allowable dimensions for the laser-cutter) of various types of paper.

phase 2 [three walls]

For the project gallery at Artists Space, we decided to create and install a freestanding paper wall using laser-cut and manually-folded units that were joined with minimal mechanical fastening. Three walls were constructed to develop the form and construction of the installation.

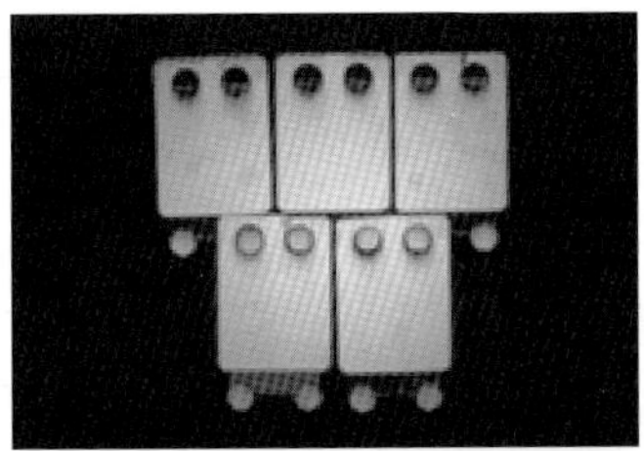

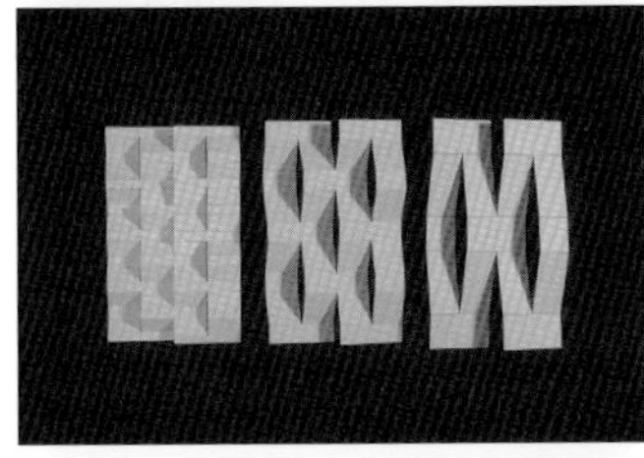

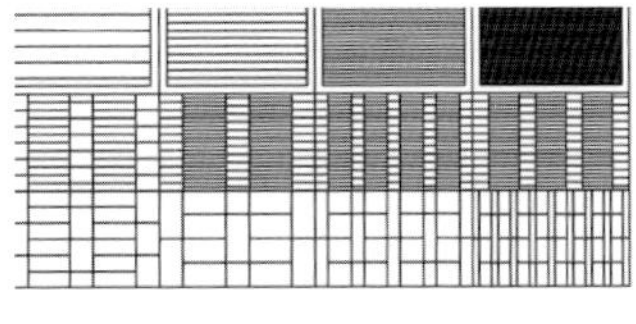

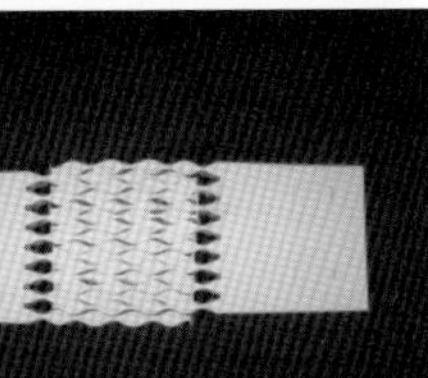

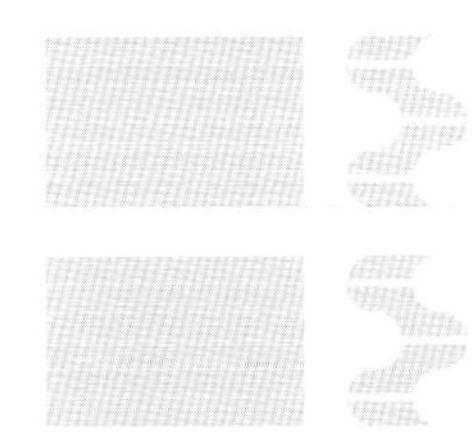

right column: CAM output;
left column: CAD drawings;
top to bottom:
"domino," "score & fold," "velcro®."

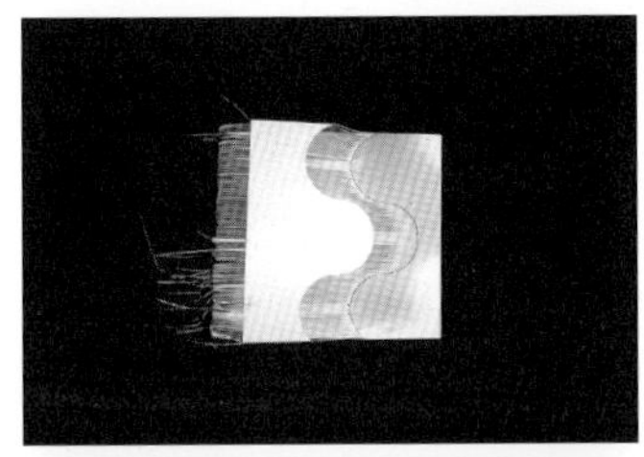

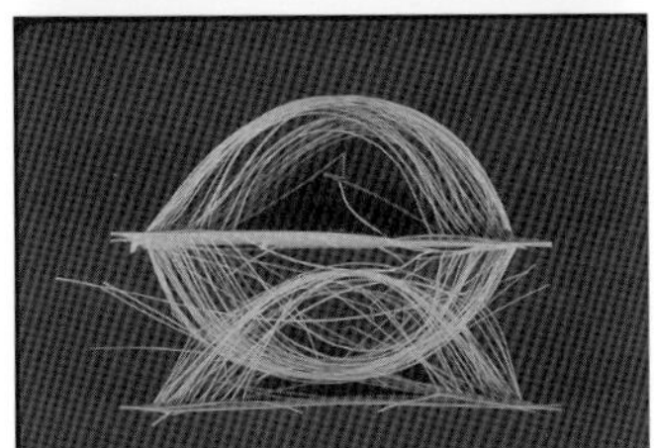

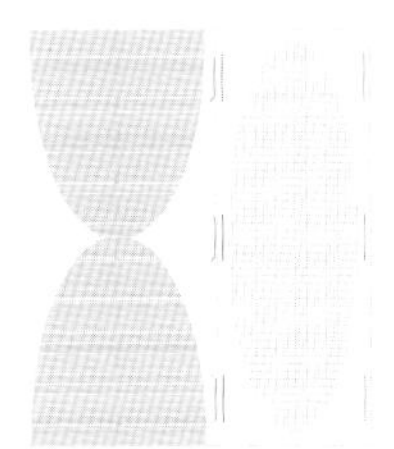

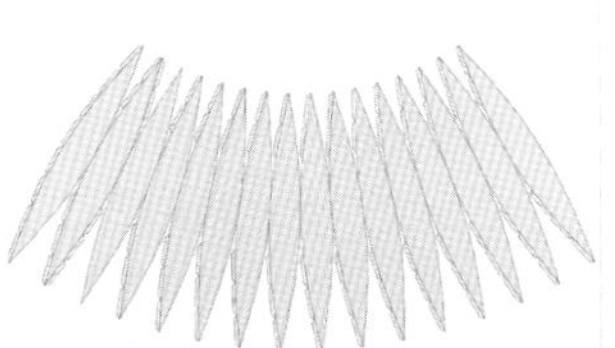

right column: CAM output;
left column: CAD drawings;
top to bottom:
"scroll wheat," "beluga," "shredded wheat ball."

phase 3 [artists space]

above, left to right:
construction at the artists space;
installation of bottom units,
construction method, wall collapse.

> The Artists Space installation allows us to explore the relationship between medium and manufacture without imposing the economic and practical necessities of function. We have control over its production, and therefore freedom in design. As with a couple of prior projects, our working method is part of the design problem. The qualities of the built installation are important, but more significant is the dialogue between process and the end result. We can build a wall that may or may not be beautiful and may or may not fall down the night before the opening. We could end up pinning the whole thing with a tack.
>
> (ARO text for Artists Space mailing, December 1999.)

The paper wall did not fall down the night before the opening. However, it did not survive the opening itself. At the project gallery of Artists Space, the collapse of the wall was for ARO a continuation of an exploration of CAD/CAM and into the characteristics of paper as a medium.

New variables introduced at the gallery had not been present at the office. Uneven and flexible wood floors at the project space made it difficult for the bottom rows of units to be a stable base for the wall. The high traffic in the gallery caused unforeseeable air currents that turned our paper wall into a paper sail.

The wall had an additional weakness, perhaps indicative of the reciprocity in architecture between appearance and function. As we got closer to the wall's final unit, we explored the unit's visual potential. The finely perforated side of the wall allowed the viewer to see into the interior of the wall, and opened possibilities for new lighting strategies. Although initially we had developed the semi-transparent unit to reduce overall mass at the upper part of the wall, we used it instead for an entire side. The structural integrity of the wall was compromised by the perforation,

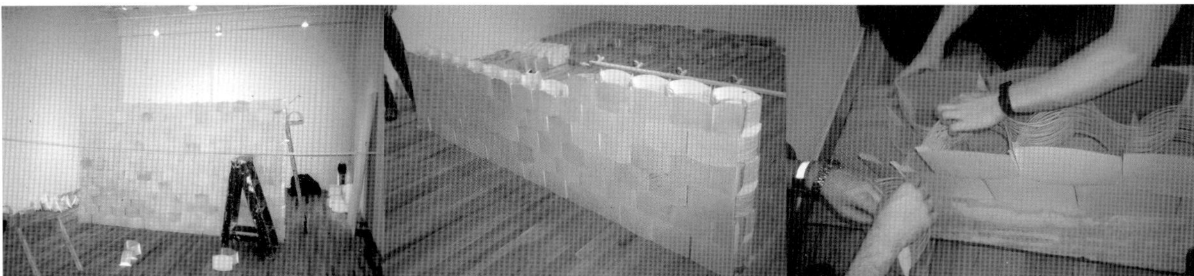

and its misuse was partially responsible for the wall's collapse.

The wall had several iterations at Artists Space. The original assembly required that each unit connect to two opposing units so an entire row would be woven together. For the first re-build, we arranged the units so every unit was connected to only one opposing unit. This created a block that could be used much like a brick.

The second iteration was a much more radical departure from the original intent for the installation. We elevated the wall on a suspended platform to eliminate its contact with the uneven floor. As we constructed the wall, we wove sisal rope through the voids that were created between intersecting units. When the wall was complete, the rope was attached to the ceiling to prevent its collapse. The installation hung for the remainder of the show.

half moon wall

The collapse of the second wall led to the design of an 8 x 6 x 5″ laser cut unit made originally of chip board with opaque and translucent variants, and adaptations for edge and base conditions. From this unit, we constructed the third wall.

Each unit had a flat exterior surface and a bowed interior, finely striated with alternating cuts removed. The straw-like result was then interwoven with adjacent units, allowing the units to shift and reposition themselves as subsequent rows were added in a running bond pattern. The success of this wall resulted from the flexibility of unit placement and positioning, which was unlike our two previous studies.

When first built, the wall seemed to have the potential to grow infinitely tall. The wall's ability to self-adjust and stabilize combined with the reduction in weight from lighter, semi-transparent units, provided the basis for the installation at Artists Space. Once we had decided on a unit to mass-produce, the unit was refined. We selected Bristol Board instead of chip board as the Bristol was less brittle, more translucent and thinner. However, choosing the Bristol Board as a medium had unique problems

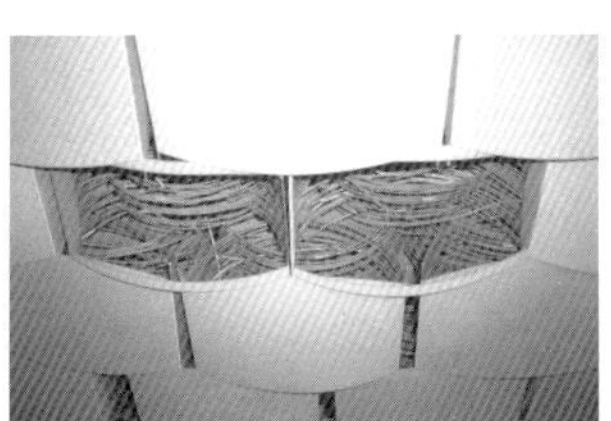

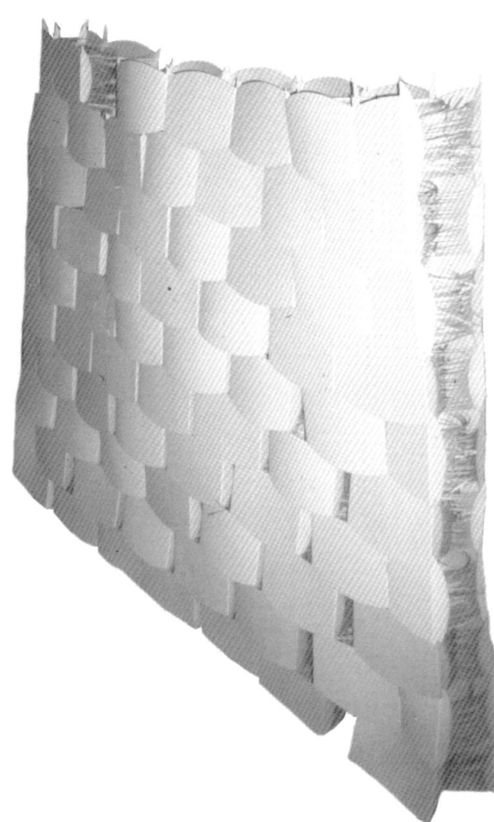

clockwise, from right:
half moon wall, unit inside, wall curved.

as well. As it was cut, the lighter weight Bristol was frequently blown into the machine's ductwork by the air that ventilated the laser cutter. Due to its flexibility, the Bristol was also more likely to deform while being cut, which resulted in unwanted breaks in the unit. Smoke resin formed in the machine and the resin stuck to and soiled the paper. For each problem, there was a solution that altered slightly the design and production of the unit. When we began our research we had discussed the possibility of exploring mass-customization facilitated by CAD/CAM. Although time did not allow us to explore this direction systematically, the quick evolution of the final unit began to touch on the subject.

Time was the biggest limitation during the week just preceding installation. We intended for the wall to fill the project room and be tall enough to block the view of the tallest visitor (approximately 8 feet). With that in mind, we calculated that the final assembled structure would consist of 480 (240 opaque + 240 perforated) cut and folded units. Each perforated unit took 24 minutes to cut and each opaque unit took 7 minutes. This meant in the remaining week it would take 5.7 perfect 24-hour-days of laser cutter production to complete the wall.

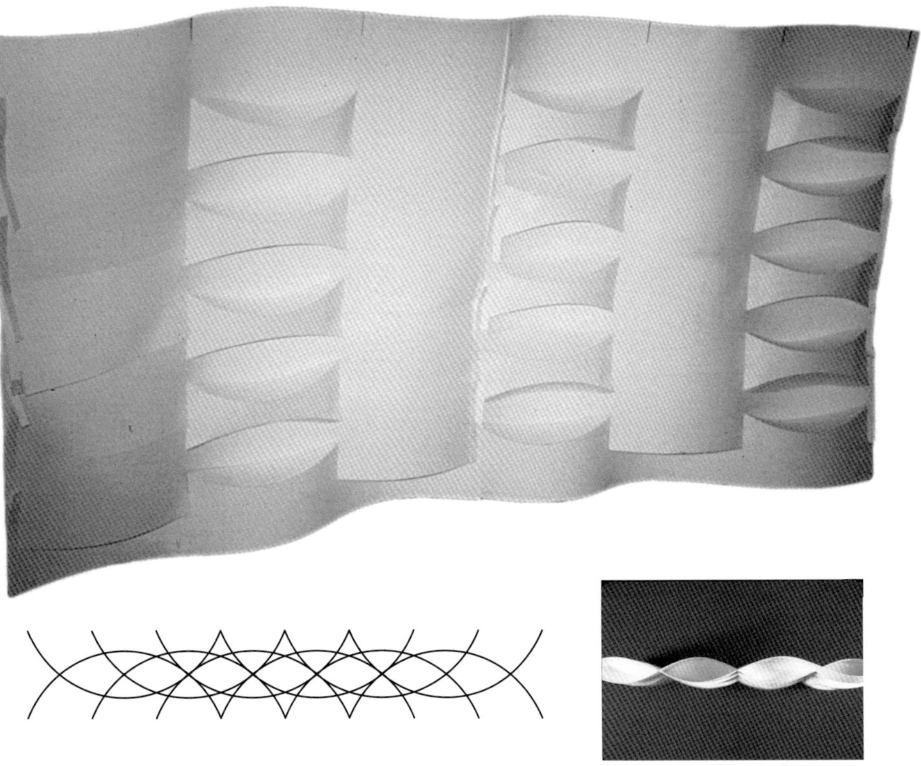

clockwise, from top:
sine curve wall, wall in plan (top view), schematic.

sine curve wall

A sheet of paper placed linearly on its edge will not stand. However when curved in plan, the sheet will stand on its own because the thickness of its base has been increased. The sine curve wall was constructed using this logic. Each 24″ sheet of paper was divided into strips that were tabbed and slotted on their sides. As each tab folded out, it would hold the next strip of paper in the approximate form of a sine curve. Similar strips were added vertically to reinforce and balance the wall's form. It reached a height of about 3 feet before it buckled. The load of the upper layer of strips was too much for the paper below to withstand. Due to time constraints, we did not investigate the complex mathematical function required to fine tune the curve in order to improve the wall.

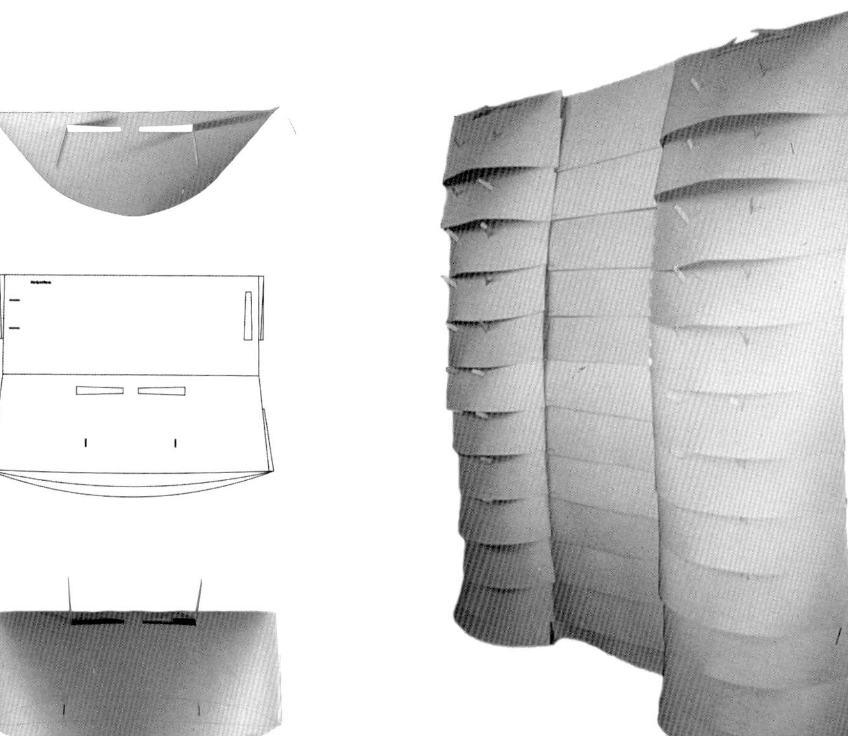

clockwise, from right:
flip flop wall, unit in elevation,
unit diagram, unit in plan.

flip flop wall

We elaborated on the first wall by developing a system that further increased the thickness of the base of the wall. We developed independent paper units, stacked them vertically and hooked them into neighboring units. Each unit was adjacent to an identical unit that was flipped in plan. The volume of each unit tapered as the wall got progressively taller. This transformation balanced the wall and distributed the load of each row to a slightly wider row beneath. To avoid internal buckling, the final variation of this unit incorporated triangulated supports for the unit above.

At this time, we explored how to reduce the load bearing on the bottom rows. Some of the earliest studies of the laser-cutter played an important role. We incorporated the laser-cutter's ability to perforate a specific material while maintaining most of its physical integrity. The semi-transparent unit weighed less than an opaque unit identical in form and size. With these lighter units on top, the flip flop wall reached a height of 5 feet before buckling.

conclusion

above, left to right:
Reid wall, wall and Abbie, elevation view of wall, wall and Matt.

Close involvement in the construction and fabrication process is a fundamental part of ARO's focus on the working process and on our material studies. We consider each project a case study, and we work empirically from the particular to the general. Intensive research informs our intuition. ARO strives to make a practice in which learning is integral to our work so that we continue to be excited and challenged about each project. ARO's research into CAD/CAM technology is ongoing.

N O T E S

Stephen Cassell and Adam Yarinsky, are partners of ARO. They presented to the University at Buffalo, State University of New York, School of Architecture and Planning on 22 September, 1999.

HADAS STEINER

LIMITS OF THE BUBBLE

ARCHIGRAM AND THE IDEAL OF THE COLLAPSIBLE INFLATABLE

Hadas Steiner teaches History and Theory of Architecture at the University at Buffalo, State University of New York.

In the decades following the second world war, soap bubbles began to appear in architectural texts, particularly in the literature promoting pneumatic structures. Now the study of bubbles had long been a feature of scientific inquiry, and it was widespread within the British tradition including the work of Newton, Brewster, Maxwell, and Faraday.[1] Scientists were fascinated with bubbles because, given the boundary conditions, they always enclosed the maximum volume with the minimum surface area.[2] The soap bubble even had a sub-history within British discourse as a theme of the popular lecture designed to introduce the general public to scientific principles.[3] The lecturers consistently evoked representations of bubbles in art to introduce the realm of scientific knowledge, from an illustration on an Etruscan urn in the Louvre,[4] to the shimmering surfaces in *Vanitas* illustrations.[5] But it was the biologist D'arcy Wentworth Thompson's *On Growth and Form* of 1917 that introduced postwar architects, particularly in Britain, to the utility of a form "so pure and simple that we come to look on it as wellnigh a mathematical abstraction."[6]

Faraday's treatment of the bubble had focused on the resilience of the envelope rather than on the perfect abstraction of the form or hollow fragility. As he wrote in 'On the Various Forces of Matter': "So great is the attraction of particle for particle in the water composing the soap bubble, that it gives it the very power of an India-rubber ball."[7] Already the connection between the natural law of the bubble and the behavior of synthetic materials was being built into Faraday's experiments with rubber, the nineteenth century version of plastic.[8] Faraday's investigations inspired other studies, including Thompson's, which explored the strength of the soap film and investigated its economy of materials as a virtue, ultimately leading to the received wisdom of the very first Archigram [1961] which made poetry out of the extreme limits of materiality:

You can roll out steel	any length
You can blow up a balloon	any size
You can mould plastic	any shape

The term 'pneumatic' stems from the Greek word for breath; the handbook of the

And to me too, who loves life, it seems that butterflies and soap-bubbles, and whatever is like them among men, know most about happiness.

[Nietzsche, *Thus Spake Zarathustra*]

British Compressed Air Society (1947) traced pneumatics back to the magical technologies of Hero and Ctesibius in the second century B.C. where air pressure was used to make statues moan and to open temple doors mysteriously.[9] The roots of pneumatics in such theatric architecture embedded it, as Vitruvius described, in a structural type that was notoriously subject to alteration and illusion. In 1917, a British engineer first patented the idea of capturing the unusual structural principles of the bubble in the shell of an enclosure.[10] The Second World War saw the development of components necessary for the realization of pneumatic structures.[11] Further, the ephemera produced by space exploration was rapidly catching up with the "geodesic nets, pneumatic tubes, plastic domes and bubbles" of the space-comic in which the speech bubble deciphered the scribbles of the inventor's pad.[12] It wasn't until after Walter Bird's Radomes of the mid-50s that pneumatic structures were extended into commercial usage by engineers.[13] When architects finally began to use pneumatic design in the late fifties,[14] those structures, because of their novelty and suggestion of transience, tended to be exiled to the arena of the Exposition.[15] Despite the cost-effectiveness of the solution, pneumatic structures were rarely seen in the street.[16] In some quarters, pneumatic architecture was met with enthusiasm: "I believe that pneumatics are the most important discovery ever made in architecture", wrote the British architect Arthur Quarmby, "that they can free the living environment from the constraints which have bound it since history began and that they can in consequence play an immeasurable part in the development of our society."[17] To most, however, inflatables exhibited a disturbing lack of rigidity.[18] Thus pneumatics remained in the domain of visionary sorts, recurring in the work of the young *avant-garde*, for want of a better word, during the sixties, appearing in the projects of Archigram, Cedric Price, Coop Himmelblau, Hans Hollein, Haus Rücker Co., and Utopie.

As Banham characterized them, these 'Zoom Wave' newcomers were "stoned out of their minds with science-fiction images of an alternative architecture that would be perfectly possible tomorrow if only the Universe (and especially the Law of Gravity) were differently organized."[19] That is exactly what the bubble offered to simulate: "The particular beauty of the soap bubble, solitary or in collocation," wrote Thompson, "depends on the absence (to all intents and purposes) of these alien forces [of gravity] from the field."[20] The bubble, in other words, provided the key for overcoming the conventional limitations of building.

The wish for weightlessness had inspired the free span, the cantilever, the piloti. In fact, the ramps of Tecton's penguin pool (1933), floating like ribbons over a diving pond, made Hitchcock finally notice modernism's foothold in England.[21] 'Lightness of materials', and the related revelation of structure, came to imply moral transparency in Britain where architecture was increasingly asked to bear the weight of sociological scrutiny. But the building wrapped in glass was still an object as the public—and the architects—understood it, with a defined parameter and constant dimensions. With the availability of materials far lighter than reinforced concrete, the young postwar architects aspired to an architecture as light as a suitcase, and in the case of Archigram, as a suit. What made the inflatable unique was that it enclosed a space with the minimum of material, with no need for columns or beams.[22] By removing the remaining slender supports, the pneumatic structure tended even more towards the goal of transparency, an architecture so well integrated in and adaptive to the needs of life that it was virtually formless.

The central fixation of the young architects, structural impermanence, was located just on the cusp of formlessness and form, from where both the strength and fragility of materials could be calibrated. Brought together in this lightweight enclosure, a resilience prone to transience tread the same territory as the desire for structural impermanence faced with the need for shelter. The tension between the formal perfection encapsulated in the

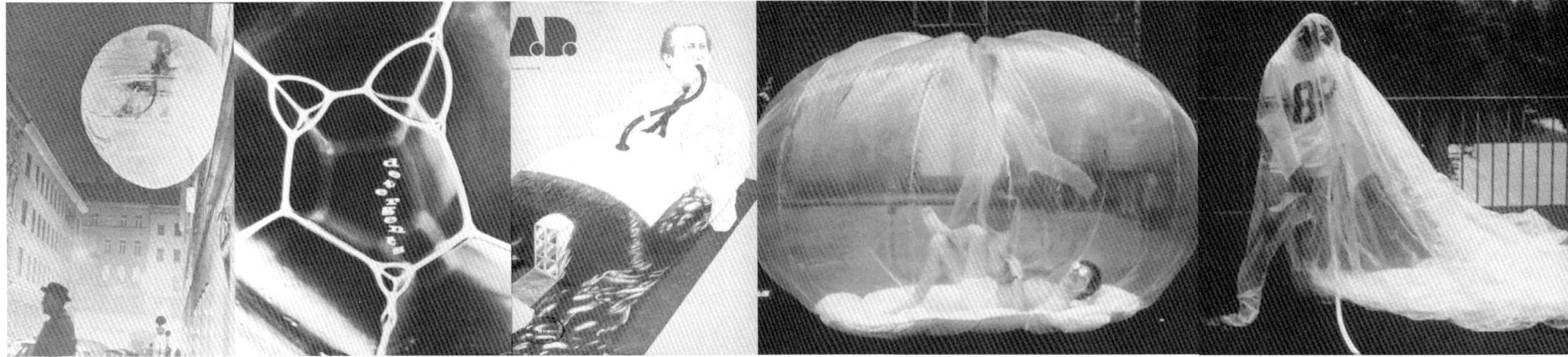

above, left to right:
Coop Himmelblau's Pneumacosm;
James Sterling [from *This is Tomorrow*];
Cover for Architectural Design, Cedric Price;
right and far right:
David Greene demonstrating Michael Webb's Suitaloon, 1968.

suspended bubble and the appealing formlessness of the pneumatic structure remained a pervasive feature of the translation from bubble to building. Although bubbles are ideal pneumatic forms in the abstract space of science, on the ground there are all sorts of forces which destabilize the fragile skin held in place by air. Broadly speaking, there are two types of Air Stabilized architectures which are sometimes used as hybrids and often mixed with conventional building techniques. The less innovative, and more common, of these, the Air Inflated Structure, functions much like other building systems, using inflatable ribs or vertical supports. In the other, as in the bubble, a membrane is supported only by air pressure. Far from exerting force on the ground, the Air Supported structure, if not anchored, floats away.[23]

This problem of a building drifting and how it might be moored raised issues that hadn't existed before in architecture above sea level.[24] "This sort of environment can never be the answer," stated an early Archigram collage with arrows pointing at generic high-rise blocks, "and it isn't even good technology."[25] Making architecture so literally transportable required a totally different conception of structure itself. Such a conception began to appear in the work of Buckminster Fuller, who denounced the tendency of architects to ignore the properties of new building materials. Fuller deployed Thompson's arguments that organic evolution obeys the laws of mathematics, sparking, in turn, a trend of curious texts written in quasi-mystical language that linked geometric design to the improvement of the human condition.[26] In these books, the soap film was represented as the "limit of aspiration". "In the soap film, the material achieves its 'moment of truth'," wrote Michael Burt in *Spatial Arrangement and Polyhedra With Curved Surfaces*, an archetypal example of these texts.[27]

Another gateway for Thompson's ideas were the activities of the Independent Group, most obviously Richard Hamilton's minimally attended 'On Growth and Form' exhibition of 1951.[28] The much larger 'This is Tomorrow' exhibition held at the Whitechapel Gallery in 1956 featured, among twelve pavilions, one by James Stirling, Richard Matthews and Michael Pine.[29] This pavilion was dominated by a sculpture which was extrapolated from photographic studies of soap bubbles undertaken by the group.[30] While these exhibitions also emphasized form, the main lesson of Thompson for the Independent Group went beyond the geometries of life to the methodology of his whole approach.[31] Thompson criticized the tendency to explain the natural world exclusively "by the teleological concept of end, of purpose or of 'design'":[32] "In Aristotle's parable," Thompson explained, "the house is there so that men may live in it; but it is also there," he continued, "because the builders have laid one stone upon another."[33] It was in Thompson's drive to study the local relations between things rather than from the perspective of an ideal final cause that the Independent Group saw its reflection. Underlying Thompson's vision of nature was a conception that viewed change and motion as the essential element for understanding the world. Moreover, Thompson dealt "with the ephemeral and the accidental, not eternal or universal things".[34] Thompson's philosophy informed Siegfried Giedion's *Mechanization Takes Command* (1948) and the art historical approach of Ernst Gombrich.[35] Together with Alfred Korzybski's *Science and Sanity* (1933) which was translated into popular terms by A.E. van Vogt's sci-fi *World of Null-A* (1948), these texts constituted a theoretical basis for Independent Group artistic practice.[36] Korzybski strove to eliminate the legacy of Aristotelian logic, the 'either-or' construction of language—day or night, land or water, life or death, etc.—in favor of a dynamic, process oriented model.[37] Using these concepts, the Independent Group criticized the modernism of Herbert Read's ICA as summed up by Ozenfant in the Purist manifesto: "But what strikes me," Ozenfant had written, "is not how ephemeral all this is, but particularly how prodigiously stable...These vast 'constants'."[38] In short, the struggle of the ICA with the Independent Group was the struggle of the Universal with the Ephemeral, the teleological view of a world versus a world of constant, random change which was taken by Archigram as a given. All this raises the question of how something that had been the icon of perfection, a 'limit of aspiration' like the soap bubble, could, in the hands of the Archigram group, transform into a model for exactly the opposite ideal, that of formlessness, in a non-teleological model.[39]

In 1963, Archigram was still illustrating hard plastic domes as 'bubbles', a form which often bore the shadow of the inflatable scaffolding used in construction.[40] These structures transformed the liquid principles of the bubble into solid. Ultimately, though, inflatable architectures made the "airy insubstantiality" of the domes seem permanent by comparison. This was in a large part due to the use of air as a structural component, but more than that, it was the introduction of time into the finished product. The Air-Supported structure was in a constant process of actively enclosing—the fans continuously churned to maintain the pressure supporting the building's form and changes arose from variations in this artificial breath. In themselves, the buildings were also subject to ambient forces, sensitive and visibly responding to "minute variations in climactic parameters and loading conditions."[41] Everything about Air-Supported structures spoke of continuous change.

Cedric Price had already used inflatables in his projects from the early sixties to express this change, not formal idealization. Price's association with Pneumatics was thorough: he collaborated with the engineer Frank Newby on handbooks for the British Standards Institution and for the Department of Environment,[42] lectured at the 'First International Colloquium on Pneumatic Structures' in Stuttgart (1967) and delivered the keynote address at the 'National Conference of Air Structures in Education' held in an inflatable at Antioch College, Maryland (1973). Significantly, Price's survey of pneumatic structures was the only one of its kind to not include the bubble analogy. Furthermore, Price avoided terms that connoted finitude. His environments took advantage of the capacity of pneumatic structures to adapt rapidly to changing conditions, introducing a "precise time factor into the process of enclosure."[43] This concept of temporality took the flip-side of the bubble's structural properties into account: the tendency to collapse, suddenly and dramatically.[44] Archigram, learning their lessons well from Price, wanted to introduce an environment where duration really mattered. By subjecting things directly to the contingencies of time, Archigram wanted to supersede the 'Mobility' slogan of the Smithsons, which amounted, in their view, to no more than the possibility of adding a bathroom.

The so-called 'mobility' associated with the Smithsons still employed hard materials like steel and concrete, glass and plastic—materials that, in the 60s, architects began to refer to as 'hardware'—as opposed to flexible membranes, which were dubbed 'software'. At this time when programs were hardwired into the computer, it was difficult for the public, including architects, to distinguish between hard and soft technology. Amongst architects, therefore, 'software' became any vehicle for change and adaptation, leading to a confusion in image and text over the domain of information and that of compliant materials. Banham exemplified this most entertainingly in 'The Triumph of Software' (1968) when he contrasted the hardware imagery of *Space Odyssey 2001* (1968) with the inflatables of *Barbarella* (1967). Banham compared Kubrick's constructions to a 'Pompeii re-excavated': "All that grey plastic and crackle-finish metal, and knobs and switches, all that...yech...*hardware*!" By contrast, he wrote, the bubbles of Barbarella were "responsive environments...curved, pliable, continuous, breathing, adaptable surfaces.

A consensus existed in the literature, abetted by the confused view of 'software', that the rounded forms of pneumatic structures offered a way out of the dead end modernism had reached by the late fifties. Banham suggested that "taste that has been turned off by the regular rectangular format of official modern architecture" was "turned right on by the apparent do-it-yourself potentialities of low pressure inflatable technology."[45] Obscurity in the domain of software, however, led to a more fundamental one in the domain of 'nature'. Pneumatics seemed to propose a synthesis of the organic world and built form that would not negate the structural dimension of architecture. In a deviation from his descriptive voice, Thomas Herzog explained in his handbook how architecture had been dominated by "orthogonal forms with hard, cold, machine-produced surfaces." Though "previous attempts to oppose this with a sensuous plastic world have meant a negation of the technical/structural dimension of architecture, building with pneumatic structures offers the possibility of synthesis." Such structures, Herzog continued, "employ forms that are technically highly developed, using soft, flexible, movable, roundly spanned, "organic" shapes, which can be of great sensuous beauty."[46] This 'organic', not to mention gendered, metaphor, implicated the biological world in the confusions of an architecture based on the bubble. Fuller went so far as to call PVC "inherently natural" because it was based on "complex structural behaviors permitted by Nature."[47] Frei Otto, in his paradigmatic study of 1962, was more concerned with how pneumatic architecture emulated plant and animal life: "We find [pneumatic principles] not only in fruits, air bubbles, and blood vessels, but also in the skin kept taut by muscle tissue and blood pressure, and largely supported, in addition, by a skeleton resistant to bending and compression. Animal and man exhibit the essential features of a lightweight structure...Pneumatic structures, developed along lines dictated by purely technical considerations, are meeting the justified and growing demand that technology abandon its abstract, antiorganic-mathematical conception, though not its scientific basis, in favor of a conception nearer to organic life."[48]

Otto's biologically based, technologically sophisticated pneumatics provide clues to how the bubble—the model of formal perfection in physics—came to symbolize its opposite in organic evolution. As a biologist, Thompson had seen evolutionary theory as non-teleological development. Nevertheless, Thompson did not totally relinquish teleological explanations—in fact he used the bubble to explain other less perfect forms. With the introduction of the element of time, avant-garde architects abandoned the bubble as a paradigm of static form in favor of a paradigm of a dynamic system.

Archigram's progressive departure from its megacity visions of 1964 wrapped architecture closer and closer around the body; in Otto's terms, the organic principles of the body were applied to enclose it. When Otto drew a detail of the layers of a pneumatic spacesuit, he included human skin as part of the outfit. But while a spacesuit was still a suit, the 'Suitaloon' (1967) blurred the boundaries between different kinds of bodily enclosures, of buildings and clothes, of inside and outside.[49] That was the point of the 'Suitaloon': when you wanted to be home, your suit increased in scale to enclose you. Archigram used what Price had called the 'time factor' and the capacity to integrate change with structure to overcome the 'either-or' dichotomies of permanence and instability, hard and soft, technological and natural—as they perceived them. With the possibilities of lightweight materials, Archigram produced an enclosure that was fully transportable, exploited the speed of expansion and deflation, constituted and reconstituted itself at will, like a lung. It was a house that was only as durable as clothing and only as natural as a second skin.

Though the suit evaded the problem of moving between inside and outside and, less convincingly, the problem of the anchoring to the ground, the internal world of the autonomous bubble for one, occasionally two, still remained. The difference between this kind of interior and that of its plastic precedent, the capsule house, is summed up by the performative images of the mock-up of the Smithsons' House of the Future (1956) which appeared in the Daily Mail and the ones of an introspective David Greene wearing Infogonk spectacles—architecture for the inside of the head—in the trial Suitaloon. This excursion to the interior of the bubble provided a glimpse at technology adapting to the biological exigencies of life, becoming, as Moholy-Nagy predicted, "as much a part of life as metabolism."[50] When compared with the 'Envirobubble', the new suburban housing type proposed by Banham, it becomes clear how this intimate container for the body forced the Suitaloon away from simple distinctions between what was on either side of the barrier. The function of Banham's hemisphere of transparent mylar was to set the inhabitant off from the catastrophic spectacle of nature. From within the comfort of your own bubble, he wrote, "you could have a spectacular ringside view of the wind felling trees, snow swirling through the glade, the forest fire coming over the hill."[51]

The bubble's tendency towards self-containment conflicted with the communal nexus of the stem and web that had been entrenched in the discourse since the fifties. "I have nothing against discontinuous domes", quipped Philip Johnson, "but for goodness sake, let's not call it architecture."[52] A plug had been provided to connect the suit with other like envelopes to circumvent enforced isolation in the design of the 'Suitaloon'. This was not a simple matter, for openings in inflated membranes are complicated things. In the handbooks, meticulous attention was paid to how bubbles clung together in groups.[53] The automatic adjustments made by the whole each time a bubble joined the collocation displaced the emphasis from the introverted realm of the individual bubble to the interaction of these self-contained units in a responsive system. The inter-connections of the system, 120 degree angles at which bubbles converge, the curvature of their shared walls, provided insight into how to overcome the exclusivity of interiority and exteriority. More than the ordered cluster of bubbles, an agglomeration made up of a multitude of bubble sizes and shapes compressed into multi-angular bodies, as in a foam, might be a better example of what emerges when there are competing ambient forces at work. In Archigram's world, the inter-relation of private and public space produced a continual series of interconnected, complex, chaotic distortions of the bubble. For an architecture that strove to abandon an "antiorganic-mathematical conception" altogether, perhaps the bubble had been a misleading archetype.

NOTES

The Limits of the Bubble was presented April 24 - 25, 1998 at *Reconceptualizing the Modern: Architectural Culture 1943-1968*, Graduate School of Design, Harvard University.

[1]The classic study is J. Plateau's *Statique Experimentale et Theorique des Liquides soumis aux Seules Forces Moleculaires*, Paris: Gauthier-Villars, 1873.

[2]This was also why architects ultimately became fascinated with them: "With regard to their surface all shapes produced with soap bubbles can be thought of as "ideal" pneumatic forms since, because of the fluidity of their film, forms always occur in which there are equal membrane stresses at every point on the surface. Within the prescribed boundary conditions the largest possible volumes and the smallest possible surface area always form. One refers to *minimal surface* areas. Thus an optimisation of form in relation to use of material takes place. The dead weight and the resulting deformation are so small in the case of soap film models with a span of less than 10cm that they can generally be ignored." (Thomas Herzog. *Pneumatic Structures: A Handbook of Inflatable Architecture.* [New York: Oxford University Press, 1976.] p. 8

[3]Two examples are CV Boys' much cited *Soap-Bubbles, Their Colours and the Forces which Mould Them*, Romance of Science series, lectures delivered to juvenile and popular audiences under the auspices of the Society For Promoting Christian Knowledge, London, 1890 and *Soap Bubbles, A Lecture*, delivered in Hulme Town Hall, Manchester, Wednesday, November 3, 1875, by Professor Rücker as part of Science Lectures for the People, Manchester (Manchester: John Heywood).

[4]Boys reported hunting for this vase in vain. (*ibid*. p. 14).

[5]The bubble paintings of Millais or Chardin for example.

[6](Cambridge: Cambridge University Press.), p. 350-351. Thompson is always cited in the pneumatic literature.

[7]Quoted in Williams, Thomas. *Soap Bubbles.* (FCS: Liverpool, 1890.) This essay, which discusses the shift represented by Faraday's theories, is another in the tradition of the popular lecture.

[8] In 1826, the British scientist Michael Faraday was the first to isolate the isoprene molecule. (Sylvia Katz. *Plastic, Designs and Materials.* [London: Studio Vista, 1978.] p. 24).

[9]Siegfried Giedion cited *The Pneumatics of Hero of Alexandria* to illustrate the 'magical' use of technology by the ancients versus our own 'progressive' view. (*Mechanization Takes Command.* [NY: Oxford University Press, 1948.] p. 32).

[10]Frederick William Lanchester submitted his patent (#119,339) for 'An Unproved Construction of Tent for Field Hospitals, Depots and like purposes' in 1917: "The present invention has for its object to provide a means of constructing and erecting a tent of large size without the use of poles or supports of any kind. The present invention consists in brief in a construction of tent in which balloon fabric or other material of low air permeability is employed and maintained in an erected state by air pressure and in which ingress and egress is provided for by one or more air locks". (Roger N. Dent. *Principles of Pneumatic Architecture.* [London: Architectural Press, 1971.] p.27).

[11]spurred on by urgencies for barrage balloons, temporary shelters, dummy buildings and compactible life boats. (Dent, *op.cit.*, p. 32-34).

[12]*Archigram* 4, 1964, p. 4.

[13]Radomes were developed to shield fragile military radar equipment from severe weather.

[14]Dent listed the Boston Arts Center Theater (Woods Hole, MA 1959), by Carl Koch and Margaret Ross with Paul Weidhinger of Birdair, as the first pneumatic construction designed by architects (*op.cit.*, pp. 39-40). Victor Lundy's sophisticated hybrid pneumatic exhibition hall for the US Atomic Energy Commission (Santiago, Chile, 1960), with Walter Bird, was noted for its innovation at the architectural level (Dent, *ibid.*, p. 41-44.; Reyner Banham. *The Architecture of the Well-Tempered Environment.* [Chicago: University of Chicago Press.] p. 270-274).

[15]The Irving Air Chute Company exhibited a two room inflatable air house—two inflatable domes connected by a tube—at the International Home Exposition in NYC, June 1957. Pneumatics were more extensively used at Expo 67, Montreal and Expo 70, Osaka.

[16]The spherical forms lent themselves to Picturesque scatter in non-urban situations. Simple inflatables proliferated during the fifties—by 1957, there were about 50 manufacturers in the US making portable air structures: Birdair, Schjeldall, Irving, US Rubber, Goodyear, Texair, Stromeyer, Krupp, Seattle Tent & Awning, and CID Air Structures, to name a few.

[17]*Plastics in Architecture.* (New York: Praeger Press, 1974.) p. 114.

[18]Anticipating his critics, Reyner Banham described their concerns: "But...surely you can't bring up a family in a polythene bag? This can never replace the time-honoured ranch-style tri-level standing proudly in a landscape of five defeated shrubs, flanked on one side by a ranch-style tri-level with six shrubs and on the other by a ranch-style tri-level with four small boys and a private dust bowl." "A Home is Not a House" in *Design By Choice*, ed. P. Sparke. (London: Academy Editions, 1981.), p. 59.

[19]Banham, 'Zoom Wave Meets Architecture' (1966), *ibid.*, p. 64.

[20]*op.cit.*, pp. 350-1.

[21]However surreal the introduction of the International Style via the zoo, the appearance of the suspension of gravitational force captivated the audience and this quality was talked about as if it resulted in a more advanced way of life: "How many citizens of London", asked a promotional publication for the zoo, "have brooded over the railings of that pool, envying the penguins as they streak through the blue water or plod up the exquisite incline of the ramp—and have wondered sadly why human beings cannot be provided, like penguins, with an environment so adapted to their needs?" (P. Guillery. *The Building of the London Zoo*, [London: RCHME, 1993.] p. 17-8).

[22] Arthur Quarmby quoted Walter Bird (*op.cit.* p.255):
"What makes the air structure so outstanding? What are its special features which it makes possible for us to satisfy requirements which can be provided with no other type of structure?
1. The air structure is the most efficient structural form available to date. It combines the inherent strength and reliability of materials used in tension with the structural efficiency of the shell. There are no problems of bending or buckling. All material is placed at the extreme fiber, where it is utilized to maximum advantage. There is no need for columns, beams, or other supports. The structural envelope is simply supported by air.
2. No other type of structure has the potential of providing free-span coverage for so large an area. Supported by air, requiring no columns or beams, great roof heights can be provided at virtually no cost premium. The Telstar dome will enclose a 16-story building.
3. As the air structure is constructed of lightweight, flexible materials, it can be made easily portable and lends itself readily to the design of demountable or removable structures.
What other type of structure offers these outstanding advantages?"

[23]"Unlike conventional structures which exert a positive loading on the ground, the pressure differential across the membrane of an air supported structure causes up-lift forces, and these must be resisted by firmly anchoring the air supported structure to the ground." (Dent, *op.cit.*, p.19).

[24]How to move between inside and outside, for example, without disturbing the balance of pressure, or how to link one enclosure with another.

[25]The collage was made for the Archigram group's first public collaboration, the 'Living City' exhibition at the Institute for Contemporary Art, London. (*Living Arts*, [2]: 1963, 81-2).

[26]For the archetypal manifestations of these see publications like Matila Ghyka's *The Geometry of Art and Life* (New York: Sheed & Ward, 1946.) which had a cult following. The text made connections between geometrical form as found in nature, art and mysticism.

[27]Other examples would be MA Guran's *Change in Space Defining Systems*, RK Thomas' *Three Dimensional Design*, J Borrego's *Space Grid Structure*, DG Wood's *Space Enclosure System*, Steve Baer's *Dome Cook Book* and M Safdie's *New Environmental Requirements for Urban Building*.

[28]The political history of how this exhibition came to be part of the ICA's contribution to the Festival of Britain is described by Anne Massey (*The Independent Group.* [Manchester: Manchester University Press] p. 42-44). Hamilton described being introduced to Thompson's *On Growth and Form* by fellow Slade student, Nigel Henderson (*Collected Words 1953-1982.* [London: Thames & Hudson.] p.10).

[29]Note the contrast of this pavilion with the 'Pop' contribution of McHale, Hamilton and Voelker or the "Junkyard Brut" of the Smithsons, Henderson and Paolozzi alongside which it stood.
[30]This is described in by G. Whitham, *The Independent Group: Postwar Britain and the Aesthetics of Plenty*, ed. D. Robbins. (Cambridge, MIT Press, 1990.) p. 143: "Pine", the catalogue quotes, "recalls the photographs as 'great fun to do' and then cites from a letter that he wrote to Jacquelyn Baas on the 20th of August, 1988: "An enlarger was focussed through an aspirin bottle containing soapy water onto photosensitive paper on the wall. This was all set up using a red filter, and when we had a good bubble image, the red filter was removed for about four seconds, and the paper immediately developed. The problem with this was the tendency of the bubbles to burst during the four seconds of exposure. However, we got enough prints for our purpose." Pine and Stirling discounted any influence of Hamilton's

On Growth and Form.

[31]Massey, *op.cit.*, p.44: "The crucial link between Thompson's thesis and the Independent Group was the rejection of teleological, universal explanations of the environment."

[32]*op.cit.*, p. 4. (quoted in Massey, *ibid.*)

[33]*ibid.*, p. 6.

[34]*ibid.*, p. 4. (quoted in Massey, *op.cit.*)

[35]Massey, *ibid.*

[36]Independent Group members received Korzybski's weighty ideas through A.E. van Vogt's *World of Null-A* (1948), a science-fiction translation of *Science and Sanity*, which imagined a society in which no rules of Aristotelian logic applied. Each chapter of the book (which originally appeared as a series in *Astounding Science Fiction*) began with a quote from Korzybski. In Frank Cordell's view, none of the IG members had read Korzybski in the original. (Massey, *ibid.*, pp. 85-9; Robbins, *op.cit*, p. 61.) Meetings and debates were held at the ICA, such as 'Were the Dadaists Non-Aristotelian?'

[37]Korzybski's resistance to Aristotelian logic was rooted in the study of language and in his view that "semantic adherence to an Aristotelian view—an either-or logic—inevitably led to unlogic, then illogic". (Robbins, *ibid.*)

[38]quoted by Massey, *op.cit.*, p. 87

[39]The Independent Group held a stronger position than Thompson on this.

[40]*Archigram* 3 (1963) was the first issue of the publication to be collaborated on by all six members and functioned as a kind of manifesto. The bubble made its first appearance on the 'Groundwork' page, nestled between the molded plastic capsule of the prefabricated bathroom and the urbanism of the system. In the move from bathrooms to bubbles, the connection to water was not trivial—the problem of the bathroom was the clash of the portable unit with the anchor of water pipes which linked back to an infrastructure of supply and waste. The sewer was one of the first places where pneumatics intersected with architecture, in the 'pneumatic sewage injector' (*Handbook on Pneumatic Equipment.* British Compressed Air Society. [London: James Cond Ltd, 1947.] p. 150). The bubble also anticipated the system: the pneumatic tubes of the postal system were a crude form of a system of information distribution—the very system which distributed the *Archigram* newsletter, for all the talk of sophisticated technology.

[41]Dent, *op.cit.*, p. 21.

[42]*Air Structure Research Report*, Department of the Environment, London: HMSO, 1971, and *Air Supported Structures: Draft for Development*, London: British Standards Institution, 1976.

[43]'Pneumatics—a key to variable hybrid structuring', in *Cedric Price, Works II.* (London: Architectural Association, 1984.)

[44]Quarmby tells a precautionary tale of his three dramatic mishaps with inflatables. (*op.cit.*, pp. 98-100) As Banham put it, "an airdome is not the sort of thing that the kids, or a distracted Pumpkin-eater could run in and out of when the fit took them—believe me, fighting your way out of an airdome can be worse than trying to get out of a collapsed rain-soaked tent if you make the wrong first move." (A Home is not a House, *op.cit.*, p. 59)

[45]'Monumental Windbags', *New Society*, 18 April, 1968.

[46]*op.cit.*, p7. See Jeffrey L. Miekle, *American Plastic*, NJ: Rutgers University Press, 1995, pp. 217-8.

[47]Miekle, *ibid.*, pp. 215-6.

[48]*Tensile Structures, vol. 1.* (Cambridge: MIT Press, 1967.) p.10.

[49]Marshall McLuhan saw housing as a "collective means of achieving the same end" as clothing. ('Housing: New Look and New Outlook' in *Understanding Media.* [New York: McGraw-Hill, 1964.] p. 123-30)

[50]*Vision in Motion.* (Chicago: Paul Theobald & Co, 1961.) p. 64.

[51]Banham, 'A Home is not a House', *op.cit.*, p. 59.

[52]'Where We Are At'. *Architectural Review.* (Sept. 1960), reprinted in *Architecture Culture 1943-1968.* (NY: Rizzoli, 1993.) p. 191.

[53]In 'Seaside Bubbles' (1966), Ron Herron's conjunction of underwater preoccupations with bubble clusters, one sees the Archigramesque version of individual units collocating as a society.

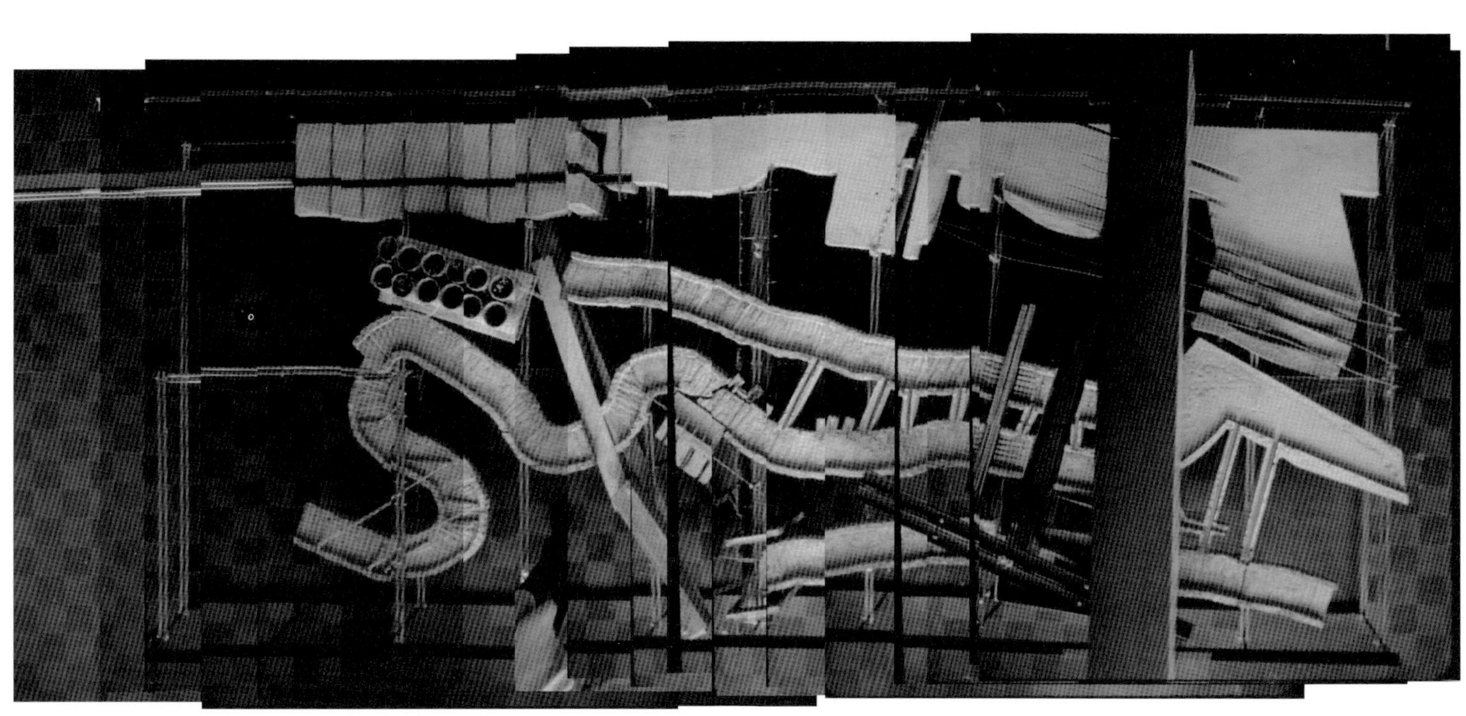

MEHRDAD **HADIGHI**

S L I P

In 25 B.C., Marcus Vitruvius Pollio wrote *The Ten Books on Architecture*, the earliest surviving architectural treatise. In it, he spoke of the architect, as the artisan, designer and builder, as the master craftsman. He argued for a triple essence to be achieved by the architect, those of constructive strength, practical utility, and aesthetic effect. The triple essences were to be achieved through the architect's first hand, mechanical, and tactile knowledge of materials, and their structural, aesthetic, and formal properties. The singularity of the piece of stone, its form, its grain, the pattern of its breakage, its material strength, and its surface texture was understood through a tactile analysis by the hand of the master craftsman, on-site and off-paper. On the other hand, this tactile analysis had to be accompanied by an aesthetic analysis, on-paper, and off-site.

Mehrdad Hadighi is an Associate Professor in the Department of Architecture at the University at Buffalo, State University of New York. Prior to his arrival in Buffalo, he taught at Cornell University, Columbia University, and Miami University. He was educated at Cornell University and the University of Maryland. Mr. Hadighi was born in Iran and moved to the United States in 1977.

> Vitruvius writes: "The architect should be equipped with knowledge of many branches of study and varied kinds of learning, for it is by his judgement that all work done by the other arts is put to test. This knowledge is the child of practice and theory. Practice is the continuous and regular exercise of employment where manual work is done with any necessary material according to the design of a drawing. Theory, on the other hand, is the ability to demonstrate and explain the productions of dexterity on the principles of proportion.
>
> It follows, therefore, that architects who have aimed at acquiring manual skill without scholarship have never been able to reach a position of authority to correspond to their pains, while those who relied only upon theories and scholarship were obviously hunting the shadow, not the substance. But those who have a thorough knowledge of both, like men armed at all points, have the sooner attained their object and carried authority with them."[1]

Architecture, for Vitruvius was conceived as a form of knowledge; a form of knowledge about the physical environment that was acquired and practiced through the active and ambulatory presence of the architect on the construction site: seeing where the sun rises, and sets, where the prevailing winds come from, and where

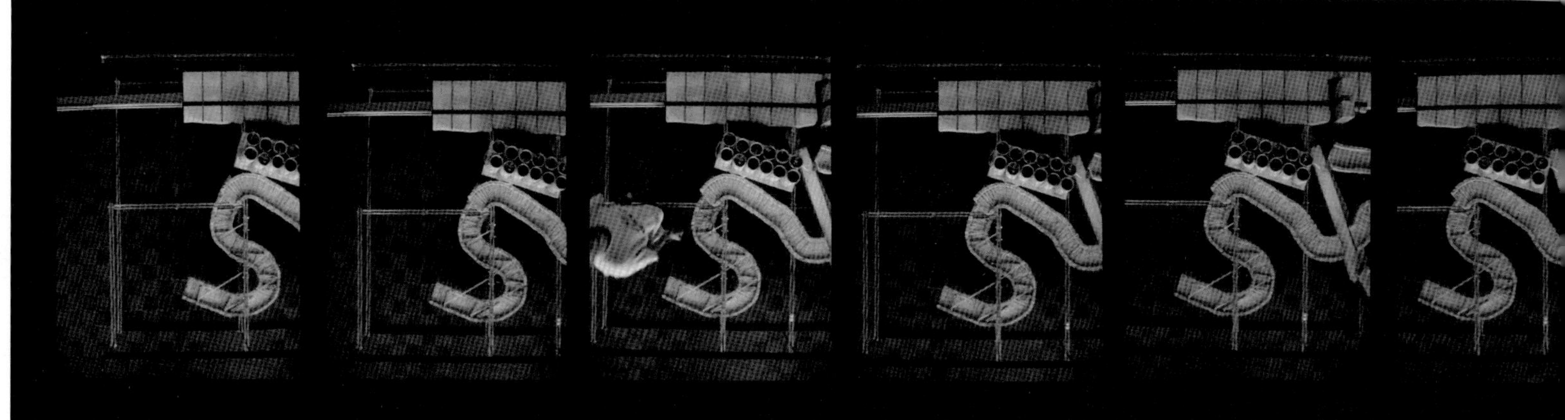

the high and low spots of the site are. The architect/builder/artisan/designer, through presence on the construction site, by handling the stone, the chisel, and the hammer, was to achieve the triple essences of constructive strength, practical utility and aesthetic effect in the building that was built.

A number of key issues arise in relation to this two-thousand year old treatise by Vitruvius:

1. Perhaps the most obvious and the most profound is the distinction, not raised, but acknowledged, between theory and practice. Vitruvius is theorizing on the practice of architecture. He is analyzing the constructive language of architecture built by other architects, and theorizing in the written language. The works of architecture referenced in The Ten Books on Architecture are representations of themselves in the books. They do not appear as language, rather described in language.

2. Perhaps not as obvious, but just as profound is the fact that the Vitruvian architect is engaged in the design, and the production of the building. Both the intellectual labor and the physical labor are a part of the architect's realm of responsibilities. The distinctions that are later drawn between design and construction, that elevate intellectual labor to the noble, and physical labor to the ordinary, are here non-existent. The two are considered as part and product of the same activity.

3. The presence of the architect on the job site, and the first-hand handling of material realities is assumed to communicate such realities to the architect.

4. Drawing, both in its techniques of construction and its use, was not a "blueprint" from which buildings were to be made; it did not exist as a representation or a reproduction in reference to the building yet to be made. Instead, it was a mode of studying and examining construction and material issues.

In 1452 AD, during the Renaissance, Leone Battista Alberti (1404-72) wrote *Ten Books on Architecture*, The most significant treatise on architecture since Vitruvius. In it he spoke of the architect as the artist and the designer, and not as the craftsman, or the builder. Yet he still insisted on the Vitruvian triple essences, rephrased to strength, convenience, and beauty. Alberti, as the pre-eminent theorist of architecture during the

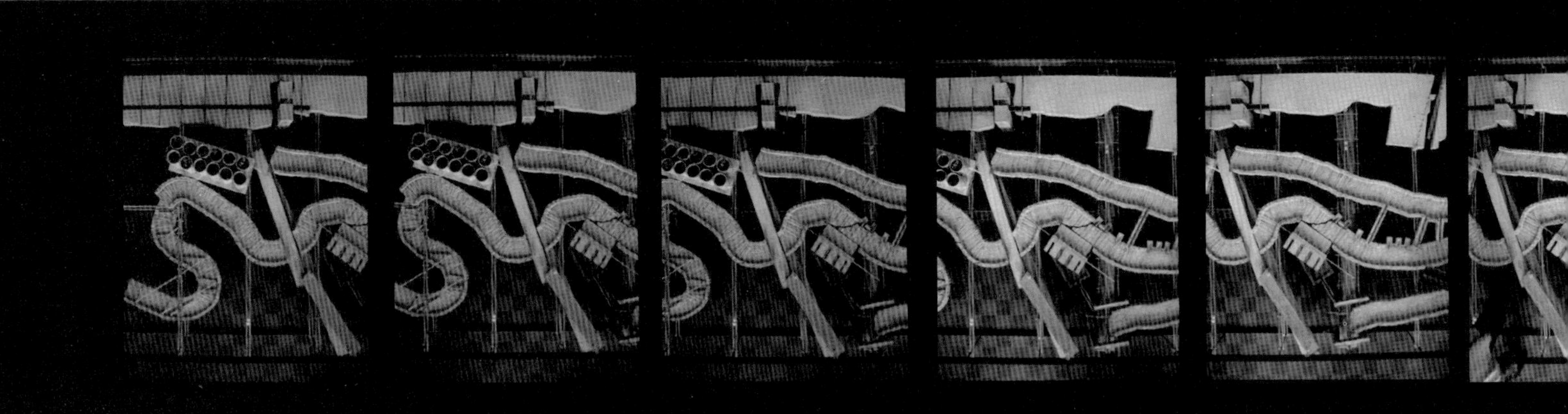

Renaissance, was reflecting on the contemporary developments in Italy. The Renaissance was associated with a growing secularism and a renewed interest in Classical Roman civilization. Patronized by merchant-aristocrat families, a new kind of architect emerged who was no longer a craftsman but a creative and a versatile artist in pursuit of aesthetic excellence. Filippo Brunelleschi (1377-1446), whose Founding Hospital and cathedral dome at Florence are the inaugural buildings of the Renaissance, was a goldsmith, and Michaelangelo (1475-1564) considered himself primarily a sculptor. Hence a new breed of architects was born: those who would privilege the aesthetic over the constructive, the on-paper over the on-site. Not only is intellectual labor separated from and privileged over the physical labor, but also a particular type of intellectual labor is preferred; that related to the oculus. The primacy of visual aesthetics has greatly altered the path of architecture since the Renaissance. Alberti as the theorist of the age, poses the relationship of the three essences to be different than the Vitruvian model. Here Alberti argues for beauty, to be of utmost importance.

> "...this part of building, which relates to beauty and ornament, being the chief of all the rest, must without doubt be directed by some sure rules of art and proportion, which whoever neglects will make himself ridiculous. But there are some who will by no means allow of this, and say that men are guided by a variety of opinions in their judgment of beauty and of buildings; and that the forms of structures must vary according to every man's particular taste and fancy, and not be tied down to any rules of art. A common thing with the ignorant, to despise what they do not understand!"[2]

The post-Renaissance architect as the artist and the designer, would have first hand knowledge of the rules of art and proportion, but would only be familiar with the craft and the constructive aspects of architecture through deferred learning.

Here, in this first major break in the conception of architecture, a number of bifurcations are introduced in the production of architecture:

1. The design and the construction of architecture are bifurcated. The Medieval architect as the designer/artisan/builder has been split into the Renaissance architect and the stone mason, or builder. The architect is responsible

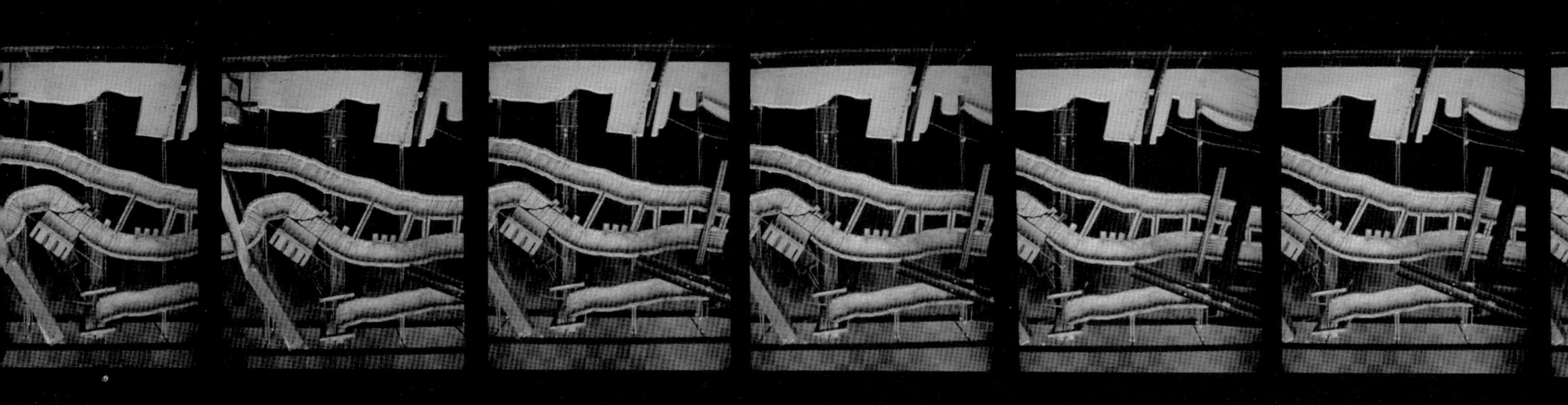

for the creative aspects of the design, the communication of that design; and the builder is responsible for the execution of the design. As a result, the architect is no longer physically engaged in the construction of buildings.

2. The simultaneity of the intellectual labor and the physical labor of the medieval architect has been split, so that the architect is responsible for the more noble intellectual labor, and the builder is responsible for the more ordinary physical labor.

3. The product of the work of the architect is no loner a building, it is a representation of the building. The architect produces drawings, the blueprints from which the builder manufactures the building. The architect works in reference to the building, and not on the building. The architect works on-paper, and off-site. As a result, the architect is primarily concerned with the appearance of the building, that which could most readily be reproduced and represented in a drawing, especially drawings of the period that would have been constructed using the rules of perspective.

4. Situations, territories, materials, and their singularities have been split apart. The Medieval architect worked with a piece of stone, as a piece of stone with all of its material singularities. The Renaissance architect works with a drawing of the piece of stone, only able to specify its shape, and dimension, and estimate its texture.

Through the separation of design and construction, theory and practice, drawing and building, and profession and discipline, the architect's work is always mediated through drawings, which are on paper, and off site. The static geometry of the appearance of the artifact is reproduced in absolute measure, on paper, with only notational or referential information to its material and constructive conditions, as they are experienced on site, and off paper. Given that material singularities, and constructive particularities do not appear visually in an architectural drawing, the whole nature of architectural drawing in relation to material singularities becomes suspect.

Perhaps the most fundamental shift in architecture that can be attributed to the Renaissance is the occularization of the practice of architecture. With Brunelleschi's invention of the scientific construction of perspective, the single, self-centered eye of the architect and the viewer dictated the primacy of the privileged position of the center in any symmetrical design. Hence the experience of architecture was profoundly limited to the visual,

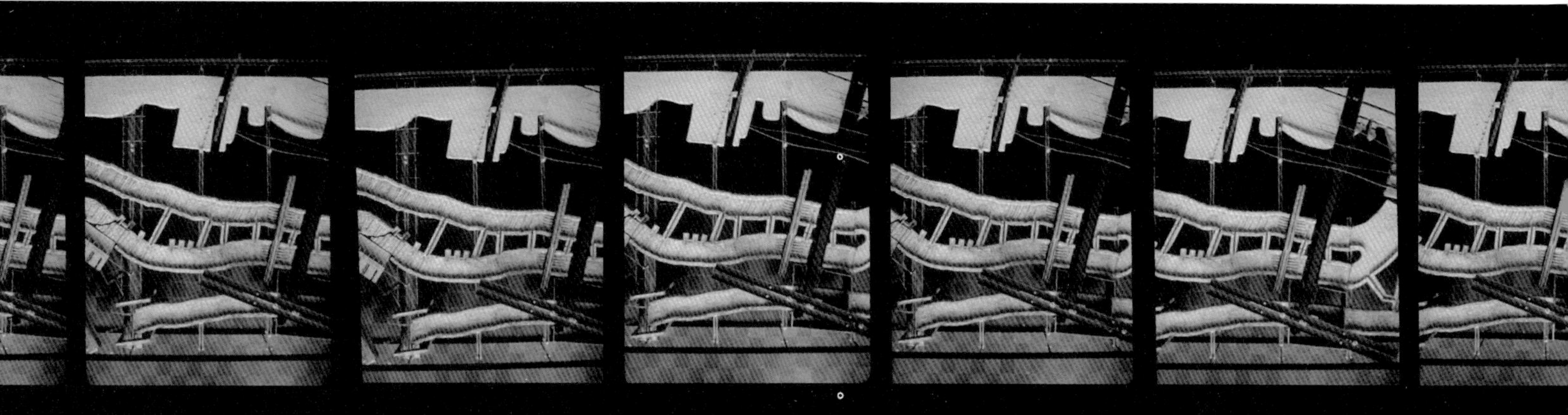

more specifically, to that governed by the fixed point of view of perspective, and not by the activity of the human body, its motion, and other senses. Medieval architecture as a form of knowledge about the physical environment was transformed to Renaissance architecture as knowledge of form, knowledge of rules and mathematical proportions that dictate formal configurations.

In the Sixteenth Century, architecture, along with civil engineering, medicine, law, clergy, and accounting became "learned professions", the first step towards the outlining of the legal within the architectural. It was not until the first part of the Twentieth Century that architects began to establish a "Code of Ethics", and eventually specialized education and licensing laws. By this time, yet another bifurcation had been introduced in the production of architecture: that of the profession versus the discipline. The profession, bound by, licensed by, and educated by the Profession's Code of Ethics, and the discipline, bound by the creative and constructive rigors of architecture.

This brief analysis of the history of architecture delineates a tendency towards the continual bifurcation of the discipline away from situational, material, and territorial singularities. This, perhaps, is not unique to the discipline of architecture, certainly not in an era when everything arrives as pixels, far from the tactile and the physical. Even the site of construction is no longer a territory to be followed and traversed in order to be studied; rather, it is a series of glowing dots of phosphorous recorded by the United States Geological Survey's Land Satellite, with digital precision, part red pixel, part blue pixel, and part green.

The Medieval architect, having to materially follow the territory of the construction site, to materially scale the surfaces and record the landscape of each piece of stone, having to triangulate the different particulars of the surfaces in relation to one another, is now replaced by a drawing, a site map, or a satellite photo, which records the territory without ever touching it, measures the landscape without ever traversing it, forms the geometry of the stone without ever lifting it, and drafts a map without ever ruling it. The Medieval architect's logic of operation could not exist purely outside of the territory, outside of the landscape, and outside of the material; it could not exist purely on paper, and off-site.

The architect had to physically engage the territory and the materials, their surfaces, and their nuances. The

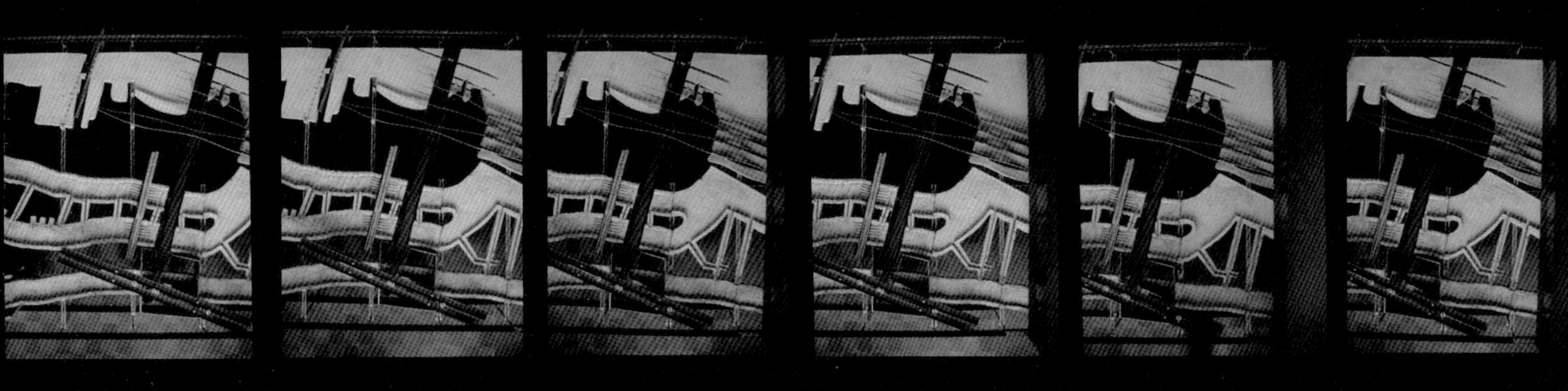

tools and the techniques of reproduction: measurement, recording, and drafting techniques, had to be continuously altered according to the terrain of the territory, and the complexity of the material at hand. On the other hand, the site plan, though far more precise in its measure, neutralizes the territory, and the participants. The same drawing technique will record a site in Buffalo, that will record the Amazon, New York City, and the Salt flats, each reproduced from a fixed position in space.

This analysis is not nostalgia for a manual, mechanical, or analog world. On the contrary, it is in search of a material hyper-tactility, and a material language with real-time engagement and real-material consequences, in a mediated, binary, always-already-reproduced environment. It is in search of a productive model that is on paper and off-site, which is mediated, and digital, yet off paper and on-site, with hyper material sensibilities. It is in search of a productive model that is mediated, yet material, which reproduces with the measured precision of the static eye, and can yet experience frenetic mobile flux as an ambulant, heuristic architect. This model is neither solely about composition nor solely about organization.

The hinge model proposes the space of architecture to be the space of projection, where the material singularities, and architecture's measured organization can be projected onto one another; a projected space for the deployment of the tactile presence as the undermining agent of resistance for the mediated reality of the drawn and the digital, and the deployment of the mediated as the undermining agent of resistance for the tactile.

The space of the hinge is a continuously moving, tense-space between opening and closure, between design and construction, between theory and practice, between profession and discipline, and between intellectual labor and physical labor. The complexity of this position is in maintaining the tension of the hinge: never to be permitted to be simply open, nor simply closed, always in fluxive tension. The complexity of this position is in engaging the potentially violent unrelieved stress of a sheet of steel without fixing it, in engaging the potential energy within the torques and bends of a piece of lumber without straightening it, engaging the unpredictable movements of vapor, and chaotic wind-blown rain without controlling it. The complexity of the hinge-position is in the mobilization of the static geometry and the absolute measure of the architectural drawing for sudden material flight. It is to make the architectural drawing move beyond its own structure of two-dimensional representation and address the possibility of the impossible-to-reproduce. It is to construct the mobile fluxive space through the

geometry of the immovable within the space of reproduction. It is to construct the ground-level plane of the medieval architect through the metric plane of the Land-Satellite image.

The accompanying project, SLIP, was produced in a graduate architecture design studio at the University at Buffalo during the Spring semester of 2000. The proposal, as the name might imply, was a slip between drawing and construction, between the precise Land-Sat accuracy of a map of Buffalo, NY, and the material consequences of slip-forming the same map in concrete. It was a slip between the physical labor of producing the slip-formed concrete structure, a continuous 96 hour effort, beginning on Friday February 25, 2000, and ending on Tuesday February 29, 2000, and the intellectual labor of programming Freudian slips. It was a slip between the production of architecture on-paper, off-site, and the production of the same on-site and off-paper. It was a slip between the studio as a construction site, and the studio as the site for drawing and modeling of architecture. It was a slip between Derrida's hinge theories in "Plato's Pharmacy", and the practical requirements for the design of a pharmacy. It was a slip between a 16" masonry circular saw, and a draughting compass; a slip between half a ton of concrete and 90 grams of mylar. It was a slip between architecture as theory and practice, as drawing and building, as discipline and profession, as intellectual labor and physical labor, and as artistic production and constructive production. It was a slip between architecture.

NOTES

1. Marcus Vitruvius Pollio, *The Ten Books on Architecture,* Translated by Morris Hickey Morgan (New York: Dover Publications, Inc., 1960) Page 5.

2. Leone Battista Alberti, *Ten Books on Architecture*, Translated by James Leoni (London: Transatlantic Arts, Inc., 1755) Page 113.

S L I P was conducted as a graduate architecture design studio at the University at Buffalo, Spring 2000 by Mehrdad Hadighi. The contribution of the following students to the development of "slippery" ideas and to the work of the studio was invaluable: Gloria Arango, Eric Brodfuehrer, Melisa Delaney, Carrie Galuski, Rami Haydar, Charlotte Kahr, Michael Maggio, Sean McCormack, Kerron Miller, David Misenheimer, Bharat Patel, Redman Toska, Ron Trigilio.

This paper was originally prepared under the title "Architecture, the Hinged Discourse" for the American Comparative Literature Association's annual meeting. It was presented at "ACLA 2000 Interdisciplinary Studies" at Yale University in February 2000. A revised version was presented at ACSA's West Regional Meeting at Arizona State University in October 2000 and appears because of conference proceedings.

Nuts!
RAVIOLI FAIR
The Original
RAVIOLI FAIR
HOT
HEROS
PLATES

THOMAS TURTURRO

X C H A N G E

INCORPORATING GROUND OF THE NEW YORK STOCK EXCHANGE

america's classical tradition

Thomas Turturro is presently completing his M.Arch degree, in 1992, he received his B.P.S from the University at Buffalo, State University of New York. He is currently a designer with Skidmore, Owings & Merrill in New York City.

There is a strong conviction in our culture today that the person who does not diverge from tradition is a slave. The leaders of our industry, politics, and architecture believe that if they can free both themselves and us from the fetters of convention, history, or precedent, true fulfillment and revolutionary well-being may be achieved. We have all seen it. It is in the endless 'brand new', the 'better' software, the 'next best thing', and the 'design of obsolescence'. Our world has become abandon itself, desperate to see or make what no one has before. When one studies the writings of our discipline's great figures, Boulleé, Ledoux, Colonna, Alberti, Vitruvius or maybe even the "modern" Wright, it seems clear they did not see the path to excellence this way. Aristotle did not either. "To live according to your country's ways of life is not slavery ... it is salvation", he wrote in *Politics*. This sentiment is quintessentially *classical,* one respecting that every modernity stands and grows out of a living past offering orientation, wisdom, and inspiration. To put it another way, a "tree's leaves and seeds could go nowhere but for its roots". In architecture this issue is easy to identify through the longstanding academic insistence on reverence for 'site' or 'context'. We are all instructed early on that a building should grow out of its site. The implicit understanding of this *contextualism* is that any place, say my breakfast table, has an intelligible network of isolatable figures (my eggs, my bacon, my juice) whose presence are due to earnest and describable forces (chickens, pigs, and trees). The diminishing visibility of these characters survey, thus betraying their *temporal* nature — 'the tip of the iceberg'. Yet as American architects we often view our larger cultural existence as context-less. It is as though we simply popped into the world *ex-nihilo.* But initially a European province and secondly an English speaking and democratic society founded upon personal responsibility, limited self-government, and technological innovation, we are a classically spawned civilization. As the literarily preoccupied in our intelligentsia can help attest, more than half of our English language's words are of Latin origin, with those of Greek roots accounting for most of the rest. Thus a fairly large part of America's mental infrastructure is grounded in, and therefore kin to, classicism. The framers of the Constitution, intellects not limited to Jefferson, Adams, Franklin, and Hamilton, all had rigorous classical educations and researched ancient

above:
U.S. Twenty Dollar Bill.

texts for guidance in their shaping of our republic. We know from Jefferson's *Notes on the State of Virginia*, Query 14, that his ideas on the subject of public education involved primary study of Latin and Greek and that full use of the traditions of democracy and science extended to us from the ancient world required mastery of the tongues that gave these traditions shape and form. Any American cultural effort, architectural or otherwise, which ignores this classical heritage, which cuts off its roots, is not only cutting off routes of legibility by its audience, but the best chance it has to honestly know itself. True excellence is always a grasp of the old in order to fashion beautiful and meaningful things for the present. If we wish not to be a culture marked by servility we must draw from the past in order to originate the new.

the site

The Corinthian façade of the The New York Stock Exchange has been called the "universal symbol for modern capitalism." A good case might be made that it probably lays somewhere between the green American legal tender which preceded it, and this celebrated wall. But it is a minor point, the resonate character both share is the neo-classical imagery adorning them. This fluted, leafy, dentiled, and stepped expression would — according to plan - stay intact and occupy a critical position facing a modern exchange built directly across the street.

This institution itself was founded just over two hundred years ago. At first one small exchange of many, it moved often, renting spaces throughout New York's financial district — even in the Merchant's Exchange on 55 Wall Street. It grew enough to build the current edifice at 18 Broad Street in 1901. Since then it has been linked to several unrealized renovation efforts, most notably those involving Henry Cobb of I.M. Pei and Associates in 1963 and Gordon Bunshaft of Skidmore, Owings, and Merrill in 1966. In 1977 it briefly considered a World Trade Center locale and now currently in 2000 is again restless — this time peering across the street to 15 Broad. Although a critical time at the New York Stock Exchange [NYSE], as the decentralization due our electronic times is eroding the physical need for a trading floor, to my reckoning it is still hard to imagine a more important American building than one unquestionably embodying our democratic country's marriage with capital. Given the now global holdings this has come to represent ... all the more so. Critique it if you like, and hope that it may evolve into something more, but market economy is part and parcel of who we are, and outside of Washington what single institution can claim such perfect effect on our collective well-being? Is there an evening newscast anywhere in America that does not flash the familiar image of those Corinthian columns and give the day's trading stats? It may not be Mecca, but at some point in their day nearly every American looks to this mask of fluted rock.

Suspicion this wall is part of a site having architectural character beyond celebrity is supported by the Frenchman Le Corbusier. He found occasion to detail this in his text *When the Cathedrals Were White*. Under the heading 'A Remarkable Architectural Sight';

> "In the intense heart of Wall Street, city of banks, at the exciting end of one of the canyons formed by skyscrapers, I experienced the shock of a remarkable architectural spectacle. There I think is the strongest and noblest plastic composition (for the moment) in the USA."
>
> Here the effect of the Doric columns on the adjacent U.S. Customs House [like Athens];
> "...takes hold of the limited open space and projects it into the air toward the skyscrapers which are like a splendid natural phenomenon, one of those places where nature or the imagination of men has delighted to place the seat of the gods."[4]

Given this 'temple' that is the U.S. Customs house, it looking south, past the Corinthian façade of the Stock Exchange, and the many other neo-classical buildings characterizing the district, is it so foolish to sense some voice buried in these stony façades? For what if their odd song which here caught Le Corbusier and Jefferson and so many of our forefathers, isn't so naive? As a modern architect working in an office on Wall Street, I must grudgingly admit to a gaining awe of the place. The endless array of column and cornice in their darn near eternal flesh draw a genuine wonder. Even though the district is incredibly compacted, even for New York, the façades somehow get past this confine in a sort of 'see-saw' manner echoing beyond a metric depth. Admittedly for building tenants this usually means little natural light, but for a pedestrian it is striking. His reward of pedaling through this dark tangle of chasm and gorge is the asphalt sea formed by the meeting of Broad and Wall Streets. Here in a place with no real retail or residential presence, the U.S. Customs House and the Stock Exchange seat the largest, and most well lit, court in the old district. On weekdays, infantries of suits, school children, heartland tourists, and local peddlers, wander about in a manner patently illustrative of a 'market'. Intermittently their eddy is parted by the northbound trickle of autos still permitted on Broad. Return on a Sunday and the peddlers are still there, although in reduced numbers, as are the tourists. And if one comes early enough a crane or two might be seen spearheading some implement about the place, or helicopter policing traffic, or chorus of workmen endlessly digging and shoring up ground — all over the rattle of those silver trains awash below. Walking along this basin one quickly realizes a harmony between his footfall and the enfilade of column. This ancient beat echoing with the place in a way that the encroaching glass and steel neighbors dampen. Something feels humane, lived before yes, but forever.

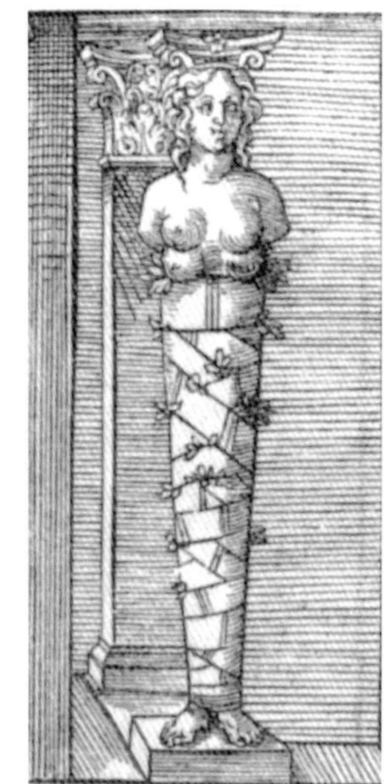

above:
Atlante.
[from Vitruvius Teutsch, 1549.]

To be direct, these stone façades seem to anticipate us. And if so, reflecting at the dawn of our new millennium, have we not figured out anything capable of addressing this gesture usually so offensive to modern architects? Clearly we cannot just copy them, even when we afford the expense of reinstituting their stone-cut techniques we know how those efforts have a sense of something borrowed. In truth, the neo-classical itself has a fair part of this fakery as well. But let's not toss the baby out with the bath water, what quality is it that they *do* have? Admittedly an uncomfortable subject to broach in the twenty-first century, maybe recent archeological advances and current scholarly review of the Hellenistic temple — lying at the root of occidental architecture - will offer a postulant architect some speedy closure[5].

trope, allegory, & myth

Little classical study is possible without some review of ancient poetic technique and its use of *trope*, *allegory*, and *myth*. Beginning by example, a *temple* is our forehead, yet also a house of worship. Such verbal play is called a *trope*. Modern dictionaries define trope as a word use other than normally proper, and it is a confusing technique dating well back past the great Latin rheoriticeans through to the ancients. Crafty, playful, and figurative, trope is the accepted root of poetry and myth as well as the fashion Vitruvius, Homer, and the epic poets used words. When Socrates in 399 B.C. argues that knowledge, episteme, is at odds with things that will not stay put — an argument trivializing the mythical first architect Daedulus — he is articulating an emerging frustration with tropos and the old-fashioned poetic reckoning they engender[6].

Confusing is a fair word to describe tropes, for, like a chimera or a horse so fast he could fly, their produce are 'con-fused', bastard children of two abruptly meeting parents. As an architectural joint amidst two wholly incompatible materials, tropes are 'monstrosities' of how the two things finally found a way to *embrace* one another. This two-fisted grasp is the trope, simply all it sucks out. For they are about qualities; or that light bulb

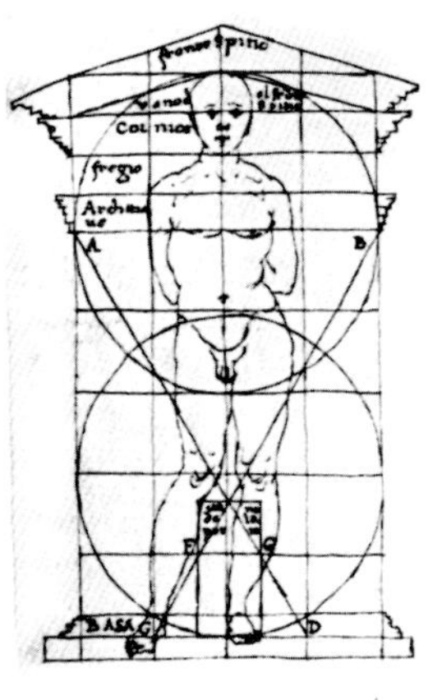

above:
Church Facade.
[from Francesco di Giorgio. *Magliabecchiano Codex*, folio 38v.]

popping discovery of the rub or frictive grain where things relate, meld, and go nova. By addressing character similarities in an earnest attempt at semantic agreement, tropes work a synthesthetic reading of the world unlike our modern more conceptually disciplined habit. Rather than discursively assigning a transparent relation between subject and object, they 'knead quality' and are thus highly invested in an embodied or corporal art of living. Soiling as it may be, understanding tropes honestly demands that one really must 'feel his way' about them.

Tropes become symbolically representative, or *allegory,* when assembled in a sort of ritual mime to express more complex relationships - such as a wine flagon portraying 'the birth of Dionysus' a naval sculpture depicting 'victory', or a temple describing 'a divinity'. In turn, the reduction of these to narrative shorthand for either oral or written transmittal constitutes an art of ***mythos*** (word) or mythology. Taking up this view, the whole corpus of lore from Archaic Greece can assume a more adult character — as *the means* a clever people used to transmit simple ideas about their history and natural world. For is it not likely that the myth of Persephone, seedling daughter of the Demetrian grain, who while out gathering flowers was swallowed up into the ground by Hades, involves an agricultural people's passing on to its youngsters a seasonal wisdom about planting? Or in life, as with the climactic narcissus bloom, a time naturally comes round for sowing young seeds into a dark but wanting ground?

on the ground

We sense from myth, historical record, and archaeological evidence, that early Greek tribes envisioned worldly fabric, their garment of *ground*, in a far more related and holistic fashion than we do today. Common in the Pelasgian, Orphic, or Olympian creation myths, this singularity found expression as a Mother-Goddess whose extent was the physical universe. Via trope within the mundane rigors of living in general, agriculture, sea-faring, battle, and worship, etc., She articulated even further. Expectedly, local and topical circumstance influenced this construal. Archaic characters like Cybele, or Gaia, were thus temporarily gleaned to portray a host of *aspects*, i.e. watery, animal, seasonal, rocky, stormy, botanical, etc. Thus a seaside community may have noticed in the oceanic waves a Poseidon, while a forest tribe saw Artemis in the hunt. Still further, these aspects themselves can expand. Thus Demeter can behave in the spring as a maiden (Persephone*) and* in the autumn more like a crone (Hecate*)*. In 'troping ground' the mythic mind never lost hold of its world as being singular in matter, yet infinitely open to articulation. Since this articulation was awareness, and awareness was this hard life's advantage, the trick was getting this ground 'pregnant' with attention.

The social organization of early Greek life (2000-1200 B.C.) was matrilineal and involved a typical Indo-European and Mediterranean sovereign leader called a wanax. Initially distinction between ground and this 'king' was not so clear-cut as legend held that humans dwelt in community with gods and even coupled together rearing spawn of half-mortal and half-divine breeding. Typically chora, or 'nursing world' in general, was construed as a womb-like earthen-mother aspect, a meter or mater, whom this ruler would annually wed after winning a laborious struggle with either the previous King or some guarding monster – serpent, dragon or otherwise[7]. Once won, the victor assumed custodianship of this living ground. Through various duties, such as leading the tilling of the soil, or initiating the harvest, he rendered her 'divine flesh' fertile to human genesis. The sense of this 'living ground' lingered through to Plato who in the Laws wrote that the legislator who forbade the construction of walls around the city of Sparta did well to "let them sleep in the earth".[8] It extended from the Hellenic mind into the Latin as evidenced by the term excitare muros, 'to awaken walls'.[9] Plainly, the occident did first see walls rising from the depths of the earth as young issuing from a parent. Classical walls, like trees, were children of the mother earth, and ever after birth, umbilically connected to her by their ontic foundations, as trees are by their roots.

This wanax sat at the apex of the social structure. He oversaw, regulation of weapons, the design of chariots, cavalry training, and location of troops. But his craft did not end there. As Divinity's shepherd, he cultivated all aspects of the community's life including: maintenance of the calendar, ritual adherence, marking of chora, and collecting sacrificial offerings from each citizen as due title. These sacrifices were usually the first picks of crops called aparche, or of animal litters, thysia, commonly 'the blood sacrifice'. In concert with priestly-magicians and a warrior-aristocratic class called basileus, who organized the georgoi (farmers), his skill in courting the natural aspects of their world left him personally liable for the existence of the community.

above:
First Female Term.
[From Sambin, Hugues. *De La Diversite des Termes.* 1572.]

temple formation

Early ritual-worship of the divine occurred at sacred groves or fields. Pliny clearly tells us that the first temples were trees, or xulon.[10] Each Greek god and goddess aspect grew a special tree aspect coming into season at a particular lunar month. For Hera it became the willow, Apollo the 'Plane Tree' or Sycamore, Poseidon the Pine, and Athena the olive. The oak sacred to Zeus bore acorns in May-June, an event coinciding with their new calendar year and the looming cereal harvest. Oak, apple, or Sycamore trees, in particular, would be important to a people limited in the agricultural arts because of their offering mast. As the tallest, most animate extension of the ground, these trees engendered the sense of a woven, temporal, and organic world. A garment where the rain soaked acorn fed both man and cow, and the annual leaf, with it's autumnal fall, compost, and April shape-shift into other crop-forms and manure, demonstrated a divine cycle of birth, death and re-constitution[11]. Given the poetic context of an archaic intellect, and the life or death consequences amidst rain, ground, cows, trees, and men, one might say these 'trees reined hold of mater, steering the fates of men'.

With cultivation the sacred groves thinned to include but one large tree, which may have been surrounded by an enclosure. In a relief of Amphion and Zethois in the Palazzo Spada, Rome, the forest Goddess Artemis stands before a tree about which a linteled ring of columns stand. It is not a difficult design move to imagine this 'rock-circle with tree-canopy' troped into a 'mud-bricked and stone bearing of timber and thatch'. This was the megaron. With the rise of husbandry and the influence of barley and grain, incorporation of thatch into a living idea of soil and wood seems likely.

The climactic drama staged at these early temples was the violence of sacrifice needed for all life. Part of humanity since hunger itself, hunting gave the first sacrificial lessons through the hunter, who, falling in love with his prey, wished to somehow save its life from complete annihilation. By leaving certain organs, claws, or horn, at the site of the kill, he secretly prayed to extend some aspect its life. The definition of trope, these were trophy — a sacrifice or offering to keep the God or Goddess from punishing the guilty stealing her flesh, and resurrection of a spoiled beauty ruined out of hunger. A trope by the resituating of the confiscated material-part (i.e. horns) in a qualitative manner echoing the whole (elk), it was intended to ally, to physically, and later legally, compensate Divinity for its initial losses.[12] In an existential sense this mortal dilemma is just what the temple allegory originates from. As a 'murder incorporated', the temple was just a dancing 'frankenstein' of stolen mater aspects – hungrily swept, invested, and held back up to Her out of love and fear. When first tree-groves, these allegory were mainly of wood with the finest oxen skinned, tanned, and hung about forming the original tympanum, or pediment, of taught hide stretched on bone. Not unrelated, hides were also the leather sails on the first ships - born too by mast.[13] When grain and barely blossomed with husbandry, thatch, the hairy

above:
The New York Stock Exchange from the U.S. Customs House Pteroma (South Porch).
[Photo by Alexander Ekuzmin.]

'tresses of the land', was put in the roofs – on the temple's head. Like night to day, spring to fall, and birth to death, Greek sacrifice taught the rhythmic decomposal and recomposal of the earthen body.

Spatially, the social organization evolved to include a central palace with administrative personnel, the surrounding basileus in townhouses, and the periphery georgoi. In sum this arrangement was called temenos. Located at its center was the temple megaron. This contained a central hearth or stone altar, where in pivotal moments, such as equinox, solstice, planting, or harvest, the wanax presented aparche and performed thysia. With jeweled stones, smithed metalwork, garlands, horns, fruit, eggs, hides, mast and masticating teeth displayed, altar was surrounded by four fluted timber-columns holding a thatched and pitched roof[14]. A stone or mud-brick wall surrounded this. Temple in turn was separated from its immediate surroundings by a stretch of bare land. This yard contained one tree, a water source, and an outcrop of rock forming the base of the altar. Insular in nature, and probably quite dark save for the always pulsing flame at the raised hearth, megaron must have felt warmly illuminating — like a matron foundry tempering its world.

This architecture all began to change with the Dorian invasions of the twelfth century. In this period, commonly known as the 'Dark Ages of Greece', the entire temenos system mysteriously collapsed. Ties with neighboring cultures slipped as well as most crafts including writing. In this historical gap a new social system coalesced with an effect on temple design. For with the bizarre disappearance of all who would be wanax, the basileus, still occupying lands, cultivating herds of horses, possessing arms, and retaining religious knowledge, were faced with keeping the peripheral georgoi organized. These two of the basic three cultural spheres so deeply rooted in early occidental culture, lacking the sovereign third, and each lacking the means and skills of the other, grew embroiled in conflict. Facing dissolution, their way to reconcile this disparity took the form of a renovated sophia or 'human wisdom'. As an unprecedented cultural aspect sophia was not concerned with the physical world or chora, but rather with the human social world so badly in need of mending. Initially the basileus assembled as an aristocracy of peers electing to choose a leader, or archon. Come to be known as arche, or 'command', this institution predicated a political-public realm previously non-existent in Greek life with a leadership founded in human choice and self-rule rather than blood or physical skill.

Emerging from this unaccounted for Dark Age, Greek culture thus reorganized its former tri-partite self in which wanax was the only one of the three who possessed the characteristics and knowledge of all the others. For originally he, having an understanding of the whole, held arche. Originally he had the broad vision to see the shaping of any one part's position within the whole cultural edifice and the nurturing chora relation to the cultural edifice. Like any good architect, wanax reckoned where something had to end and begin, a required job skill supported by derivative uses of the term arche which include: a 'circular ring or wall around a city'; a 'circular or cyclic chorus danced around an altar'; 'wreath'; and 'a ring to pass the reins through'. Thus he could knowingly site at divisions on chora edges, horus, or 'boundary stones'. Arche was firstly an original and exquisite understanding about where grounds had to begin and end by virtue of their broader context. An Atlas of familiarity, only the educated wanax could bear (up) the visionary arche allowing him to see his entire world's footings and peaks.

But with arche no longer the educated vision of any one person, and turning on elected officials, this 'broad sight' became a topic of public debate. Arche now bent on the opinions of the basileus become 'a common group', called demos, with each member now standing in equal relation to his fellow.[15] Spatially the old megaron centered arrangement was rearticulated to favor a plateau or outcropping upon which was sited the temple, and alongside of it at the plane of the ground, this new group's 'conference-space' or agora (meeting place). It is here in the eighth to seventh centuries that a bureaucratically occupied class of urban dwellers called politae emerged. For having no absolute monarch, the older temenos organization had to grip around the decision-making demos increasingly obliged to be away from the stable or the shipyard — their active participation in a democracy mandating proximity. As a new cultural weave, this lifestyle as urban polis, or 'city', more and more so became one marked by real feelings of passion in the agora rather than in the fields, battle, or the temple. Speech became the craft and skill needed to play in debates regarding arche which slowly aired previously cloistered areas of knowledge. With a collective council called strategos put in charge of locating all horus on the chora, religious ceremony, agricultural practice, military tactics, and personal conduct all began to undergo a related public surveillance. Institution would now thus hinge on polemic and open debate. The architectural effects of this new social-spatial arrangement would unavoidably impact the temple and its configuration to the transparencies of an urban society as polis, and the inherently mysterious and gritty mater nursing it.

above:
Nike of Samothrace,
after 308 B.C.

the winged temple

Originally the summit of humility, a 'gift' built to the mater or ground casting mortality, temples slowly contorted to continue embodying Her sacrifice and to incorporate political accessibility. It was here in the eighth to seventh centuries that temple design troped the megaron into a core naos housing a divine image or goddess-head, draped in turn by an exterior forest of evenly spaced columns. These veiling avenues were called ptera, or 'wings'[16]. Termed peripteral, an early one to make this transition was of Hera at Samos. Home to a wooden image of Hera, a xoanon or 'bound animate-sculpture', the temple in sum was sited in a swamp thick with the lygos or willow tree sacred to her.[17] First a collection of limestone and mud brick walls with a pitched roof supported by an interior row of fluted-timber, it was all of a hundred feet long. But in the middle of the eighth century, it's column turned outward with roof extended to cover them. Pausinias records a description of this shift – one helpful not for just identifying the new columnar frames character, but for reinforcing it's precursor as one of xulon or wood. [18] Originally built to Apollo Daphnephoros (Laurel-Bearer) out of laurel-wood and twigs, when redesigned the temple was said to have been rebuilt by a man called Pteras. Pteras name means 'wingy' with pteron meaning 'wing' or 'sail' and its derivative pteroma the term for the new porch around the temple.

Now the most famous form, temple still upheld the matter of Divinity. Slowly incorporating more stone, it rose from a typically three-stepped base. This was composed of krepis (shoe) and stylobate (upright standing place). Although stylobate has modernly come to mean this whole podium, this was not the case. Stylobate referred only to the uppermost surface of the krepis. Analogous to one foot in front of the other, day following night, the furrows of the field, Boreas (the 'wind-serpent') in the grain, the lyrical waves of the flute, lunar tides, a choppy sea, and the oars of a ship, this krepis is usually misconstrued as 'steps'. This was not the case either. In dimension krepis 'steps' were far too large for human use. Worshippers availing the temple had to use intermediate blocks dividing them at specific points. By their very size krepis were thus a serious gesture. If any thesis that the temple is a recollection of the mater is fair, then these massive 'steppings' bear a remarkable resemblance to the nature of the Mediterranean landscape, one designated 80% 'mountain country'.[19] Was this land to be cultivated, it would have had to been done so by terrace farming, a stepped means still widespread.[20] The orchestrated impact of this vast civic grooming upon the mater must have seemed, like the seasons and the furrows themselves, a 'rhythmic courtship'. As a riveting seduction upon which so much of their existence hinged, prone to devastation by drought, disease, and flood, the worship paid to this 'earth-folding' must have been staggering.

Rowed and astride this 'wavy basis', the krepis, were the ax-carved columns - they still again with the enfilade sense due fluting. Perhaps ax-carved because the chord-shaped edge of an ax sinks perfectly into a flute.[21] Homer helps us to consider such kinship amidst ax and timber in The Illiad where when Ajax strikes down Imbrios,

> '... he fell like an ash which is cut with the bronze axe on the peak of a mountain seen from afar and brings down its *tender leaves to the ground."*[22]

A trope *Homer* uses repeatedly, it appears again when Asios is slain by Diomedes.

> "... he fell as an oak falls, or a poplar, or a tall pine, which craftsman cut down in the mountains with their newly whetted axes..."[23]

The notorious poetic implication of a X, and its means as a fluting tool, is now seeming all the more conspicuous against the often-cited passage of Vitruvius who said flutes were meant to resemble the folds, or ptux, in a chiton or robe.[24] With chiton as woven material sliced and made integral by thousands of little X or chi, Vitruvius's point although maybe poetic of the timber as a 'garmenting of the ax' carving into it, seems to imply a more mortal involvement. After all, chiton are worn by people. If timber-column are aspects of the mater, might fluting then somehow be a rhythmic axis or weaving of not just mortal about Her, but Her about mortal? In other words, fluting as not just mortal harvesting mater, but mater harvesting mortal? With temples being firstly about sacrifice - and we know the thysia performed on the temple steps always involved the smiting of an oxen forehead with ax - fluting may simply involve a reciprocal instance of trophy.[25] For temples were not only about the past sacrifice of the mater fabric to hungry mortals, they were equally about the current mortal sacrifice to mater. With timber-felling for column as a theft, or a hunt, carving them well may have thus been a sacrifice of the first-born fruits of mortality, their lives won or labor. The rhythmic 'chop-chop-chop' of the tree-felling fluted into Her wooden flesh, thereby demonstrating the most immediate offering possible by a mortal hand snarled in Her flesh of bronze and timber. In this grooming 'exchange', mater scarring wrought by this tragedy, as either ugly disfigurement or handsome grooming, was thus of their making. As murder or sacrifice, it was thus both of theirs. A tricky little twist, somewhat like a crow eating a 'coy oat' and then depositing it in some far away valley, such mortal/ immortal incorporation was imagined to provide both the mater with brute labour for ontic complexity, as well as divine material for the brutes to build their own bodies. Chora, as a cultivation of this event of ceaseless mending and ammending of the mater, their known world as 'garment of ground', was thereby one they participated in; and was as well, one she would hold them liable for.

A Greek myth illustrating the proper use of a 'X change' is found in Ixion. Proposing to marry Dia (light) and provide rich bridal gifts, he invited her father Eioneus to a banquet. But Eioneus did not make it to the feast for Ixion had laid a pitfall in front of the palace — into which the father fell and perished. As retribution Zeus later commanded that Ixion repeat the words 'benefactors deserve honour' and be eternally bound to a fiery wheel wobbling aimlessly through the sky. Like a kid not owning up to having just cut down a cherry tree, this short-sighted Ixion's prison-wheel had no axle, no orientation. His story tells about exercise of not just the ax, the healthy exercise of human appetites, but making amends to that yielding this ax well. By possessing flutes, timber-column thus recommended how they came to be.

Atop these 'wave-tossed children', or krepis born column, was the two-part capital. Sitting on a trachelos or necking, the Doric example had on top an echinus or a bristly sort of flower. In both the later Ionic and Corinthian, this echinus grew to involve volutes or horns, fronded hair, and prickly acanthus foliage. Bearing atop all of this, as capital, was the hefty epistylum or entablature. It was composed of triglyphs (thighs), metopes (brow), and guttae (body drops). Biting outward of the epistylum were the dentils (teeth) and lastly crown (corona).

With the rise of the polis and its growing cultural life in the agora, these newly sprouted ptera, while still redressing and giving stature to ground, added an interstitial space for the now equalized Greek citizenry to dwell. In the sacrificial rites they add a new moment to the temple experience, one engendering independent reflection. Like the oars of a ship, the wings of an eagle, or the roots of a great oak, this also was leverage.

classic design seed

Through researching the ground, a fecundity, with little tricks like coyly propping up grain, berry, and acorn in May, only to have them bitten off and scattered to broader sites by an August wind, crows, or hungry men, peripteral temple designers reckoned paradeigma, or 'eternal pattern'. For it was through that veiling forest of ptera they sprout up about the core naos, that their own little mortal version would be staged. These ptera of the temple, divisively the ax in-between the cultural life outside and the thysia climaxing inside, benefited ground and mortals both because it was in their frame worshippers would be saddled by a magical realization – the fitful humility of'unity. For to catch any sight of the tremendous sacrificial procession parading up to the temple, our now equalized citizen would have to first take up a position allowing him to see. This means he would have to peer out by moving under that massive lintel. It in turn straddling those two fluted bearers. Like great oaks in a summer wind, or deckhands at sea, with our trio atop the outcropping and all precariously surfing krepis under-foot, they proudly wavered in unison. But he even more so. Like the wing of a great gull, or the gape of a ship, his jaw dropped between a mysterious and dynamic holding up on the one hand, and the fore ground majestically welling this offering up toward altar on the other. The chora! That venous and circulatory nurse with stony walled route, bearing mud-brick and wooden frames, his very culture itself suckling grain and olive, which in turn sap the distant loam and spring of the stepped horizon. Under a life-crushing entablature dripping guttae, our worshipper stood there caught. Donned in chiton, a clay-footed patriot transfixed alongside those interminable flutes, he fought to gather and bear the weight of this all, his very person's possibility. Then in this quiet suicide, he bravely crept inward from amidst his own two feet. He examined his own mortality. Xenophon records for us that this introspection would have included thousands of garlanded livestock kicking up dust as they were escorted and marched in from the outlying chora. As great civic thysia, a procession of musicians, calvary, wine, and all manner of produce (male and maiden too), this must have seemed a river of divine secretion pulsing floods of earthenware heralded in from every heading[26]. With pied eyes made of this river, he and his like could glean these ptera remand to bear their own arche — to under-stand. Like the very columnar frame itself, the ground they stood upon was what they should turn to gather and hold up. Astounded each reckoned the original meaning of twisting chora into mortality, and mortality back into chora — and thus on the heels of this vision ... sinister prospect of devising ever more subtle ways to further it.

For after this ritual, pondering one foot in front of the other, each would travel home to their distant, little expert sites of dwelling. Out there, deep in their 'home field' of this great chorus of Life, be it the georgian farm or the agora, they could now see through this arche, through the daily disguise, to dig out more sense, more advantage ... more Life. Like autumnal grains on a gust, or bees thieving pollen from a rose, the lascivious patrons of the ptera would sweep simple ground to new heights. Out of a desperate and violent hunger they were forced to devour that which they worshipped most – but they struggled heroically to give it back stature. These building wings were a communion and a genesis, an original font of mortal wonder and divine fluting of life's one true song — architecture.

Unquestionably we no longer live in a world where the experiential elements of our ground, the hard two-fisted phenomena like light, dark, rocks, water, tree, or wind, really matter in daily life. Born along in this state of cultural vision, it is difficult to spot fonts of our mortality in a manner at all synchronous with that of our classical fathers. After all, how many of us will stand on a porch tomorrow worrying about having to go out and plow for our daily bread? Our concerns have grown discursive, more thought — less material. We as architects do not draft graphite lines anymore; we coolly depress televisual keys. But do our chests still not pulse? Don't we breathe? We are happenstance, biologic beings, mnemonically inhaling a ground both of and upon which we act. Our sun still rises, our winds still sweep across us, and our seasons have yet not to change. Still putting one foot in front of the last, we are living in an immediate and defining ground we could bite off, and then hold up to the light of our mortality. A down to earth and earnest architecture hungry to eat from a 'classical plate' could begin by listening to it, perhaps just dancing out, or echoing, its 'sense and sounds'. Like classic archon and flute-maker of old, our modern aim is to honestly breathe the animate material freely at play and on our site. Then, skillfully handle it through our mortal appetites into an organization of resounding interests – an amendment. In other words, like the early hunter desperately hungry yet hopelessly fallen in love with his prey, who immortally prays for a meaningful way to spare it from complete extermination, the architectural disruption which our mortal program demands might configure in a manner to savor 'the horns of the beast'. Given that there is a desirable, nourishing, and thus material site, it must have a depth to its attraction. Like the apple it must have a tree with roots. A sensible design would research exactly this quality. Wholly self-interested, thoroughly subjective, it would decadently couch itself ever deeper into the garment of the native beauty. For this rabid architecture, a building simply makes the site, rather than ignorantly numb atop it. Realizing that this rule applies to all the materials, means, and tools of the effort, gesturing in the mediating tongue of trope, and then allegorical thematic, an archaeological hunt to slyly snare these branches secret 'ways of being' amidst ours, might be a good start.

the exchange

A stock exchange, at best a sort of chora caretakers association, is not a temple. Yet although rites ancient or modern will not be enacted in it — no cows will parade up to it, incense will not be burned, hymns to a deity will not be sung — unmistakably it does have a vast piece of world marched into and organized by it. Rain forests in Chile, coal mountains in Tennessee, oceans of fish in Maine, banana plantations in Mexico, oil refineries in Arabia, electric companies, HMO's, tanneries, canneries, desalination plants, and all of the dirt, steel wood, and sweat that goes into them, are there. It is just that because of some bad architecture their sense is nearly undetectable in the march of contracts, inked checks, trade slips, and e-things, which should be troping them. Others incompetence never excuses our own.

Granted the role of the Exchange, with the archon or leadership of countries within its effect, may be beyond today's scrutiny. Honest address of the life, the folks, and the lands it involves, is not. The apples of Upstate New York farms are not. Neither is the really big apple at 15 Broad Street — 'the neo-classical' built in earnest by our ancestors. Even of imaginable architectural projects few approach the extreme importance of housing this

ground of the living order. Architects, like an Ancient Greek citizen peering out from between the columns, need to make feel and understand the wonderfull humility of this.

> According to tradition, the NYSE was founded under the leafy canopy of a buttonwood. We know little about the origins of this famous tree, but we do know a great deal about its colorful past.
>
> The buttonwood was located on the north side of Wall Street toward the eastern end, between William and Pearl Streets. It undoubtedly was an outstanding representative of the species of plane tree, or sycamore, known as Platanus Occidentalis. The plane tree is the largest hardwood in the eastern United States, often reaching a height of 150 feet with a diameter of 8 to 15 feet. The fruit of the plane tree is a hard brown ball that looks like a button — whence the name buttonwood... Buttonwoods are solitary trees and often grow in isolation from others of their kind. Soaring and majestic, the Wall Street buttonwood would have been all the more striking in a lower Manhattan largely devoid of any type of tall timber ... whether it actually happened that way is less important than the buttonwood's symbolization of a time when the NYSE trading post was a living tree on a busy commercial thoroughfare.[27]

Perhaps Aristotle may have liked 'according to tradition' as it expresses the research aspect of classicism. 'The allegorical symbol of a living tree on an urban avenue is echoed in the "foundation myth" of Apollo's 'broad leave tree' aspect. That in the neo-classical culture of America, a mind open to this local tree — seeing it as a similar to it, and later erecting a Corinthian façade, was fairly well educated and thus acted *accordingly*. Beyond spinning institutional character, these founders went further and helped recollect and seat a parent-like culture. indicative of true civility. Classical architectural expression has always incorporated the tree as a divine aspect demonstrative of a living universe. The above citation, extracted from a full 'tree' chapter in an biographical text commissioned by the NYSE, must be seen as further indication of its classical character. Pursuing not only a native force of the original site and institution which organizes so much of our worldly ground, this myth feasts upon a deeply originating one of our whole occidental world. Clearly the NYSE and its founders have strong ideas about the incorporation of ground, the roots of classicism, and their "X" changes.

above, left to right:

The Cow Byre faces south on the cool meadow. c. 1792 [Jean Jacques Lequeu.]

Head of Demeter. Terra-Cotta panel. Museo Nazionale Romano delle Terme. Tome, Italy. [Photo courtesy: Art Resource.]

The earth is its (Wisdom) Nurse. *Nutrix ejus terra est.* 1618 etching by Michael Maier.

1940 publicity shot of Veronica Lake, for Paramount Pictures *I Wanted Wings*.

the allegory of 15 broad street – pesephone's sea

Exhausting all them year of industry,
Stepped in an oily tangle of manhole, tailpipe, and howly backsteet
that Cadillac tide rolls again
School kids craning for a view,
try your brickpile shores of soot, asphalt, and sweat
- damn concrete aisle now grown so rotten with mice
but boy how they do make fast prayers for the dirty weave

Come out now Steffi, croon them radio siren,
casting it all the way out to the deserts of Cali
The aurora is fast rising behind you,
New England rays is runnin across your beach and apple

Darn Darn Darn
Yeah, wonderful stainless train, John Wayne ratchet'n up in that dark
nightclub worm for some tender white bait
yet never really catching on to your little hitch
He'll most never know it's there
just a blind cigarette dragon of rose and ivy tongue

Come out now Steffi, croon them radio siren,
casting it all the way out to the deserts of Cali
The aurora is fast rising behind you,
New England rays is runnin across your beach and apple

Purple mountains majesty, Lord I hungered to have ya out
Aw Steff
I knew you had barbs and thunderous route
I'd wouldn't a scared
I had mustang, falcon, and hog gassed out back

If only I'd made it to your porch
at least I might have told ya, till next time darlin,
good luck, goodbye ... Stephanie

- Wall Street, New York City, Autumn 2000.

NOTES

[1] Joan Warner, "Trading Places" in *Grid* (1:4, Fall 1999).: 79-81.

[2] *ibid.*, p. 79.

[3] Le Corbusier [Charles-Edouard Jeanneret Gris]. "A Remarkable Architectural Sight" pt. 2, sec. 2 of *When The Cathedrals Were White,* trans. Francis E. Hyslop Jr. (New York: Reynal & Hitchcock, 1947). p. 73-74.

[4] *ibid.*

[5] With Michael Ventris 1952 decipherment of the Mycenean Linear B scripts a flurry of new examinations of archaic Grecian culture has been put in play. Prominent figures effected (to varying degrees) by this include: Joseph Rykwert, George Dumezil, Jean-Pierre Vernant, Alberto Perez-Gomez, George Hersey, and Indra Kagis McKwen.

[6] Plato, *Meno.* 97d-98a.

[7] The Greek word for mother is *meter*, however Michael Ventris' decipherment of the Mycenaen Linear B scripts, suggest that certain dialects would transliterate as *mater*. A more comprehensive review can be found in Paul MacKendrick. *The Greek Stones Speak.* (New York: W.W. Norton & Company, 1981). p. 90.

[8] Plato, *Laws.* 6.778 D.

[9] See J.J. Bachofen's essay "Sanctum and Sacrum" in *Myth, Religion, and Mother Right: Selected Writings of J.J. Bachofen,* trans. Ralph Manheim. (Princeton: Princeton University Press, 1967).

[10] Pliny, *Historia Naturalis.* 12.1, 12.2.

[11] Both oak and beech mast use as food is born out by archaeological evidence, contemporary literature, and modern practice. Furthermore the nutritional value of dried acorn versus barley is higher on every count except albumen.

[12] Greek law would later embody this metonymic principle by declaring a specific divinity as titleholder to a *chorion*, or parcel of land. Xenophon records the following inscription on a stele he placed on a *chorion* of his custodianship, *"This area is consecrated to Artemis: whosoever has it in his possession and makes use of it, must offer a tithe every year. From the profit he will maintain the sanctuary in its proper condition. Should anyone neglect this, it will not pass unnoticed by the Goddess."* Xenophon, *Anabasis.* 5.3.4-13.

[13] see Indra Kagis McEwen. *Socrates' Ancestor.* (MIT Press: Cambridge, 1993).

[14] examples include: the Mycenaen *Palace at Pylos* containing a *megaron* in which the hearth is surrounded by four timber columns of 32 flutes each; and the Minoan *Palace at Knossos* in the *Hall of the Double Axes* the throne is surrounded by four timber columns of 28 flutes each. An in-depth study of timber use in the ancient Mediterranean can be found in Russell Meiggs. *Trees and Timber in the Ancient Mediterranean World.* (Oxford and New York: Oxford University Press, 1982).

[15] My examination of Democracy was in no small measure critically begun through my participation in Dr. Arthur H. Chen's research project entitled *'Democracy Machine: A Monument to Celebrate The Twenty-five Hundredth Year of Democracy'*. Published as "Democracy Machine" in *Intersight: The Journal of The School of Architecture and Planning.* (3, 1995) 33.

[16] Pliny, *Hist.* p. 36.31.

[17] An excellent modern description this temple's landscape refer to Vincent Scully. "The Temple. Hera" chap. 4 of *The Earth, The Temple, and the Gods.* (New Haven and London: Yale University Press, 1962).

[18] Pausanias, *Description of Greece.* 10.5.1.

[19] An in depth study of ancient Grecian geography may be found in Signe Isager and Jens Erik Skysgard. "The Geopgraphical Background", chap. 1 of *Ancient Greek Agriculture.* (London and New York: Routledge, 1992). p. 17.

[20] *ibid.*, p. 15.

[21] This possibility of flute crafting was first made aware to me in Joseph Rykwert. *The Dancing Column.* (Cambridge: MIT Press, 1996). p. 177.

[22] Homer, *Illiad.* 13.178.

[23] *ibid.*,13.389-91

[24] Vitruvius, *The Ten Books on Architecture*, 4.1.7.

[25] A very detailed description of the great civic sacrifice *thusia* may be found in Louise Bruit Zaidman and Paulibe Schmitt Pantel. "Rituals." chap. 4 in *Religion in the Ancient Greek City,* trans.Paul Cartledge. (Cambridge: Cambridge University Press, 1997). p.34-36. This possibility of flute crafting is in Rykwert. *op. cit.,* p. 177.

[26] According to Xenophon, in the year 370, more than 1000 oxen and more than 10,000 other animals were delivered from Thessaly for offering at the Pythia. *Hellenica.* 6.4.29.

[27] from: "Whatever Happened to The Buttonwood Tree?" in chap. 1 *The New York Stock Exchange: The First Two Hundred Years.* ed. James E. Buck. (Greenwich Publishing Group, 1992). It is critical to regard that the *NYSE commissioned* the research and publication of this book, implying an architectural sense.

jackson

herzberg

kempf

ellin

buscaglia

G E O

INTRODUCED BY ALEX BITTERMAN

Do boundaries separate or do boundaries envelop? Geographic boundaries — boundaries "of" the map — divide populations, but also help to define community and identity for those same populations. Boundaries can be desolate — "no man's land" — or can be zones of convergence as is the case with Niagara Falls, New York and Niagara Falls, Ontario, Canada.

This section investigates the notion of boundary. Whether geographic or urban, natural or political, boundaries are the "invisible" constructs of the human mind which allow us to define place as well as space.

In this section: David Herzberg examines the historical genesis of the Niagara Region and centered about the international divide marked by the Niagara Gorge. Petra Kempf considers the urban boundary and its potential as an incubator for architecture. The "imaginary" maps of José Buscaglia graphically portray a rich history of cultural identity based on geographic separation. Bruce Jackson chronichles the effort to, literally, bridge two countries and the complications which ensue. Nan Ellin discusses the impact of boundaries and division on the urban fabric.

print at left:

Puerto Rico, U.S.A.

by José Buscaglia. Mr. Buscaglia's contribution, *14 Imaginary Maps of Precision/14 Mapas de Precisiones Imaginativas* begins on page 114.

BRUCE JACKSON

BEAUTY & THE BRIDGE

beginnings

There had been conversations about and attempts at building a bridge between Fort Erie and Buffalo going back at least to 1851. For a variety of political, economic and technical reasons nothing happened until 1919 when a group of twenty-five Americans and Canadians led by Buffalo steel magnate Frank Baird, set up the Buffalo and Fort Erie Bridge Corporation. They put up $50,000 of their own money to get the corporation going, and then set out to raise $4,500,000 in bonds for the actual construction. The bonds were mostly sold locally, and the offering was oversubscribed before the first offering day was out. People on both sides of the river really wanted the bridge, they liked the idea of the bridge, they were willing to invest their own money to have the bridge.

Some people wanted to name the bridge after Baird, but he'd have none of that. It would be called the Peace Bridge, in commemoration of the century of peace between Canada and the United States following the end of the War of 1812. Had it not been for the assassination of the Grand Duke Ferdinand in Sarajevo and the Great War, they probably would have gotten the job done closer to the real anniversary.

The first automobile to make an official crossing was driven by Edward J. Lupfer, the bridge company's chief engineer, on March 13, 1927. The Bridge opened to the public on June 1 of that year. Some people say that when the Peace Bridge opened for business the happiest Americans were those who liked summering along Lake Erie's sparsely populated Canadian shoreline but hated waiting to board the ferry that was the only way for them to cross the swift Niagara river between Buffalo and Fort Erie. Others insist that the happiest were the Americans who wanted the pleasures of booze without the sordidness of bootleggers and revenue agents.

Frank Baird and other men of vision surely understood the long-term commercial implications of easy traffic across this part of the border, but for most people the opening of the Peace Bridge was, well, just really nice. The original toll schedule had rates for trucks — but it also had rates for pedestrians, bicycles, horses, horse-drawn carriages, automobiles, and hearses.

opposite:
Peace Bridge
(from Fort Erie, Ontario)

Bruce Jackson is SUNY Distinguished Professor and Samuel P. Capen Professor of American Culture at State University of New York at Buffalo. Before joining the UB faculty in 1967 he was a junior fellow in the Harvard Society of Fellows. He has received grants or fellowships from the John Simon Guggenheim Foundation, American Council of Learned Societies, National Endowment for the Arts, National Endowment for the Humanities, New York Council for the Humanities, and other agencies and foundations. He is the author or editor of 21 books. His articles have appeared in many scholarly journals, as well as *Harpers', Atlantic Monthly, Antioch Review*, *New York Times Magazine*, *Nation*, *New Republic, Society, Rolling Stone*, and other general interest publications. His documentary films have been shown at the Museum of Modern Art, the Library of Congress, at major international film festivals, and have been broadcast in the United States, France, and Germany. He recorded and edited eight ethnographic sound albums, one of which, *Wake Up Dead Man*, was nominated for a Grammy. Between August 1998 and March 2001, he wrote 49 articles about Peace Bridge politics for *Artvoice*, a weekly newspaper in Buffalo, New York.

above, left to right:
all photos, The Parker Truss

Edward Lupfer's design was simple and elegant: a series of six steel arches would support the two-lane cobblestone roadway that would cross from Fort Erie, Ontario, to Fort Porter on the northern end of Front Park, the crown jewel of the park and parkway system Frederick Law Olmsted had designed for Buffalo. The bridge, Lupfer thought, would complement Olmsted's landscape.

Would that it had been so. Lupfer's design was spoiled from the beginning. Over the years, the various roads and processing buildings linked to the bridge made Olmsted's fine park all but unusable. The Peace Bridge turned the crown jewel into an eyesore.

The U.S. Coast Guard insisted that the segment of the bridge crossing the Black Rock Canal and making the landfall in the U.S. would have to be one hundred feet high from corner to corner — not just in the middle or in most of the middle, but all the way across. Tall ships had once used that canal and tall ships might come again, so the bridge had to be ready for them. No steel arch going to the Fort Porter high ground could possibly accomplish that. So Edward Lupfer's elegant design was mutilated before the first spade of earth was turned: instead of a sixth arch making the American landfall there was the looming dark box of a Parker truss supporting the roadway from above, rupturing the smooth line of the border road.

That's why the Peace Bridge has always been nicer to look at from the Canadian than the American side. The Canadians had the arches and open sky above the bridge; Americans had the big ugly truss.

But a lovely design spoiled by bureaucratic intransigence wasn't the only thing to interfere with Frank Baird's dream. Within a few years of the bridge's grand opening (attended by the Prince of Wales, the vice president of the United States, and thousands of swells and ordinary folks) there was also a matter of grim economics. The Great Depression reduced traffic across the bridge by pleasure seekers and by people engaged in ordinary commerce, and the repeal of Prohibition ended traffic across the bridge by the merely thirsty.

In 1933, the Bridge Company sought and got governmental salvation. Over the next year, three separate pieces of legislation in Ottawa, Albany, and Washington, D.C., created the Buffalo and Fort Erie Public Bridge Authority, a public benefit corporation. The corporation was supposed to operate the bridge until it made enough money to pay off its bonds and turn over the bridge to the ordinary transportation agencies in Ontario and New York. The corporation made money, a huge amount of it, but it never did pay off its bonds, and it is now not one bit closer to turning over its worldly goods to the governments that created it than it was on the day it came into being.

above, left to right:
Peace Bridge
(from Fort Erie, Ontario)

neither | nor

New York public benefit corporations exist in a land of deliberate legal ambiguity: they're set up by governments but they behave like private corporations. They can partake of benefits of government status — their property and bonds are tax exempt, for example — but they control their own resources. They can make contracts that state legislators cannot subsequently undo or even meddle with[1]; they needn't engage in competitive bidding (unless more than half the board members were appointed by the governor and/or are on the board because of New York public offices they otherwise hold); except for annual financial reports their records are not open to public inspection (as are the records of ordinary government agencies); they can refinance their outstanding debt by issuing replacement bonds; and, in many instances, they don't have to hold public hearings before beginning new construction.

Public authorities are designed to build something — a bridge, tunnel, roadway. They collect tolls from the public for the use of what they've built. When their construction bonds are paid off, they are supposed to go out of business and whatever they built is to be turned over to the people. In practice, dissolution rarely happens. Public authorities are like any other animal: their first instinct is self-preservation. Once established, most of them find ways to keep going and going and going.

The two most common devices for authority self-perpetuation are refinancing old bonds and engaging in new construction that justifies issuing new bonds. "If an authority ceased to build," wrote Robert A. Caro in his magisterial biography of Robert Moses, "it would die; if all it did was collect tolls, the tolls would pay off its bonds and when the bonds were paid off it would have no choice but to go out of existence. Only by continually embarking on new projects — which would require new bond issues—could an authority remain viable."[2]

For the Buffalo and Fort Erie Public Bridge Authority, there has always been what seemed a good reason for refinancing and always a demonstrable need for expansion. The major banks in the region have been their allies in these endeavors because the commissions on the new and reissued bonds are huge and, from the point of view of the general public, invisible.

raiding the cash

The Authority at first had nine members, six from the US and three from Canada. It acquired all the assets and debts of the financially-strapped Buffalo and Fort Erie Bridge Corporation. With the debts restructured and almost no taxes to pay, the Authority was immediately on firm financial footing, which it has never lost.

In 1957, New York State created the Niagara Frontier Port Authority (subsequently the Niagara Frontier Transportation Authority) and tried to tuck the by-then-profitable Peace Bridge into it. The board members of the Buffalo and Fort Erie Public Bridge Authority balked. They asked New York Attorney General Jacob Javits for a ruling: could the New York Legislature take over an organization created by the government of New York, the government of Canada and the U.S. Congress? Javits said no, the state's reach wasn't that long.

So the ownership papers were redrawn once again. There were four key changes:

· The bridge would be directly tied to no other agency, which meant it would remain fully independent.

· The two countries would divide excess revenues equally.

· The sunset, the date everything would be turned over to the two governments, was extended from whenever the outstanding bonds were paid off to 1992.

· Total board membership would increase to ten, with five members from each country.

The five Canadians are by law residents of the Province of Ontario appointed by the federal Minister of Transport in Ottawa. Two of the Americans are appointed by the Governor of New York, and three serve *ex officio*: the board chair of the Niagara Frontier Transportation Authority, the New York attorney general, and the director of the New York Department of Transportation. The three New York *ex officio* members usually appoint senior staff members to represent them, but sometimes they appoint instead people who made major campaign contributions to the party controlling the New York governor's office. That means at least seven and as many as ten of the board members are political appointees. In theory, the PBA is a nonpolitical board; in fact, it is anything but.

The 1957 restructuring would turn out to be of key importance at the century's end, when the PBA's expansion plans focused on a $200 million bridge and plaza construction project. Because the ten-person board had five Canadian members, the PBA was not longer subject to New York's laws on open and competitive bidding on construction contracts. Henceforth most of its most critical business would be handled in closed rooms.

expansion

In 1970, the New York Department of Transportation decided that bridge capacity would have to be expanded before very long, which meant the Public Bridge Authority would get to issue new construction bonds. The several governments extended the life of the Authority to 2020 and raised the Authority's debt limit. The Canadian government and the State of New York, agreed that, instead of splitting whatever cash was left over after payments were made, they would each get a flat $200,000 each year, and the Public Bridge Authority would keep the excess for development.

The Peace Bridge is a very profitable operation, so that excess is considerable. The PBA made a good deal of money from increases in ordinary passenger and truck traffic over the years, but after the North American Free Trade Alliance (NAFTA) went into effect on January 1, 1994 and the volume of truck traffic exploded, revenues from trucks quickly surpassed revenues from passenger vehicles. In 1998, the Peace Bridge reported income of $25,040,401 ($5,996,828 passenger tolls, $13,952,982 commercial tolls, $4,866,212 rentals, and $224,379 "other") and what their accountant terms an "excess of revenues over expenses" (what you and I would refer to as "profit") of $9,180,378. After paying all operating expenses and debt service, the Bridge made a 36.6% profit. If the Peace Bridge were a private corporation, this would be a joyous rate of return.[4]

Equally important is the fund balance, which is what they've accumulated. When you want to know how rich someone is, you don't look at what came in or what went out, you look at the fund balance. In 1998 the Authority had a fund balance of $64,668,291, up from $55,487,913 the year before. Absent some new and very expensive construction, the PBA was in danger of profiting itself out of existence. No way were they going to permit that to happen.

Except for the time the Americans tried to scoop up the cash reserves and the board representation was changed, hardly anyone ever paid attention to the Buffalo and Fort Erie Public Bridge Authority. Its job was simple: maintain the bridge and keep tolls at a level that kept the corporation in the black. They met once a month or so and did mostly dull business, like deciding who would get paving, painting and derusting contracts; setting the terms of retirement and medical plans; occasionally voting special death benefits for the families of longtime employees; deciding which banks would get the commissions for handling their bonds. They went along for years with a single engineering consultant handling all their major planning and maintenance, they doled out sweetheart maintenance and purchase contracts on both sides of the border, they spread the bond commission money around. They did small or medium-sized construction projects, like building a duty-free shop on the American bridge plaza (which caused messy traffic problems, but it was a moneymaker) and they worked hard to keep Fort Erie unambiguously happy: the Bridge Authority built a huge duty free store in Fort Erie, as well as a commercial truck processing plaza, a new courthouse, a new city hall, a new two-surface skating rink and a new community center. A lifetime resident of Fort Erie said: "This is a small town. You throw $100,000 around and it's a big deal. These people are throwing millions. The courthouse. The town hall. The double-surface rink. That's $20 million in a town the total real estate assessment of which is maybe $58 million. If you were mayor what would you do when they told you they wanted something?" And another said, "The Bridge contributes to everything over here. Whatever Fort Erie wants, they get. And whatever the PBA wants, Fort Erie gives."

Had the PBA been an ordinary government agency rather than an authority there would have been public hearings about the justification for and placement of all that construction, but it *was* an authority so the PBA's ten directors just met and did what they thought best. The NAFTA-driven tolls were pouring in, Fort Erie would agree to any plan the PBA had, Buffalo hardly paid attention to the PBA at all. Things were going very well indeed.

Then they decided to expand the bridge itself, and everything went haywire.

the center does not hold

Because of the increase in truck traffic and the likelihood that the truck traffic would continue increasing for the next decade, the PBA decided to expand bridge capacity. This meant adding more lanes to the crossing and improving customs and immigration facilities at the American plaza. Critics would later argue that all of the current congestion problems could be handled by computerizing the customs and immigration operations and moving them to an international zone on the Canadian side, but the PBA insists that would be ameliorative, but sooner or later more lanes would be needed.

They decided to build a second steel bridge, a copy in all details but one of the bridge Frank Baird and Edward J. Lupfer had built three-quarters of a century earlier. Since the U.S. Coast Guard still held firm to its 100-foot-clearance requirement, the PBA and its engineering consultant, Parsons/DeLeuw, designed a truss a little less bulky than the original. They said that after the second bridge was up they'd shut down the old bridge for a while and they'd redeck it and they might redo its truss to match the one on the new bridge. The new bridge with its new links to the New York Thruway would of course require an expanded processing plaza, which meant it would consume even more of the surviving remnants of Olmsted's Front Park.

The PBA insisted that the plaza and bridge expansion projects were independent of one another, and said they were still considering bridge design options. They even had some public hearings about design. Opponents were quick to point out that once you build a plaza with all its connecting ramps and roads, and you're committed to keeping things on the Canadian side as they are, you've pretty much limited what kinds of bridges might be built linking the two plazas.

Later evidence revealed, and one of the two bridge administrators admitted, that they'd decided to ignore all expansion alternatives other than a companion span and, failing at that, widening the present bridge, years before they went public with any of this.

This is documented in the *Peace Bridge Capacity Expansion: Draft Environmental Assessment,* a report prepared by the Public Bridge Authority in September 1996. Chapter three, "Bridge Crossing Alternatives," reports on a structural design conference held in September 1994. "The Conference was attended by the Bridge Authority and representatives of the four consulting engineering companies." Nobody from the general public, no designers with other ideas, nobody but the PBA, its staff, and the engineering firms it was paying to provide advice.

Here is the key paragraph, the one that articulates the policy decision that caused all the trouble:

> The Structural Conference concluded that capacity expansion of the existing bridge would be required within the very near future. Therefore, the group of consulting engineers collectively prepared and identified preliminary alternatives for expanding the bridge's capacity. The alternatives included widening the existing structure, or alternatively constructing a parallel structure either to the north or south of the existing bridge, that would be visually compatible with the existing bridge.

There was no consideration at all of entirely replacing the old bridge. The consulting engineers were never asked or allowed to deal with that possibility.[3]

Jack Cullen, a Buffalo businessman, and Clinton Brown, a Buffalo architect, thought something much better could be done with a new crossing. Rather than duplicate the anachronistic steel structure with a design that had been spoiled from the beginning by the Coast Guard's fantasy of the return of tall ships, they said the PBA should put

above, left to right:

The Peace Bridge, 1945, George J. Hare

Buffalo toll plaza and the Parker Truss.

Postcard of Front Park bench, trees, grass and paths, circa 1907.

Front Park cracked asphalt, garbage mound, and bridge offices, 2000.

up a totally new six-lane bridge that would celebrate the significance of the border crossing, a bridge that incorporated twenty-first rather than nineteenth century bridge-building technology, a bridge people might like to look at. They got hundreds of people to endorse a group they called "SuperSpan Upper Niagara PLC." SuperSpan never had a bridge design, just the idea that a well-designed bridge made far more sense than a badly-designed bridge. The most important thing about the SuperSpan group was, they got people to think about possibilities. And about the possibility of one more architectural disaster if something weren't done to get the PBA to alter course.

why buffalo balked

Most people in the Buffalo area who are involved in or concerned about public affairs can recite a litany of public works and private construction projects that promised much but wound up subtracting substantially from the quality of city life:

· the Niagara section of the Thruway cuts the city off from the waterfront and routes high-pollution diesel trucks through populated areas;

· the new football stadium for the Buffalo Bills was located in a suburb 15 miles out of town;

· the Amherst campus of the University at Buffalo ripped a huge middle class population group and its associated services out of the city and deprived the university of the rich resources a city environ ment can provide;

· an expressway was built to make it easier for people to get into the city (route 33) with no thought given to the fact that it also made it easier for people to *get out* of the city, to work in the city but live elsewhere;

· a dark, squat, and inadequate convention center breaks one of city-designer Joseph Ellicott's functional radii;

· a huge office building squats across the foot of Main Street, literally blocking out the light;

· a light rail system designed to increase access to downtown stopped halfway to its destination because some people felt it would make access to the wealthy suburbs too easy to the nonwhite poor, and the construction process dragged on for years, destroying downtown retail business.

above, left to right:

PBA board member John Lopinski standing in front of an artist's rendition of the proposed twin span (devoid of the diesel trucks that would be its primary users).

Senator Charles Schumer listens to his aide, Jack O'Donnell, during a presentation by representatives of the Detroit Bridge Company.

PBA chairman Victor Martucci, flanked by Buffalo Common Council President James Pitts and Buffalo Mayor Anthony Masiello, announces that the PBA will obey Judge Eugene Fahey's order that it conduct a full environmental impact study, 15 November 2000.

Public Consensus Review Panel member Rev. Ivery Daniels inspects engineers' model of bridge options, WNED-TV studio, Buffalo, 7 March 2000.

Buffalo is probably not special in this kind of public works stupidity. Other cities at other phases in their history made the same kinds of blunders. But Buffalo did it a lot and did it over a brief period of time. The city isn't very big, and the blunders were coterminous with a decline in the city's economy because its major heavy industry—steel — moved to Asia. Because of that accumulation of wounds, the city is like someone riding a motorcycle on a busy highway: there is no such thing as a minor error. Do anything wrong now and it will hurt big.

What happened this time was a citizen's revolt. With only a few exceptions, the politicians were caught by surprise and had to play catchup. Two politicians were ahead of the curve: Senator Daniel Patrick Moynihan, long the most sensitive of U.S. senators to the importance of public works for the human spirit; and Buffalo Common Council President James Pitts. Anthony Masiello, the city's mayor, waffled, but finally came down on the side of those who wanted a rational bridge. Al D'Amato, New York's other U.S. senator during the early part of this battle, pretty much ignored it, but D'Amato's successor, Charles Schumer, joined Moynihan in aggressively working for something other than the twin span. (The area's congressman, John LaFalce, for reasons he has still never explained, sided with the Canadians and the steel bridge supporters.)

A group of young professionals looking for ways to make the area more viable, the New Millennium Group, took up the bridge issue as one of their projects. They knew the steel twin span wasn't good enough, but it wasn't until Bruno Freschi, dean of the UB School of Architecture and Planning, joined with San Francisco bridge engineer T.Y. Lin, and produced a spectacular design that the New Millennium Group had an image to accompany their passion.

Freschi is an internationally-known architect who holds the Order of Canada, that nation's highest civilian award. He is a Fellow of the Royal Architectural Institute of Canada, he was elected to the Royal Academy of Art, and he is an Associate Member of the American Institute of Architects. Lin is one of the world's most accomplished bridge makers.

They came up with a curved single-pylon cable-stayed bridge, made of concrete. It wasn't only gorgeous, it also avoided a mass of problems the steel-bridge promoters were trying very hard to obscure. The steel-bridge plan called for building one new three-lane bridge, then shutting down the 1927 three-lane bridge for two or three years of redecking and other repairs. During all that time heavy truck traffic would be rerouted through Buffalo's city streets, through Olmsted's Delaware Park, along expressways ordinarily full of passenger cars. City traffic would be a mess for most of a decade. Furthermore, the piers of the old bridge hadn't been inspected for more than two decades and many engineers are convinced that the entire 1927 bridge will need replacement before very long; they say any rehabilitation work will be of only transient value. Even if they're only partly right, in the not-too-

above, left to right:

Postcard of the Peace Bridge postmarked 1953, when the bridge was still two-lane and used primarily by passenger vehicles, and the New York Thruway had not made the waterfront inaccessible.

Wrong Way sign with Peace Bridge in the background.

Peace Bridge Duty Free Store, Fort Erie, Ontario.

Inside the Parker Truss, heading into Buffalo.

distant future, the crossing would be back to three lanes and the city would once again suffer years of disruption while the major construction of a second replacement bridge went on.

The Freschi-Lin bridge — or something like it — could be built with no interruption in ordinary traffic, with little disruption of the city's life. On the day it was finished, Freschi said, "You cut the ribbon on the new bridge and shut down the old bridge." For some opponents of the twin span, the Freschi-Lin design was what *had* to be built in that space; for others, it was an example of what *could* be done if the PBA would step back and think about the possibilities. Very soon, the names of other bridge builders were being bruited about, most notably the great Spanish architect Santiago Calatrava and the much-honored American engineer Eugene Figg.

For the Buffalo and Fort Erie Public Bridge Authority, the Freschi-Lin design was a nightmare come true. Before it appeared, people opposed to the twin span could only say, "It's ugly, we need something better." Once Freschi-Lin was on the table, people could say, "Tell us how and why your anachronistic steel bridge is better than this." And neither the PBA nor its most relentless supporters — the Buffalo Niagara Partnership (the current name for what used to be the Chamber of Commerce) and the *Buffalo News* (the city's only daily newspaper) — had an adequate response.

A small group of arguments against Freschi-Lin and any other concrete cable-stayed bridge were repeated again and again by PBA spokesmen: cable-stayed bridges are no good in this climate because they accumulate ice and fall down, all those cables would confuse birds and they'd crash into them at night, the single pylon would negatively alter Lake Erie's water levels, concrete bridges were far more expensive than a simple tried-and-true arched and trussed steel bridge, we're ready to go right now...

None of those arguements was true. None of them.

why were they like that?

There were two sets of interests involved in the decision to improve services at the Buffalo-Fort Erie border crossing — one local, the other distant — and they had virtually nothing in common with one another.

The distant interests — those beneficiaries of NAFTA in Ontario and much of the U.S. outside of Buffalo — were concerned about the flow of truck traffic across the border, nothing else. They had a single desideratum: as many trucks should make the trip as quickly and as cheaply as possible. The local interests — people who lived and worked in Buffalo and Fort Erie — were concerned about the impact of that truck traffic on their lives.

For Fort Erie, the trucks mean jobs and public structures. Fort Erie is almost totally dependent on the Peace Bridge. The Peace Bridge is the heart of Fort Erie's economy. The Bridge provides jobs directly and indirectly, and it provides swell buildings that the town could not otherwise afford. For Buffalo, it's not so simple. The area around the Peace Bridge Plaza has the city's highest incidence of lung disease, a result of diesel trucks slowing down and idling, many think. Those NAFTA manufacturing jobs don't come to Buffalo.

Someone on the PBA staff assumed or decided to act as if the old bridge had historical value. It had no significant historical value. There is nothing remarkable about its architecture and nothing significant about its existence. It is an aging bridge that will in a few years begin to have serious structural problems. It is a geriatric steel bridge that is becoming more and more expensive to maintain. The bridge staff and the Authority's directors assumed that, or chose to act as if, the bridge had to be maintained at any cost and, when they set about finding ways to increase bridge capacity, they assumed that the most aesthetically pleasing way to do it would be to twin the current bridge. Probably they had reasons that made sense at the time, but in retrospect the decision was absurd. And irresponsibly costly.

So they selected a klutzy design and an anachronistic technology. Nothing wrong with that: new projects often begin where the old one left off, What usually happens then is you give serious consideration to design and impact issues, look at the new technology available since the last time you did this, and then you go on from there. But the PBA never took that next step: they settled on a twin span made of steel using a bridge technology no one had used for decades and they fought for it in every forum they could find, expending vast sums of public money, opposing any one and any idea that conflicted with theirs.

vox populi

At least seven interlinked factors prevented the Buffalo and Public Bridge Authority from erecting their steel companion bridge:

opposite:
Model of the bridge designed by Bruno Freschi and T. Y. Lin.
[image © Bruno Freschi].

· The New Millennium Group organized forums, gathered and analyzed data about the current bridge, presented information about other bridge projects in other cities, contravened the PBA's claims about costs of its bridge, disruption to local traffic patterns, and so forth.

· Buffalo's mayor, Anthony Masiello, refused to issue easements the PBA needed to begin construction. Robert Moses famously said that once one of his shovels broke ground his projects were all but unstoppable. The mayor's refusal to issue the easements kept the PBA from getting that first shovel into the ground.

· Two highly-respected local service organizations, the Olmsted Conservancy and the Episcopal Church Home, filed suit in New York State Supreme court to force the New York Department of Environmental Conversation to withdraw its approval of the segmented project and instead to require the PBA to do a full environmental impact study of the combined bridge and plaza projects.

· The Community Foundation and the Margaret L. Wendt Foundation, two of the area's largest foundations, funded, in collaboration with Erie County and the City of Buffalo, the Public Consensus Review

Panel. The Panel, which everyone soon referred to as the PCRP, included representation from a wide range of commercial, governmental, and civic agencies, as well as neighborhood groups. (Fort Erie officials refused to join the panel because there weren't any Canadians on the panel, one of its officials said; John Lopinski, a Canadian and then-chairman of the Public Bridge Authority refused to take part for the same tautological reason.) The PCRP held several public hearings, at which scores of people gave ideas, provided technical information, testified about the impact of the proposed projects on them, offered suggestions for alternatives. The hearings were broadcast live on one of the city's two public radio stations and on the public television station, WNED. The PBA boycotted the proceedings until it seemed as if Judge Eugene Fahey was about to rule against the segmented project, whereupon they proposed to send Canadian engineers to join the engineers the PCRP had evaluating various designs. That turned out to be little more than a delaying and muddying operation. Several months later, the Public Consensus Review Panel recommended that the Public Bridge Authority build a six-lane signature bridge and that it move its operations out of Front Park so the Olmsted Conservancy could restore Olmsted's mutilated design. The PCRP had no status in law, but it provided a forum in which opposition to the steel companion span could develop focus and find support. The Public Consensus Review Panel gave voice to people the Public Bridge Authority wanted kept silent and kept the whole enterprise in public view long enough for legal opposition to take shape and become effective.

· One of the city's independent weekly newspapers, *Artvoice*, took up the bridge issue and, over a two-year period, published more than 60 articles on various aspects of it by several different writers (I was one of them). During most of this time *The Buffalo News*, the city's only daily newspaper, mostly endorsed the proposals of the PBA, and ignored or underplayed opposition to the PBA's plans. Tom Toles, the paper's Pulizer-Prize-winning cartoonist, regularly took tough looks at Peace Bridge politics, but the paper's critical thinking stopped there. "We had an editorial board decision and decided that the bridge is a dead issue," *the News*'s editorial page editor said in July 1998. "*The News* is not interested in the bridge question any more and we won't be running any more editorial comments on it." And they didn't, save for editorials saying the city should accept the PBA's decision—until there was so much opposition to the twin span they could no longer avoid it.

· New York Supreme Court Judge Eugene Fahey refused to grant the PBA's request that he order the city to issue the easements, and he agreed with the Episcopal Church Home and the Olmsted Conservancy that the PBA would have to stop everything it was doing until it did a full environmental impact study. His order meant the PBA could do nothing without paying heed to the very people who had been taking part in the Public Consensus Review Panel, which the PBA had boycotted so assiduously for more than a year.

· Senators Charles Schumer and Daniel Patrick Moynihan kept applying very public pressure on the PBA about its continued inaction after Fahey's decision. Fahey's decision became final in June 2000. The PBA did nothing about it all summer and fall except to file a notice of intent to appeal. Moynihan's chief of staff, Tony Bullock, visited Buffalo and told the Common Council's Bridge Task Force that the only thing holding up progress on the bridge was the PBA's intransigence. Senator Schumer invited the operators of the Ambassador Bridge in Detroit to town to explore their idea of building with private funds a new bridge a mile down river from the Peace Bridge.

It was a dazzling variety of individuals, community groups, and public officials working, from their different perspectives and in terms of their different needs, toward the same end. It was public power so strong that, even with the extraordinary walls of secrecy and autonomy created by New York's public corporation law, the Buffalo and Fort Erie Public Bridge Authority could no longer continue ignoring all voices other than its own.

the end of the affair

On November 15, 2000, Victor Martucci, chairman of the Buffalo and Fort Erie Public Bridge Authority, shut it all down. He called a press conference and announced that the PBA was voiding the several American and Canadian permits it had obtained, it was dropping all plans for appealing Judge Fahey's ruling, and it would, in a new partnership with Fort Erie and Buffalo, undertake a fully open all-inclusive environmental impact study.

His remarks were followed by celebratory speechifying by his fellow board members and by several politicians from Buffalo and Ontario, and if you didn't know any better you'd have thought it was the beginning of a sensitively-designed public works inquiry rather than the end of a long, bitter, and very expensive public policy war. But that's the way things are in politics: you start from where you are now, not from what you thought last week.

When asked why, after all this time, the PBA had reversed itself, Martucci said, "The judge's order made it a new landscape."

There is a fundamental irony to the Peace Bridge War that cannot be lost on the Public Bridge Authority. Had they not tried the gambit of a segmented project so they could avoid community involvement in an environmental impact study early on, the EIS they would have had then would have been far simpler and gentler and quicker than the one they face now. Now, the public is alerted to and knowledgeable about alternative designs. There are serious and infromed questions about whether or not this is the proper place for an expanded truck crossing at all. Had the PBA been willing to abandon the ego satisfaction or profits to steel manufacturers, and had it embraced rather than fought the consistently-escalating opposition to the steel twin span design, had it opted for a more economical and more aesthetically pleasing bridge of the kind being built nearly everywhere else, then in all likelihood construction would already be underway.

And there is another irony that cannot be lost on the Canadian officials who fought so hard to suppress American public opinion and push this project through without the full environmental impact study American law requires. Only because of the long delay did Americans come to learn about the obscure Canadian law that exempts all Canadian government offices from rental payments on tolled border crossings. At every tolled bridge and tunnel crossing along our three-thousand-mile border from the Atlantic to the Pacific, Americans pay rent for the space used by immigration and customs and other agencies and the parallel Canadian agencies do not pay any rent at all. At every one of those crossings, the Canadian share is taken out of toll revenues, half of which are paid by Americans. Every year, Americans pay millions of dollars more to support these bridge and tunnel border crossings than Canadians do — a fact that would have continued to languish in bureaucratic obscurity had not the Buffalo and Fort Erie Public Bridge Authority spent so long fighting for its steel twin span project and trying to avoid American environmental law.

was it worth the fight?

"I don't see what the fuss is about," a Canadian official said a few months after public opposition to the steel twin span developed. "A bridge is supposed to get people from one side to the other. Beauty has nothing to do with it. If it gets people from one side to the other it's done its job. That bridge in Detroit is ugly. It gets people from one side to the other and you don't hear anybody complaining about that bridge, do you?"

He missed the point. The Ambassador Bridge in Detroit, like the Peace Bridge in Buffalo, is old. No one complained about the old Peace Bridge in Buffalo either. What people complained about was the plan to build another just like it. They couldn't control what happened 75 years ago but they thought they should influence what happened next year or the year after that. Rational people make a fuss when a fuss is useful.

The Canadian official, and others who are similarly tone-deaf to the melodies of architecture at its best, might take instruction from the great Spanish architect/engineer/artist Santiago Calatrava. "I love being an architect of bridges," Calatrava told a *New York Times* reporter last year. "Take the Golden Gate Bridge, a perfect work of art. Without it, San Francisco would be just one of many beautiful bays along the Pacific coast of the Americas. Instead, it makes the bay unique in the world. The idea of a bridge adding dignity to a place is very important. That's why every bridge has to be different. It is made for different people, above all for different surroundings. It can be in a horrible urban spot, but it can rescue its environs."[5]

Events like the Peace Bridge War are instructive. I think it unlikely that any industrial group or public officials will, in the foreseeable future, simply try to push through a massive project in Buffalo. Shortly after taking office in January 2000, the new County Executive put on hold all plans for a new convention center; he said before anything more was done there would have to be a full environmental impact study. The intensive community involvement in a project to replace an aging bridge in Rochester, New York, 90 miles away from Buffalo, was consciously structured to avoid the kind of imbroglio that happened at the Peace Bridge. There's a generation of young-to-middle-aged professionals who made their political bones in the Peace Bridge War and they're not likely to sit in silence when other large public works projects come into view.

I love Santiago Calatrava's notion that a fine bridge can "rescue its environs," but the statement about the importance of the hand of man in the human landscape I like best of all is in Wallace Stevens's poem, "The Anecdote of the Jar":

> I placed a jar in Tennessee,
> And round it was, upon a hill.
> It made the slovenly wilderness
> Surround that hill.
>
> The wilderness rose up to it,
> And sprawled around, no longer wild.
> The jar was round upon the ground
> And tall and of a port in the air.

It took dominion everywhere.
The jar was gray and bare.
It did not give of bird of bush,
Like nothing else in Tennessee.

In that poem, the simple placing of the jar imposes or reveals an order to the universe that was not there previously. For Stevens, the joy of nature is not violated by that human act; rather a point of order, a place where the imagination can take hold, is established.

Architecture doesn't just occupy space; it also helps us understand and experience space, it organizes space. Architecture at once joins and redefines the order of all other things in sight. It is organic. That's what Stevens' poem is about.

The chorus of voices opposing ugliness and secrecy at the Peace Bridge stayed the advocates of ugliness from setting to work. In this place. This time. This won't be the only place and it won't be the only time. "The building of a public work," wrote Robert A. Caro, "shapes a city perhaps more permanently than any other action of government. Large-scale public works shape a city for generations. Some public works—most notably the great bridges and highways... — shape it for centuries if not, indeed, forever" (p. 753).

These are wars worth fighting.

NOTES

1. No state shall....pass any bill of attainder, ex post facto law, or law impairing the obligation of contracts...." United States Constitution, Article I, Section 10.

2. *The Power Broker: Robert Moses and the Fall of New York*, Vintage, NY 1975 (1974), p. 631. Not much has been written about public benefit corporations. I never fully understood their potential until I read Caro's instructive and fascinating chapter on how Moses manipulated New York public benefit corporation law ("The Warp on the Loom," pp. 615-636). The specific legislation establishing the Buffalo and Fort Erie Public Bridge Authority can be found at *New York Consolidated Law Service, Chapter 149.*

3. [Dollar(s) refer to U.S. dollars] *Ed.*

4. Their full report is *The Peace Bridge: Structural Conference, Report of Findings*, Buffalo and Fort Erie Public Bridge Authority, October 1994.

5. Riding, Alan. "Santiago Calatrava: Architect, Artist, Engineer", New York Times, 31 December 2000, Section 2, p. 36.

All photographs by Bruce Jackson, except for the two postcards reproducted on page 75 and page 77.

Bruce Jackson's "The Peace Bridge Chronicles" which originally appeared in *Artvoice*, are available online at: http://www.acsu.buffalo.edu/~bjackson/allbridge.html.

clockwise from top right:
Whirlpool at Niagara Gorge; Niagara Gorge; View of skyline Niagara Falls, Ontario, Canada; Population distribution map of the Great Lakes; Horseshoe Falls.

Photographs by Michael Richards, site study for Upper Level Graduate Studio.

DAVID HERZBERG

THE NIAGARA FRONTIER

BORDER ZONE OR MIDDLE GROUND?

If we were to stop thinking about the Niagara River as a boundary that divides two nations and start thinking of it as the center of one bi-national region, what would we think about? And if we were to think about this bi-national region as one of the world's most attractive places to live, as well as one of its most popular visitor destinations, what would we do? These are the kind of questions The Urban Design Project, a center in the School of Architecture and Planning at the University at Buffalo, has been exploring with its partner organization, The Waterfront Regeneration Trust, of Toronto, Ontario, Canada. The vehicle for the exploration has been an ongoing bi-national forum attended by senior stakeholders in the region. The article to follow was commissioned by the Urban Design Project to help establish the historical foundations of our continuing cross-border collaborations.

Robert Shibley

Director, Urban Design Project

The Niagara River does nothing by half measures. It hardly can. Think *your* "in-box" is full? Imagine this: after descending only 30 feet along the 1,000 mile stretch from Lake Superior to Lake Erie, the entirety of the water collected by the 87,000 square miles of the four upper Great Lakes then pours into the Niagara, where it plunges the next 325 feet to Lake Ontario in the river's scant 35-mile length. And even this rapid journey is telescoped, with the last 160 feet or so of descent accomplished in one spectacular leap at Niagara Falls. This is not just a river. It is a brute fact carved upon the landscape, an elemental force that animates and defines the region around it.

Indeed, it also divides that region. The easiest way to imagine the Niagara River is as a natural border given added symbolic power by the thunderous and impassable majesty of the Falls. Certainly the history of the United States and Canada, rife with conflict and punctuated by the occasional war, offers much to support such a vision. This perspective, tempting as it is, captures only one element of the complex and dynamic history of the Niagara Frontier. If the river is a border, it is also a crossroads, a place of connections. Its roaring waters make the Niagara a potent symbol of separation – but why are the waters roaring? Because the river links the

David Herzberg, a sometime resident of Buffalo, NY is a Jacob K. Javits Fellow and Ph.D. candidate in American History at the University of Wisconsin - Madison.

While living in the Niagara Frontier Region, Mr. Herzberg consulted for the Urban Design Project, a research center at the University of Buffalo, State University of New York, School of Architecture & Planning, as well as for Downtown Buffalo 2002! He has served as a research associated with the Bruner Foundation's Rudy Bruner Award for Urban Excellence.

vast Great Lakes watershed to the Atlantic ocean. What divides also connects. With a little imagination, one looks at the Niagara and sees not a border, but a nexus — a "middle ground" where cultures, economies, and even geologies have encountered each other, creating a dynamic history and a unique regional identity. This is the great opportunity presented by borders: when different peoples come into contact, they do not necessarily compete with each other for dominance in a zero-sum game. Rather, something new can be created, something that represents not a victory of one side over another, but a joining together of efforts to achieve common goals that could not be reached — or perhaps even be imagined — separately.

Of course, encounters between peoples do not always produce cooperative middle grounds. They can be destructive as well. The Niagara River is no exception; it has witnessed its share of bloodshed. But the Niagara Frontier's best moments have occurred when the people living on both sides of the river have pragmatically recognized their common stock of cultural, economic, and environmental problems and opportunities. Some of these have been obvious, such as tapping the potential of the Falls to power industry and tourism, or building canals and railroads to establish the region as a center of trade and transportation. Others have been more subtle, such as building upon regional solidarity to foster a durable and surprisingly peaceful international zone of cultural and economic interdependence. Each instance represents a successful effort to transform shared problems into shared opportunities through cooperative effort — to imagine the region as a middle ground instead of a border zone.

The Niagara Frontier today faces a slate of issues that do not, in some respects, differ so much from what has always confronted the region: how to reap the benefits of a unique cultural heritage; how to further facilitate trade and transportation; how to adapt to economic and technological change by re-using old industrial sites ("brownfields"); how to take advantage of the region's many natural and built attractions; and how to encourage the growth of new industries, especially in the arena of information technology. These are fields of endeavor that call for region-wide action. They are problems that become opportunities if considered from the vantage point of the middle ground. As the recent Peace Bridge controversy illustrates[1], the prevailing tendency today is to pursue separate processes even when goals are essentially the same. Nonetheless, the history of the Niagara Frontier is one of cooperation hard-won against just such backdrops of tension and conflict. It offers hope, and concrete precedents, that can sharpen our vision of today's opportunities for collaboration even as we recognize the realities of division.

As you read the next pages, keep in mind this image Niagara Falls in 1859. The waterfall is monumental – it will be decades before any water is diverted for hydroelectric power. It is only seven years before a renegade band of Irish-Americans will actually launch an invasion of Canada from Buffalo. And yet, what do we see at the Falls themselves, if we jostle through the thronging crowds close enough to get a glimpse? Jean Francois Gravelet, better known as "Blondin the Great" to his audience, walking on a tightrope across the Niagara. He is the first of a series of fearless entertainers who will walk, run, dance, bicycle — even eat leisurely breakfasts while reading newspapers (!) — along ropes strung across the great cataract. These playful but also deadly serious spectacles embody the paradox of the Niagara Frontier: without the power and danger of the border that they dared to cross, the feats would have meant nothing. Can you imagine looking at the Falls and seeing, as Blondin did, a path between the U.S. and Canada? Ludicrous! Americans and Canadians have been doing this, in one way or another, throughout history — and, with luck, will continue to do so.

the niagara frontier: a history of connections

The line dividing Canada from the United States is only the most obvious evidence that the Niagara Frontier sits upon a crossroads. Other borders have run through the region in the past, and even in modern times the area has been primarily shaped by its location at a nexus of cultures, economies, and geographies. Indeed, the central defining theme of the Niagara Frontier's history can best be characterized as "connections": on the one hand, the destructive and often bloody encounters of antagonists; on the other, the trade, transportation, and communication that have been the main engines of the region's development. When conceived as two sides of the same coin, these two kinds of connections have defined the Niagara Frontier, for better and for worse, since the beginning of the region's recorded history.

the first middle ground: native americans and early europeans

When Louis Joncaire first led the French into the Niagara Frontier in the second half of the seventeenth century, a terrible and bloody war waged by the Iroquois confederacy (who had armed themselves with advanced weapons through trade with the Europeans) was driving out the Hurons, Ottawas, Algonquins, and other native tribes from the area they had shared around Lake Ontario. This calamity struck peoples whose numbers had already been devastated by European diseases. The refugees headed west where they eventually formed an alliance with the French that successfully put an end to the Iroquois war effort in the late 1690s. The alliance was premised in no small part upon a lucrative fur trading partnership developed between the allies. This cooperative economic underpinning laid the groundwork for a complex middle ground in which a distinct syncretic culture flourished. Despite their very different agendas, the two peoples came together and forged a common ground to serve both their needs. If that common ground was far from equal — the French's guns and gifts gave them quasi-"paternal" status according to the system's logic — it was also far from the brutality of open conflict and war.

Throughout the first half of the eighteenth century the French-Algonquin alliance maintained — not without difficulty — a fairly stable and profitable economic trading region bounded on the east by the Niagara Frontier and encompassing the Upper Great Lakes region to the west. But by that time they were no longer the only players in the Niagara region: the British, led by Sir William Morris, had begun to arrive, eager for their own share of the fur trade. As the stakes grew higher for the two competing empires in the 1750s, the French lost their faith in the hardy middle ground that they had helped create and gambled instead on a unilateral military solution. In the Seven Years' War with the British that followed, the French and their Native American allies were defeated. The middle ground at least temporarily survived, however, as the result of Pontiac's Rebellion in 1763. In that year Senecas and Chippewas led by Chief Pontiac occupied all the British forts in the area except Niagara, Detroit, and Pitt. The ensuing military stalemate gave Pontiac the leverage he needed to force the British into a role similar to the one previously held by the French.

The next chapter in the Niagara Frontier's history is brutal and all too familiar. During America's Revolutionary War (1776-1783) many Indians fought alongside their British allies, and as a result were treated as conquered or to-be-conquered enemies by the new nation. The new cash-poor American government sold land that it barely controlled, if at all, to restless and aggressive backcountry settlers whose hunger for lands ensured constant conflict with local Indians. Despite heroic efforts by such famous Native American leaders as Red Jacket, Cornplanter, and others, most of New York State save a few reservations had come under the ownership of U.S.

nationals by the end of the century. On the Canadian side of the river, the Mississaugas fared little better. After having been relatively unbothered by European encroachments in the sparsely settled Niagara peninsula, their territory was suddenly flooded by British loyalists fleeing the newly independent (and somewhat vengeful) United States. These loyalists established the peninsula's first townships, small farming outposts like Niagara, Queenston, Chippawa, and Fort Erie along the Niagara River. Despite the Mississaugas's official protection under Britain's Royal Proclamation of 1763 (the Indian rights document that brought an end to Pontiac's Rebellion), the tribe was negotiating from a position of weakness and ceded nearly all of its land to the incoming loyalists. Ultimately the Mississaugas retained only small reserves and fisheries at the mouths of the Twelve and Sixteen Mile Creeks and the Credit River.

a new borderland:
canada, the united states, and the economic middle ground

The complex world constructed by the French, British, and Native American peoples had fallen apart, but the Niagara Frontier still remained a place of encounters and connections. The Niagara River, the new border between the United States and Canada, lay at its heart. And as European settlement continued to stretch westward the Niagara Frontier became an important nodal point in the trade routes connecting the great resources of the Midwest with the great business centers of the east. The region, over the next century and a half would once again witness both successful efforts to create a peaceful and profitable middle ground; and troubled times when conflict and division temporarily derailed the cooperative spirit.

The most well-known rupture in these relations was the War of 1812. When U.S. President James Madison declared war on Britain that year, his bravado masked a profound military weakness in the United States. Utterly incapable of waging war directly against Britain, American nationals eyed a closer and — to their minds — easier target: Canada. Since America outstripped Canada in population (25 to 1), militia (9 to 1), and regular soldiers (7 to 5), and three out of every five settlers in Canada were Americans from New York, Pennsylvania, and Connecticut, the conquest seemed to former U.S. President Thomas Jefferson "a mere matter of marching." But after a failed invasion launched from near Niagara Falls and a series of hard-fought but ultimately inconclusive battles, the war ended with no change of territory but with great devastation. In the Niagara region where the hopeful young cities of Niagara, Ontario, and Buffalo, NY had been burned entirely to the ground in December 1813.

This picture of division and antagonism should not, however, be over-emphasized. Why did the American invasion north of Niagara Falls fail? Many reasons, but for our purposes one in particular stands out: the New York militiamen refused to join the U.S. regular army in crossing the border. Contending that they had volunteered only to protect their homes, not to undertake invasions, they simply watched as their nation's army was pulverized on the other side of the river.

Ironically, this act of apparent respect for the international border in fact reflected a deeper, more pragmatic local understanding of interdependence across that very boundary. Since the onrush of American settlers to the Niagara Frontier after 1783, the area had witnessed the efflorescence of a "borderland economy" characterized by strong ties between American and Canadian frontiersmen. Far from the developed markets in the east, residents in this frontier land depended upon each other for markets, friendship, and family alliances. Borrowing heavily from America's Enlightenment-derived philosophy of "natural rights" and free trade, pioneers in the

above, left to right:

In 1770, Indians and French fur traders shared the site of the future Buffalo, on the banks of Buffalo Creek, with a view of Fort Erie across the lake. [Howard, p. 114].

In 1859, Jean Francois Gravelet, "The Great Blondin", was the first of many daredevils to construct a path across the gorge from one nation to another – on a high wire. [Berton, p. 214].

Historian Donald Braider called the Battle of Lundy's Lane, July 25, 1814, the "most savage and costly engagement" of the War of 1812. "Both sides claimed a victory when, in fact, both sides lost." [Braider, p. 182]

Lake freighters and railroads brought ore and coal together in Buffalo in the second half of the 19th century and lured Lackawanna Steel – later Bethlehem Steel – to Lake Erie in 1900. [Eberle and Grande, p. 165.]

W.E.B. DuBois led the founding of "the Niagara Movement" – precursor to the National Association for the Advancement of Colored People – in Fort Erie, 1905. [Eberle and Eberle, p. 98]

Niagara Frontier worked hard to keep the border free of harassing customs officers, restrictive trade regulations, and legal complications in the conveyance of their goods across the river. These efforts were embodied early on in such documents as Jay's Treaty of 1794, which called in principle for free trade between America and Canada. Literally days after the cessation of hostilities in 1814, citizens of the two nations eagerly returned to the whirring mechanics of a regional economy, hiring each other, selling to each other, and following each other's culture and fashions. The very elements that, in some situations, were a recipe for war — different peoples encountering each other under conditions of hardship and necessity — had instead served as a catalyst for creativity and productive interconnections. Ironically, the War of 1812, fought over free trade and shipping rights, was itself an unwanted impediment to free trade in a Niagara Frontier already committed to interdependence and cooperation.

This mostly informal regional solidarity almost plunged the United States and Canada into a second war nearly three decades later. In 1837, Canadian Scotsman William Lyon Mackenzie led a failed revolution against the British government in York (Toronto). After he and his followers were routed, Mackenzie fled to the Niagara River and was smuggled across to Buffalo. There he gathered sympathetic Buffalonians and, under the benevolent blind eye of Buffalo officials, took his new 100-strong army and occupied Upper Canada's Navy Island and proclaimed a provisional government. Events took another lurch toward war when the British sank the American steamboat *Caroline*, which, in the tradition of "innocent" American ships, had been brazenly transporting American volunteers for Mackenzie's Patriot Army to Navy Island all day. The situation threatened to escalate to all-out war until President Martin Van Buren dispatched Major General Winfield Scott to Niagara to defuse the crisis. Despite its quick settlement, the brief skirmish continued to echo through the region in the following years: Mackenzie supporters formed secret societies called Hunter Lodges along the waterfront, and the U.S. and Canada fortified the border against each other at Fort Niagara (U.S.) and Fort Henry (Canada). It was the same pattern again: obvious divisions inseparably linked to informal but powerful bonds of solidarity.

the canal era: the economic middle ground ascendant

Shortly after the end of the War of 1812 it became clear that New York State would finance a canal to connect the Great Lakes with the eastern seaboard. Such a project would instantly transform a situation of hardship and necessity into one of enormous potential – another recipe for conflict. Indeed, the famous competition between Black Rock and Buffalo over who would receive the terminus of the Erie Canal reveals just such dynamics. This competition was not destructive. Instead, it spurred Buffalonians to come together in a broadly-based community effort to dredge Buffalo Creek and create a harbor so that the city would be more attractive to the Canal designers. Across the border in Canada, canal-borne dreams of plenty produced more anticipation of increased prosperity than jealousy. Just as the American side of the river, and Buffalo in particular, grew astronomically in economic activity and importance after the 1825 opening of the Erie Canal, so did the Canadian side. Evidence suggests that many Canadians, especially businessmen, were perfectly aware of the source of their windfall. The "borderland economy" that had sustained them through the pioneer days would now, all hoped, make them rich.

That they expected to benefit from the Erie Canal did not detract from a healthy competitive spirit among Canadians. Determined not to allow the Niagara peninsula to become a mere adjunct to a successful Erie Canal corridor, William Hamilton Merritt of St. Catharines sheparded the construction of the second great waterway construction of this era, the Welland Canal, which connected Lakes Erie and Ontario to the west of the Niagara River. The Canadian canal builders, who completed their project in the winter of 1829, relied heavily on Americans for inspiration, know-how, and ultimately for capital. They also envisioned, correctly, that the Welland would boost the already thriving north-south trade with the United States. Americans agreed, applauding any development that would increase trade and trading opportunities in the region. Indeed, U.S. investment along the Welland Canal in the decades to come would be so heavy that some observers later described it as "an American industrial outpost in Canada." These American regional boosters, like their Canadian counterparts, recognized that trade was not a zero-sum game. Instead of focusing on the potential competition the Welland opened up between the Lake Ontario-St. Lawrence channel and the Erie Canal, they chose to view the new waterway as expanding the regional economy. Even though the Welland had been spurred by competition across the border, it was ultimately about addition, not subtraction: the Welland extended the reach of the system north as well as west and south to the ultimate benefit of the region as a whole.

They were right. The canal years rank as one of the Niagara Frontier's glory periods, when, with Buffalo as its "Queen City," it established itself as a regional center of trade, navigation, and communication between the heartlands of North America and the great economic centers of the east. The transshipment of grain was a major engine of this development, especially after Buffalo's Joseph Dart invented the steam-powered grain elevator in 1842. In 1836, the first year that Ohio's grain production outstripped New York's, Buffalo relayed 1.2 million bushels of oats, barley, corn, wheat, rye, and soybeans. As the American Midwest continued to grow into "the world's bread basket," grain shipments grew at a fantastic rate: 5.5 million bushels by 1842, and 22 million bushels in the early 1850s. Along with the grains came a torrent of other raw materials transferred from Great Lakes barges to canal boats heading east: pork, bacon, beef, whiskey, lumber, tobacco, lead, oil, hemp, furs, sugar, potatoes, iron, leather, ashes, lard, butter, cheese, cotton, wools, beans, fish tallow, cranberries – the list was practically endless. The city's role as a link between east and west was highlighted in 1850, when W.G. Fargo and Henry Wells merged their famous transportation and communication holdings to become American Express.

On the Canadian side of the river growth was less explosive but still measurable. St. Catharines, the premier Welland Canal city, housed a growing trade of grain, apples, nails, salt, fish, potash, glass, and virtually anything else that could fit in a barrel. Meanwhile the tiny settlement of "Aqueduct" on the canal transformed into the small mill town of Merrittville in 1847, and in turn became the city of Welland in 1858. Still no metropolis, it plied the canal trade with sawmills and brick and cloth factories working from regional raw goods. Meanwhile, in the 1830s the Shickluna family continued a Niagara peninsula tradition with their famous boat building opera-

above, left to right:

The Great Depression sent thousands of workers to the bread lines and put local governments in Western New York on the federal dole. [Eberle and Grande, p. 195]

In 1959 the St. Lawrence Seaway opened, providing a new water route to the Atlantic, and depriving the Buffalo economy of crucial geographic advantages. [Eberle and Grande, p. 215]

Bethlehem Steel was a mainstay of the regional economy through much of the century, but by 1982 nearly all of its works were closed. [Eberle and Grande, p. 215]

New York Governor Nelson A. Rockefeller turned the ceremonial first shovel of dirt on construction of the new University of Buffalo Amherst Campus. [Eberle and Grande, p. 214]

tions. (The first Great Lakes steamer, the *Walk-In-Water*, had been built there.) Outside these and a few other proto-industrial outposts, the Canadian Niagara peninsula continued to rely on its healthy farming and fruit agricultural base.

Heavy manufacturing (especially iron processing) began to join grain storage and shipment in the regional economy, the built environment of the Niagara Frontier began to take on a new and distinctive look. In constructing the grain elevators, factories, warehouses, and processing plants that kept the engines of trade humming, local architects established a new vocabulary of enormous, forthright, and "functionally honest" building styles. Graced with an undeniable purity and authenticity, these massive structures of the new industrial economy helped shape the stylistic vocabulary of modernist architecture. Indeed, the buildings have in more recent years been recognized as one of North America's highly successful and internationally influential native art forms along with modern dance and jazz.

The hum of activity and innovation led to a rapid growth in population in the Niagara Frontier. By 1855 Buffalo alone had 74,000 residents, up from 2,500 in 1825. The Canadian side posted less spectacular but nonetheless solid growth as well: St. Catharines, for example, more than doubled its population from 1,700 to 4,000 between 1828 and 1851. Welland grew from a scant few hundred to over 2,000 residents by 1885. Much of this growth was due to a surge of immigration from Europe, German and Irish on the U.S. side of the river, and Irish on the Canadian side, especially during the canal-building years. In 1855, 60 percent of Buffalo's residents were foreign-born, a full half of them German and another fifth Irish. This first wave of immigration provided the muscle that powered the Niagara Frontier's growing economy, and also inaugurated a strong tradition of ethnic culture that has played no small role in shaping the region's identity. Even though the tightly-knit ethnic neighborhoods have since dispersed, landmarks such as St. Joseph's Cathedral on Franklin Street in Buffalo, built by Irish Bishop John Timon in the 1850s, remain to testify to their still-powerful legacy.

Like most of North America, the region's prosperity was temporarily derailed during the Panic of 1837; that year, for example, Benjamin Rathbun, the preeminent capitalist and urban pioneer who essentially created Buffalo's downtown business district and its hardworking Mechanic Street, went bankrupt and actually landed in debtor's prison. Four years later, in 1841, the county legislature took over a bankrupt Welland Canal. But the Niagara Frontier bounced back, and trade figures for both American and Canadian canal regions leaped up over the years as more or less friendly competition spurred improvements in both waterways. Much of this economic elasticity was due to a regional phenomenon easy to overlook amidst the flood of transcontinental commerce: trade between Americans and Canadians on either side of the Niagara River. This local economic activity continued to provide a bedrock of common interests and common profits.

Ultimately, Canada and the United States recognized the synergistic potential of the region's trade in the Reciprocity Treaty of 1854. This agreement, which lasted until America's Civil War, provided for limited free trade, American access to the provincial fisheries, and American navigation of the St. Lawrence River and the Canadian canal system. The benefits were immediate and obvious, particularly on the Canadian peninsula where a slow but steady growth transformed into an economic boom powered in part by a thriving cross-border cotton and timber trade (St. Catharines first cotton mill opened the same year as the Treaty). The "borderland economy" had, it seemed, come of age with the Treaty. A formal acknowledgment of aspirations long held by Niagara Frontier peoples, it marked an era of exponentially expanding trade between the two nations.

niagara falls

The Niagara River's dual role as the dividing border and unifying heart of its region is perhaps best exemplified by spectacle of Niagara Falls. As a tourist attraction and as a source of endless cheap power, it has fundamentally shaped and defined the communities that surround it. And this has held true not only for the cities that grew up on its Canadian and American edges, but also for other regional locales which, for example, have advertised "come to Buffalo and see the Falls" while building up healthy processing and manufacturing industries based on hydroelectric power. The Falls' plenitude of potential riches has engendered divisions – competing tourist attractions, for example, or international maneuvering over who would profit from its hydroelectric power – but it has also produced connections, as personal as those made by visiting honeymooners and as grand as the bridges that span it and the regional economy it has powered.

Niagara Falls today remains one of the most-visited tourist spots in the world, receiving nearly 20 million visitors yearly. And yet, planner Ernest Sternberg argues, the spectacle has been poorly exploited as a tourist destination. Relying solely on the (carefully staged) drama of the falling water itself, little effort has been made to place the cataract in the context of a broader narrative that could sustain a visitor's experience beyond the 20 minutes that it mesmerizes the average tourist. Before transportation improved with the advent of the Erie Canal in 1825, the Falls' inaccessibility gave it an air of exotic profundity, and early tourists often spoke of their visits there as pilgrimages to an otherworldly realm where anything at all seemed possible. For decades afterwards, the cataract maintained its mysterious and magical aura for visitors. The awful and terrifying spectacle of the so-called "River of Death" invited contemplation of the sublime, of the meaning of nature and the frailty of human accomplishments, and, perhaps most profoundly, the meaning of death. At the same time, of course, the fame-seeking acrobats like Blondin and Farini drew crowds by braving the horrors of the Falls on seemingly flimsy ropes. Ultimately, historian Patrick McGreevy argues, honeymooners were drawn to this liminal boundaryspace where the ordinary rules of everyday life might be suspended for the equally otherworldly rituals of passion.

The Falls also inspired other dreams, no less grandiose but certainly less otherworldly: dreams of electric power and the fortunes that could be won with it. The majestic profundity of the cataract had already suffered the degradation of commercial exploitation as business took every advantage of the spectacle's growing tourist value in the post-Erie Canal era. "Attractions" that had elbowed right up to the precipice were swept away by popular movements to recapture the natural beauty of the Falls. Ready to take the place of these merchants were the dreamers and speculators of an economy that had just begun its meteoric rise through industrialization. Rather than seeing a sublime statement about the nature of existence, men like Edward Dean Adams, president of the Cataract Construction Company of Niagara Falls, New York, saw "a power almost illimitable, constantly wasted, yet never diminished – gazed upon, wondered at, but never hitherto controlled." By the end of the 1890s, eleven major electric companies had located in Niagara Falls; by 1909 there were twenty-five. Meanwhile, development on the Canadian side had been stymied by a stubborn belief in steam power and the not-accidental ownership by American companies of the exclusive rights to develop electricity from the Canadian falls. It was not until after the great coal strikes of 1902 that Canada, made suddenly aware of its dependence on American coal, dug a tunnel under the Falls to generate hydroelectric power. By 1908, however, production on the Canadian side had surpassd that on the U.S. side, with Ontario Hydro advancing a public ownership model that was to set the example for organizations like the Tennessee Valley Authority.

Thus began Niagara Falls' domination by industry and economy. Although some careful planning was evident during that era – for example, U.S. water diversions were limited under President Theodore Roosevelt in 1906, and a treaty with Great Britain similarly limited Canada's siphoning – it was also a time of extravagance and excess. Humanity's limitless imagination envisioned future utopias entirely powered by a conquered Niagara Falls. The popular American comic strip "Buck Rogers in the twenty-fifth Century," for example, cast the fictional city of "Niagara" as the capital of the futuristic nation. For a while such visions won out over careful planning, and industrial pollutants invisibly poisoned a natural wonder that was already being undermined and obscured by power and processing plants. In the mid-twentieth century, when the industrial strength of the region sagged, Niagara Falls would be bereft of transcendent meaning: no longer a meditation on the sublime, no longer an exotic outpost of the otherworldly, no longer the centerpiece of an imagined industrial utopia, the Falls became simply a mass of falling water to be witnessed for as long as it entertained the visitor.

the importance of the border: race and nation

The national border marked by the Niagara River has meant many different things at different points in its history, but its most important role may well have been played out in the roughly seven decades between 1793 and the American Civil War. In 1793 Canada abolished slavery, and while New York State was also slave-free since the early nineteenth century, U.S. law made escaped slaves fair game for headhunters even after they had reached free states. This state of affairs eventually helped propel the nation into Civil War, but in the meantime it ensured that freedom's true home lay across the Niagara in Canada.

Although reliable documentation is difficult to find for the American side of the river, it is clear that one of the two main branches of the Underground Railroad directed escaping slaves through the Niagara region and over the river to Canada. Harriet Tubman, for example, crossed the Niagara River in 1851 and established a family home and base of operations in St. Catharine's, an Ontario town that housed many other escapees. She lived there for six years, working to finance her activities as a "conductor" on the Underground Railroad and attending the Salem Chapel B.M.E. Church on Geneva Street.

The role of Buffalo and other sites on the U.S. side of the river in the history of race relations was a more complex and ambiguous one at best. On the one hand, the Underground Railroad did undeniably pass through the region.

On the other hand, Buffalo was never too congenial a home for abolitionist activity in the nineteenth century. Racial tensions were excacerbated by a history of economic competition on the docks between white ethnics and African Americans, who, largely excluded from white labor organizations, often had little choice but to accept work as strikebreakers. Like many other American cities, draft riots erupted in Buffalo during the Civil War. Immigrants from Germany and Ireland saw little reason that they should fight for the freedom of the same African Americans who they felt threatened their livelihoods on the docks. Perhaps for these reasons, or merely from the habit of secrecy, little in the way of reliable information about the Underground Railroad in the region survives.

The Civil War and its aftermath revealed that the border still mattered even during the heyday of the "borderland economy." While Canada maintained its neutrality during the conflict, at least some Americans did not return the favor. The Fenians were a group of Irish immigrants centered in Buffalo who hoped to invade and capture Canada and then ransom it for Ireland's freedom from Great Britain. On June 2, 1866 they invaded their northern neighbor from Buffalo while the U.S. Army turned a blind eye. The fight was short and one-sided, as the Canadian army quickly repulsed the invaders. It would be the last skirmish along the Niagara border between the two nations, but it left a lasting imprint: Canadian defenses would be designed to foil U.S. attack until after World War II, nearly a century later.

The Civil War settled the matter of slavery in the States, but did not end the significance of the Niagara as a border for African Americans. When W.E.B. DuBois brought together black activists in 1905 to start a more active, confrontational advocacy organization, he planned to hold the meeting in Buffalo. When the hotel with which DuBois had made arrangements refused to deal with black patrons, he followed the old freedom trail across the river to Ft. Erie, Canada, and founded the "Niagara Movement." Within a decade it merged with White liberal activists, it changed its name to the National Association for the Advancement of Colored People (NAACP) and pioneered the powerful tactic of focusing on litigation and legal rights.

boom times: the steel belt

By the beginning of the twentieth century, the Niagara Frontier had reached a point where its natural advantages, augmented by human efforts such as the canals, left it poised to become an even more important center of financial and transportation activity. The age of the canals had been short – as early as the 1850s, for example, the Erie Canal had ceased to turn a profit and railroads had begun encroaching on the shipping business. But despite the worries of those narrowly fixated on canal traffic, the area easily adapted to the evolving economy. Still boasting the largest inland port in North America, and still conveniently located at the terminus of Great Lakes shipping routes, the Niagara Frontier was as attractive to railroad builders as it had been to canal diggers. A network of railroads linked Buffalo to New York, Philadelphia, and other points east that had formerly been served by the canal. By 1869 the city's railroad freight tonnage exceeded canal traffic for the first time, and by the turn of the century, Buffalo was second only to Chicago in the number of railroads terminating in the city. On the Canadian side, the Great Western Railroad linked Fort Erie to Detroit in 1854, the national "Grand Trunk Railroad" linked up to the peninsula's lines in 1882, and in 1893 tracks joined Toronto, Hamilton, and Buffalo.

Along with the railroads came a new industry: ironworks. Iron had long accompanied grains and other raw materials through the Welland and the transportation hub at Buffalo, but in the 1850s railroads connected the Niagara Frontier to coal producing regions. This made it significantly cheaper to process iron in the region. Two decades later, the iron deposits in Lake Superior began to be seriously exploited by entrepreneurs like the Goodyear brothers, and the influx of raw ore quickly transformed the Niagara Frontier into an industrial center ready to challenge Pittsburgh as the iron capital of North America. Soon the landscape was dotted with great ironworks, many of them in Buffalo: Jewett and Root; Hart, Ball, and Hart; Buffalo Architectural Iron Works; Buffalo Iron and Nailworks; and others. In 1900 Buffalo granted Lackawanna Iron and Steel Company a virtual fiefdom south of the city, and they relocated their entire operation from Scranton, Pennslyvania. The industrial giant soon became the region's economic lodestone, employing over 6,000 people. In 1922 Bethlehem Steel bought Lackawanna, and in 1938 retooled it for the growing automobile market. This drew in automobile industry giants like General Motors, Dunlop, and Studebaker. Meanwhile, smaller metalworks factories sprouted up in Canadian cities like Welland (the Welland Iron Works in 1860, for example, and Welland Iron and Brass Company in 1918) and St. Catharines (particularly the McKinnon Dash and Metal works plant in 1901, bought by GM in 1928, and the Packard Electric Company, which began producing Oldsmobiles in 1905).

By the end of the nineteenth century, the cheap and plentiful hydroelectric power provided by the Falls made the region an irresistible location for processing all kinds of raw materials, not just iron. Industrial growth acquired its own momentum, and new power-dependent industries began to congregate: Buffalo, for example, welcomed Ketchum Mowing Machines and Reapers; Forbush and Brown's Shoe and Boot Manufacturing; Gerhard Lang Company brewery; Kittinger Furniture; the Larkin Soap Company (in an office building designed by Frank Lloyd Wright); National Aniline Chemicals; Pierce automobile manufacturers; Conrad Steam Motor Carriage Company; and the list could go on.

Across the river, the Canadian peninsula was also seeing its most rapid growth after recovering from a post-Civil War slowdown caused in part by the demise of the Reciprocity Treaty. American Byron J. McCormick masterminded Welland's rise by organizing the Welland Realty Company, which played a hand in luring branch plants of important U.S. firms like the Welland Plymouth Cordage Company (from Massachusetts) and a variety of forging, lumber, knitting, metalworking, and shipbuilding concerns. In St. Catharines, coal powered industries like Warren Knitwear and the Welland Vale Manufacturing Company put their shoulders behind the region's economic growth as well. In 1898 a hydroelectric power plant was installed at DeCew Falls in St. Catharines and underwrote the widespread of industrial expansion with the promise of more far-reaching power from Niagara Falls. Some of this Canadian growth, ironically, had been an unintentional result of high tariffs during the 1890s, which spurred American companies to expand onto Canadian soil to maintain their traditional trading patterns across the Niagara — an unlikely and unlooked-for benefit of the "borderland economy"!

Just as the canal era had been powered by the muscle of immigrants, so this industrial era relied on a seemingly endless stream of European migrants. Most poured into the American side, to Buffalo, adding the distinctive flavor of eastern and southern Europe — Italians, Poles, and Jews — to the city's ethnic mosaic. After the turn of the century the Canadian side, too, witnessed an influx of immigrants, the first time in the overwhelmingly British peninsula that a substantial number of residents were not Anglophones.

Once again, the Niagara Frontier was reaping the benefits of its role as a middle ground — a place where the Old World and new met through immigration; where the North American heartland linked up to the eastern seaboard; where raw materials were transformed on their way to market; and where waterways, railroads, and communications lines intersected in a great web of connections. But this role had not come easily. The region had grown into it through active efforts to create, nurture, and sustain an infrastructure that capitalized on natural advantages.

the end of boom times

The good times were not to last. The Great Depression of the 1930s hit the Niagara Frontier hard, and federal support could only mitigate the disaster to a limited extent. What could a region reliant on manufacturing and trade do when factories stopped producing, goods stopped shipping, and people stopped buying? Go on federal government relief, was one answer, and many individuals and even the city government of Buffalo proceeded to do so. But the booster spirit was not entirely moribund. Buffalo, for example, landed a new Chevrolet plant that began production in 1938, right after Bethlehem Steel modernized its facilities to produce steel for automobiles. The city's workers, long active in the periodic waves of organizing and protest that accompanied industrialization, put together durable and powerful unions under the aegis of the New Deal's friendly labor laws. Meanwhile in 1932 the Canadian ship building industry reached its apex with the creation of the Port Weller Dry Docks, which still is in operation today.

Despite its troubles, therefore, the region was in good shape to welcome the enormous boom that followed the start of World War II. The conflict jump-started both nations' economies and flooded the industrial Niagara region with contracts and work. A series of trade agreements between the U.S. and Canada beginning in 1938 quickly erased four decades of high tariffs, the most recent of which had been the disastrous 1930 Hawley-Smoot levy by the U.S. that had devastated Canadian farmers. And, like all of the region's other booms, the postwar expansion was accompanied by a new wave of immigration. This last one, the third, took place primarily on the American side of the border and constituted an intensification of a decades-old migration of African Americans from the south to the industrial centers of the north.

But if the war was enough to re-inflate the Niagara Frontier's economy, it was not enough to set the region on a path of long-term stability. Changes in technology, environment, and the economy were slowly but surely undermining the area's hard-won position as a central nodal point for trade and communication. Interstate trucking, begun at a small scale in the 1920s, had continued to grow but now blossomed in the frenzy of highway building that followed the war. Unlike the railroads, these highways had no compelling reason to steer through the Niagara region. To make matters worse, the grain belt had begun to migrate southward even as early as the late nineteenth century, and the situation evolved to the point where it became economical to ship grain directly by train or truck instead of first sending it to Buffalo across the Great Lakes. Even the Welland Canal, improved on three separate occasions to keep pace with current technologies since its inception had its troubles: the 1933 improvement had enabled ships to pass through without stopping, effectively marooning the canal-based industries that had grown up along its banks. Manufacturing alone could not make up for the loss of the transshipment hubs, as soon became clear. After the war, as government contracts were canceled or not renewed, entire industries began to leave. Curtiss-Wright, Bell Aircraft and Westinghouse were some of the biggest.

The final blow to the river region's importance as a trading hub came with the opening of the St. Lawrence Seaway in 1959. Like the Welland Canal, the Seaway had initially been conceived as a joint operation between the U.S. and Canada. But it was not to be. Railroad and private industrial interests, as well as Buffalo and other port areas that would be affected, lobbied hard against American involvement. During the Depression years they successfully turned federal interest away from international development schemes of that sort and toward internal opportunities like the Tennessee Valley project. By 1951 Canada had decided to act unilaterally, and in 1959 the St. Lawrence Seaway opened an alternate (and vastly superior) water route to the east. With no regional logic or cooperative imperative driving it, the Seaway dramatically upended the Niagara economy. Although the Welland Canal continued to service this route to the east, the antiquated and little-used Erie Canal — and its terminal city Buffalo — were now bypassed by water traffic. In the past, Buffalo had flourished because of the shipment transfers that had occurred there, from Great Lakes barge to canal boats or railroads. The improved Welland offered no such stopping point and no new trans-shipment hub or manufacturing center sprang up along its banks to take Buffalo's place. Indeed, very little shipping volume either originated or had a destination in the canal.

Denuded of its historic role as a vital link between east and west, the Niagara Frontier saw its shipbuilding industry collapse and grain storage and milling contract. Other industries followed, devastating most of Buffalo's steel mills and prompting many residents to leave the area in search of employment. In the wake of these departures, the region became better known for the poisonous fallout of industrial activity than for industrial activity itself. The biggest headline to come out of the area in the second half of the twentieth century may well have been the Love Canal disaster, in which a school and neighborhood built on land contaminated by Hooker Chemical back in the 1940s had to be evacuated in the 1970s because of seeping toxic waste. The Welland suffered no public relations disaster of this magnitude, but the canal and its related industries had given birth to its own unaddressed environmental problems.

the irony of regional peace in the twentieth century

It would be easy to ascribe the region's economic decline to uncontrollable or "natural" forces, but the Niagara Frontier's history suggests otherwise. Little that might appear natural in the Niagara Frontier has been entirely untouched by human effort. Buffalo's advantageous positioning at the terminus of the Erie Canal, for example, relied not on an existing harbor but on a community-wide effort to dredge and build an artificial one. The "natural" gravitation of the steel industry to the city had to be well-greased through negotiation and tax abatements. The railroads threaded through the region because of tireless efforts by locals to make themselves invaluable as a trading hub. Virtually all economic development from Niagara Falls tourism to Niagara-powered industry, has been the direct result of active efforts to shape and then market the region.

When successful, these efforts have been undertaken by people who correctly gauged the direction of economic and technological change, and who were brilliant at transforming what was available to them – a waterfall, a border, a creek — into the "natural" and obvious advantages that secured the region's future: a power source, a regional trade zone, an inland harbor and canal terminus. And the most successful efforts have been those that understood the Niagara Frontier as a diverse but unified region, with a distinct regional culture and a distinct role to play. Or, to put it another way, the region has been at its best when the *de facto* community of interests that extends across the border has been reflected and embodied in formal commercial and political activities and organizations.

The Niagara Frontier today is beset with new challenges. In the Falls it boasts one of the world's largest tourist draws, but the region around the spectacle is so under-interpreted and poorly presented that visitors are there and gone too quickly to influence the economy as they could. The area has a proud heritage of creatively reinventing itself as a nexus of trade and transportation, but still seems dazed by changes in shipping patterns that happened half a century ago. A similarly noble heritage of adaptability is marred by unused brownfields that testify only to decay, not rebirth. The environment features a wealth of truly remarkable natural and built wonders, but they are underappreciated, undermarketed, and sometimes even demolished for little apparent reason. Finally, the region has been taking tentative steps toward remaking themselves as a communications hub in the new information economy, but no region-wide collaborative efforts in the Niagara Frontier's historic style have been initiated to propel these steps forward.

The irony of this failure of regional vision is that barriers to cooperation would seem to be lower now than at almost any other time in history. No garrisons line the Niagara on opposing sides; instead, the U.S. and Canada are joined in one of the world's most successful military alliances. No high tariffs block trade across the river; indeed, NAFTA far exceeds the 1854 Reciprocity Treaty as a facilitator of international trade. True, the controversy surrounding replacement of the Peace Bridge has presented a thorny problem in international cooperation, but the very inadequacy of the existing bridge only underlines the volume of people and goods that constantly travel over the border.

If we conceive of the Niagara Frontier as a distinct bi-national region with its own unique and dynamic cultural, economic, and environmental history, then each of its problems suddenly presents itself as an opportunity: an opportunity to invest in heritage and cultural tourism; to implement new technology and creative facilities to encourage trade and transportation in the modern economy, especially across the border; to develop a new and purposeful sense of place by reusing old industrial brownfields; to integrate natural and built landscapes into a single, world-class destination; and to reinvigorate the region's historic "economy of connections" by investing in knowledge-based industries. Considered from only one side of the border, or from one town or city, the logic that sustains these opportunities disappears. As always, the Niagara Frontier's future will in large part be determined as a region, and especially in these times of peace we ignore that at our peril.

NOTES

Additional information on the regional bi-national forum and on the Urban Design Project is available at: http://ap.buffalo.edu/~urbandesignproject.

Sources Referenced:

[1]Baglier, Janet. "The Niagara Frontier: Society and Economy in Western New York and Upper Canada, 1794 – 1854." (Ph.D. diss., State University of New York at Buffalo, 1993.)

[2]Banham, Reyner. *A Concrete Atlantis: United States Industrial Buildings and European Modern Architecture.* (Cambridge: MIT Press, 1989.)

[3]Berton, Pierre. *Niagara: A History of the Falls.* (Toronto: McClelland & Stewart, 1992.)

[4]Braider, Donald. *The Niagara.* (New York: Holt, Rinehart and Winston, 1972.)

[5]Craig, Gerald. *Upper Canada: The Formative Years, 1784-1841.* (Toronto: McClelland and Stewart, 1963.)

[6]Creighton, Donald. *Canada's First Century, 1867-1967.* (New York: St. Martin's Press, 1970.)

[7]Denison, Merrill. *The People' Power: This History of Ontario Hydro.* (Toronto : McClelland and Stewart, 1960.)

[8]Eberle, Scott and Grande, Joseph. *Second Looks: A Pictorial History of Buffalo and Erie County.* (Norfolk and Virginia Beach: The Donning Company, 1987.)

[9]Engel, Gerrit. *Buffalo Grain Elevators.* (Verona: EBS, 1997.)

[10]Goldman, Mark. *High Hopes: The Rise and Decline of Buffalo, New York.* (Albany: SUNY Press, 1983.)

[11]Graham, Lloyd. *Niagara County.* (New York: Duell, Sloan & Pearce, 1949.)

[12]Howard, Robert. *Thundergate: The Forts of Niagara.* (Englewood Cliffs, NJ: Prentice-Hall, Inc., 1968.)

[13]Jackson, John. *St. Catharines Ontario: Its Early Years.* (Belleville, Ontario: Mika Publishing Company, 1976.)

[14]Jackson, John. *The Welland Canals and Their Communities.* (Toronto and Buffalo: University of Toronto Press, 1997.)

[15]Jackson, John. *Engineering, Industrial, and Urban Transformation.* (Toronto and Buffalo: University of Toronto Press, 1997.)

[16]Jackson, John and Burtniak, John. *Railways in the Niagara Peninsula.* (Belleville, Ontario: Mika Publishing Company, 1978.)

[17]Jasen, Patricia. *Wild Things: Nature, Culture, and Tourism in Ontario, 1790-1914.* (Toronto and Buffalo: University of Toronto Press, 1995.)

[18]Johnson, J.K. *Historical Essays on Upper Canada.* (Toronto: McClelland and Stewart, 1975.)

[19]Johnson, J.K. and Wilson, Bruce. *Historical Essays on Upper Canada: New Perspectives.* (Ottawa, Canada: Carleton University Press, 1989.)

[20]Martin, Virgil. *Changing Landscapes of Southern Ontario.* (Erin, Ontario: The Boston Mills Press, 1988.)

[21]McCalla, Douglas. *Planting the Province: The Economic History of Upper Canada, 1784-1870.* (Toronto: University of Toronto Press, 1993.)

[22]McGreevy, Patrick. *Imagining Niagara: The Meaning and Making of Niagara Falls.* (Amherst: University of Massachusetts Press, 1994.)

[23]McIlwraith, Thomas. *Looking for Old Ontario: Two Centuries of Landscape Change.* (Toronto: University of Toronto Press, 1997.)

[24]McKinsey, Elizabeth. *Niagara Falls: Icon of the American Sublime.* (Cambridge and New York: Cambridge University Press, 1985.)

[25]Moore, Christopher. *The Loyalists: Revolution, Exile, Settlement.* (Toronto: Macmillan Canada, 1984.)

[26]Pentland, H. Clare. *Labour and Capital in Canada, 1650-1860.* (Toronto: James Lorimer & Company, 1981.)

[27]Pitegoff, Peter, ed. "Buffalo Change & Community: a symposium." *Buffalo Law Review* (39:2, Spring 1991): 313-607.

[28]Power, Michael and Butler, Nancy. *Slavery and Freedom in Niagara.* (Ontario: Niagara Historical Society, 2000.)

[29]Severance, Frank. *Old Trails on the Niagara Frontier.* (Cleveland: The Burrows Brothers Company, 1903.)

[30]Shipley, Robert. *St. Catharines: Garden on the Canal.* (Windsor: Windsor Publications, Ltd., 1987.)

[31]Sternberg, Ernest. "Staging a natural wonder," chap. In *The Economy of Icons: How Business Manufactures Meaning.* (Westport, CT: Praeger Publishers, 1999.)

[32]Thomas, Owen. *Niagara's Freedom Trail: A Guide to African-Canadian History on the Niagara Peninsula.* (Thorold, Ont: The Corporation , 1996.)

[33]Wallace, Anthony. *The Death and Rebirth of the Seneca.* (New York: Vintage Books, 1969.)

[34]White, Richard. *The Middle Ground: Indians, Empires, and Republics in the Great Lakes Region, 1650-1815.* (Cambridge and New York: Cambridge University Press, 1991.)

[35]Wyckoff, William. *The Developer's Frontier: The Making of the Western New York Landscape.* (New Haven: Yale University Press, 1988.)

[36]Young, N. Richard. "Welland to World War I: A case study of economic development and population expansion in the Niagara peninsula." in John Burtniak and Patricia Dirks, eds., *Immigration and Settlement in the Niagara Peninsula: Proceedings of the Third Annual Niagara Peninsula History Conference.* (St. Catharines: Brock University, 1981.)

at far left, top:
critique at installation, *pictured: from left to right:* Bonnie Ott, Petra Kempf, Brad Wales, Mike Webb, Kent Kleinman, Magda Cordell Mc Hale, Hadas Steiner.

second photo:
critique at installation, *pictured: from left to right:* Kenneth Frampton, John McCumiskey.

third photo:
critique at installation, *pictured: from left to right:* Bonnie Ott, Kenneth Frampton, Brad Wales, Kent Kleinman.

bottom photo:
critique at installation, *pictured: from left to right:* Bonnie Ott, Petra Kempf, Brad Wales, Mike Webb, Kent Kleinman.

large photo at right:
pictured: from left to right: from left to right Jim Churchill, Petra Kempf, Kenneth Frampton.

PETRA KEMPF

TERMINAL CITY

studio description and background

This studio confronted issues facing the future of an under-utilized stretch of railway property in New York City's borough of Brooklyn. The site is located in the district of Brooklyn known as Fort Greene. The boundaries for this project were the blocks bounded by Atlantic Avenue, Flatbush Avenue, Dean Street, and Carlton Street. This stretch consists primarily of vacant unpaved land, and suppressed railyards of the Long Island Railroad (LIRR). The area serves as an interchange point for the Metropolitan Transportation Authority (MTA), the Long Island Railroad (LIRR) and the New York City Transit. Located In the immediate vicinity of the site are the Williamsburgh Savings Bank, the Brooklyn Academy of Music, the Brooklyn Museum, the Brooklyn Technical High School and a number of government agencies. The composition of the population is wide ranging. Originally, the neighborhood was originally settled by the Spanish, today the area is home to large Latino and African American populations.

After several years of decline, downtown Brooklyn is experiencing an increase in both commercial and institutional investment. The studio challenged issues and problems facing the future of the Fort Greene neighborhood as a potential transportation hub for downtown Brooklyn. The main objective of this studio was to integrate a transportation hub into a diverse urban environment and to focus on the issue of how to deal with an underutilized railway property in the urban landscape. In addition, the studio investigated the hypothesis that re-using this particular railway property, coupled with the appropriate programs, would have beneficial effects for the city itself, as well as for the general renewal of this particular neighborhood. The students developed new programs to accommodate the spectrum of uses which a terminal of the twenty-first century should provide to serve not only its customers but also the neighborhood in which it is to be built.

Petra Kempf is an Assistant Professor of Architecture, at the University at Buffalo, State University of New York. She Received a Diplom Engineer Degree in Architecture from the Fachhochschule Darmstadt in 1996 and a M.S. in Advanced Architecture and Urban Design from Columbia University in 1997. In 1996 she was a recipient of an academic fellowship for Graduate Study Abroad DAAD (German Academic Exchange Service).

She has worked for various groups in the public and private sector, including the New York City Department of City Planning, the Van Alen Institute, The Project for Public Spaces, and with Richard Meier & Partners. She has taught at Parsons School of Design and is currently teaching at the University at Buffalo, and at the Pratt Institute in the Department of Architecture and Urban Design. Most recently, she won the 2001 annual Design Competition "City Limits" for Young Architects sponsored by the Architectural League in New York City.

The studio was divided into three parts: During the first part the students visited New York City in order to research and document the site from an urban point of view. The studio met with city agencies such as Brooklyn Office of the Department of City Planning and the Transportation Division in the Borough of Manhattan. Based on the students' discoveries, each student then took the assigned program, transformed it according to his/her findings and applied it then to the site. In the last stage each student incorporated a responsible building design.

exhibition

The studio concluded with an exhibition, produced and organized by students at the end of the semester. The exhibition was accompanied by a lecture given by internationally renowned architectural critic and Ware Professor at Columbia University, Kenneth Frampton. Professor Frampton is the author of numerous books including his most recent publication *Studies in Tectonic Culture*. His lecture "Megaform as Urban Landscape" focused on the discourse of Urban Megaforms throughout the modern urban landscape.

column 1, top to bottom:
projects by:
top: Steven Haardt;
middle: Ramsey Danham;
bottom: Steven Haardt

column 2, top to bottom:
top and middle:
Jorge Chang &
John McCumiskey;
bottom: Jason Herriven

column 3, top to bottom:
all images, project by:
Richard Maklary

column 4, top to bottom:
all images, project by:
Chris Siano

column 5, top to bottom:
all images, project by:
Benyu Yang & Mike Schwallie

column 6, top to bottom:
projects by:
bottom: Benyu Yang &
Mike Schwallie

column 7, top to bottom:
top and middle:
Leanne Vater;
bottom: Richard Maklary

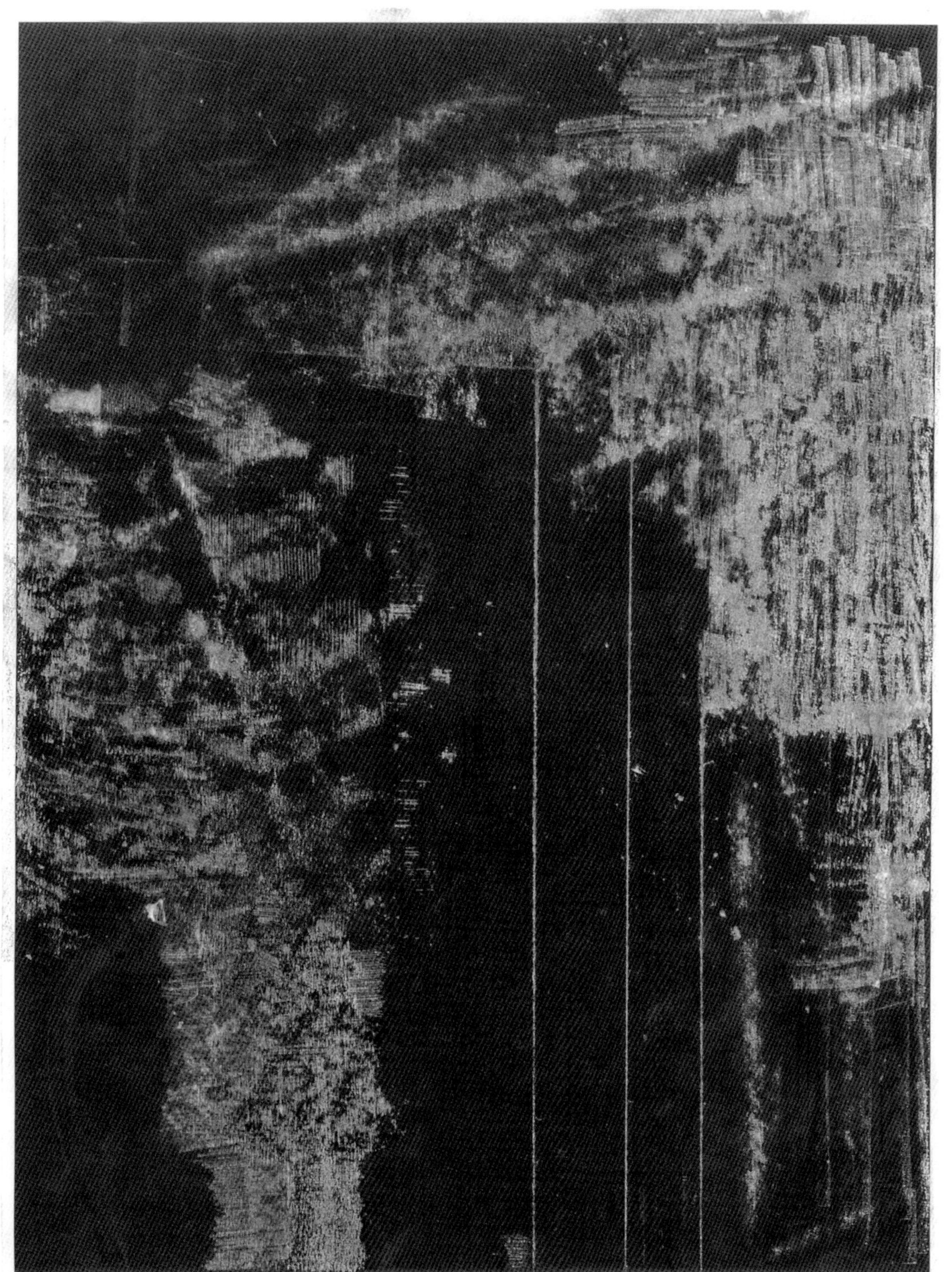

image at left:
"Displeasures"
Images completed by Joseph Sevene during first-year graduate study at the University at Buffalo, State University of New York. The images shown are scratched carbon on bond paper.

Mr.Sevene holds a B.S. in Philosophy and Art from the State University of New York.

INTERVIEW: NAN ELLIN

Nan Ellin is Associate Professor in the School of Architecture at Arizona State University. She holds an M.A., M.Phil., and Ph.D. from Columbia University and a B.A. from Bryn Mawr College. Ellin was a Fulbright Scholar in France where she carried our research for her dissertation on the European New Urbanism.

She is the author of *Postmodern Urbanism* (revised edition, Princeton Architectural Press, 1999) as well as numerous articles. Ellin is the editor of *Architecture of Fear* (Princeton Architectural Press, 1997). Having explored degenerative and reactive trends in urban design, she is now exploring reconstructive and proactive alternatives to these in a forthcoming book entitled *Integral Urbanism*. She is also writing a monograph on New York architect and urban designer Deborah Berke (Princeton Architectural Press).

ab **Nan, thank you for agreeing to speak with me today.**

Boundaries are constructs of the human mind which assist us in the definition of place and space and help us to include as well as to exclude. While these constructs can take physical form, what do you feel are the fundamental underpinnings with regard to the persistence of "boundary" throughout urban history, or for that matter, throughout history in general? That is, which reasons perpetuate the notion of boundary today and throughout history?

ne There is a haiku which expresses this eloquently:

but for the boundary
the mind is still
trapped within a frame
the mind exerts its highest creativity

Without boundaries—or limits—we would not have a frame of reference for thinking, acting, or building. Culture itself is a set of boundaries. But culture is inherently dynamic and so then are boundaries. Sometimes boundaries are regarded as too restrictive, so may be transgressed, transforming the nature and location of the boundary, whether it is a cultural boundary or a physical one. From inside the boundary, it can be a security blanket, a blinder to what is outside, or a restriction against which to rebel and bring about change. Regarded from the outside, a boundary can be a source of wonder and mystery or a source of frustration and anger at being excluded. Modernism sought to eliminate boundaries but this was its Achilles heel. Postmodernism reacted by erecting walls both real and metaphorical everywhere, a fortress urbanism. Now, we are witnessing many efforts to acknowledge the human need for boundaries but to ensure their permeability, allowing movement through them, and flexibility, allowing change through time.

ab **In the new Foreward to Postmodern Urbanism, you write, I'm paraphrasing here...,: " ... borders or edges may be geographically situated ... They may also be the conceptual membranes that separate ... it has grown increasingly clear that our** ab **future depends on the ways in which we negotiate the challenges posed by this condition." Could you elaborate on this observation, specifically, what do you see as the most recurrent challenges, and what potential outcomes might you foresee?**

ne It is important for us to learn from the mistakes of modernism and postmodernism and not fall into the same traps. In order to do so, we must go beyond their superficial manifestations and look deeply into their underlying presuppositions. Although outwardly very different, postmodernism did not really challenge the modernist tendency to think in binary oppositions, to deny certain changes taking place, and to insist upon architecture's separate-ness from and "superiority" to the rest of the landscape. While modern architecture and planning denied change by retreating into essentialisms and universalisms, postmodernism denied it by seeking inspiration from the past or from fiction. But the denial of change and the elitism that went along with that only further challenged the legitimacy of the profession in both instances. What postmodernism did challenge was modern idealism and aspirations for betterment. But this was a setback. Anxious to avoid the pitfalls of modernism, its criticism of it was truly misplaced. It should also be noted that the time was not yet ripe.

Now perhaps it is. Over the last decade, we have been witnessing a shift away from the modern logic of binary oppositions (expressed in the dialectic and in structuralism generally) in many fields from medicine and business to the academic disciplines and the design professions. Though perhaps still tentative, it is undeniable, expressed as challenges to traditional oppositions such as mind/body, reason/emotion, spirit/flesh, masculine/feminine and culture/nature. The shift away from binary logic is apparent in the displacement of linear, hierarchical, static models (the tree metaphor) by holistic, multi-centric, nonhierarchical, dynamic models (the web/network metaphor). In the case of the city, it is no longer center v. periphery, but a network of hubs with connecting spokes extending indefinitely through physical and virtual space. Culture and boundaries are not obliterated, not in the least, but it is no longer a condition of being strictly inside or outside. Rather, these are characterized by flux or flow, a fluidity of identities and of movement through space as well as time. There are opportunities for making connections between places and people but there are also opportunities for preserving distinctions. It is not the fortress city but nor is it bland homogenization.

The modern view of space as objective, homogenous, and neutral (or Euclidean space) is being superceded by an understanding which acknowledges and celebrates subjectivity, heterogeneity, and value-laden places. These shifts are apparent in the evolving models for buildings and cities. From the machine, to cities of the past, we are now seeking models simultaneously in ecology and new information technologies, for example: webs, networks, the world wide **web**, the inter**net**. This reorientation carries deep implications for the way in which urban design projects are conceived and implemented.

ab **Boundaries are usually regarded as those areas which make possible separation, while the marginal area adjacent to the border generally acts as a physical reinforcement or buffer zone. Given the change inherent to the notion of boundary, should these areas be redeveloped or meshed into the existing urban context or should these areas remain in some way as physical memory of the social differences they represent?**

ne OK, how do we translate these concepts into built form? One important thing to keep in mind is that each boundary is unique. Boundaries have their own reasons for being; programmatic, social, ecological, symbolic, etc. So if we are to intervene, we should understand the particular place in some depth through research into the physical site and its history and through ethnography. There will likely also be a client and some new program to engage. What we choose to do will depend on what we discover. The synthesis of our research may suggest that we reinforce, erase, or modify aspects of the boundary through our intervention. And it will suggest how we modify it.

Presumably, this solution would neither be "meshing it into the urban fabric," a somewhat modernist tendency to suppress difference. But nor would it be preserving the area as a "physical memory of the social differences they represent," a postmodernist tendency to suppress change. There is no set formula or recipe. I don't mean to be evasive, but one thing I can say for certain about this approach is that it is case-specific. In contrast to master planning which dominated most of the 20th century, this approach is not about controlling everything. Instead, it proposes more punctual interventions that contribute to activating places through the creation of thresholds or places of intensity. And it seeks to allow things to happen, things that may even be unforeseen. Gilles Deleuze and Felix Guattari in *A Thousand Plateaus* might describe this process as liberating the natural flows of desire which perpetually seek connections and syntheses from the repressive and hierarchical modern city. This approach might also be regarded as a form of "urban acupuncture" that liberates *chi*, or the life force; Ignasi de Sola Morales and Kenneth Frampton have suggested this. In the best case scenarios, these interventions have a tentacular or domino effect by catalyzing other interventions in an ongoing never-ending process. They can be applied to existing built environments as well as new development.

ab **As a follow up, in what way could, or should these "no man's land" spaces be reused to mend or heal some of the social difficulties they manifest?**

ne We have become very interested in these "no man's land" spaces, also described as in-between, interstitial, leftover, dead, or lost spaces. I think that part of our fascination with them is that they are the spaces that have somehow evaded planning, that are free of architecture. Appropriated by local people in response to their needs or completely abandoned and left to the elements, they can seem exotic to us. The spontaneous, haphazard, and collective quality of these places refreshes, soothes, and inspires our hyperrational souls. So, we are sometimes moved to celebrate them and leave them as they are. Other times, if the place is desolate or somehow causing harm to people or the environment, we may choose to "mend the seam" in the urban fabric or "heal the wound" in the urban organism.

The way in which we go about mending or healing would be informed by doing the research into the larger area first. The process of doing the research is not separate from the product, the intervention itself. For instance, if the place is contested and/or the people who use it feel disenfranchised, the process would bring them together to discuss solutions while empowering them. It is not strictly community design or participatory architecture since the designers become another constituency. They clearly bring their own views to the table based on their knowledge of the site, structures, materials, personal biases, and other issues while also listening carefully to the views of the other constituencies. Of course, there needs to be an attitude of openness toward learning from the others and a sincere desire to enhance this place. This will to betterment combined with the designers' skill can ideally generate a synergy among constituents and an intervention that enlivens a dead space or finds a lost one.

ab **I very much like your observation: "form follows fiction, fear, finesse and finance". It, in a sense, illustrates the limits or boundaries of creativity for design professionals within the urban realm. Which organizational strategies do you envision that may allow form to truly walk "hand in hand" with design intentions?**

ne I suppose that organizational strategies are important, but there is something deeper going on which is more significant. It has to do with a more holistic understanding of function. When form was to follow function throughout much of the last century, function was understood in a mechanistic way. Even the medical profession was understanding the body and anthropologists were interpreting cultural behavior as machine-like, each piece functioning to keep the larger whole (the body or culture) working efficiently. This twentieth-century tendency to elevate the machine and to see it as a metaphor and goal corresponded to the expansion of the factory system, mass production, and mass consumption. In the last decade, however, the information revolution, the new economy, and globalization have been transforming the contours of this political economy along with our ways of thinking. In addition, unfortunate urban, social, and ecological outcomes of the modern emphasis on separation and efficiency have reared their ugly heads. As a result, the attitude is shifting, slowly perhaps but definitively. In the larger sweep of history, the twentieth century may appear as an aberrant blip in its tendency to understand all in mechanistic and instrumental terms. We are not moving away from this exactly, but including it in a larger vision that is not embarrassed to include needs that may be symbolic, emotional, or spiritual. In fact, we now find the distinction between these and "purely" functional needs very difficult to make.

The postmodern tendencies for form to follow fiction, fear, finesse, and finance were largely reactive and failed to look at the big picture. Now we are returning to form follows function but function is defined much more broadly. The cynicism, arrogance, and glibness of much postmodern work might all be understood as a retreat from (or fear of) getting to the heart of the matter. This lack of engagement was ultimately not sustaining and not inspiring for a younger generation that is responding with a renewed idealism, this time imbued with a pragmatism and ambition to enlarge the scope and impact of architectural interventions.[1]

The result is a revision in architecture and planning theory and practice ranging from small-scale interventions to regional plans that I've been calling **Integral Urbanism**. An Integral Urbanism runs counter to our prevailing urbanism characterized by freestanding single-use buildings connected by freeways along with rampant sub(urban) sprawl and their attendant environmental, social, and aesthetic costs. In contrast to the master-planned functionally-zoned city which separates, isolates, alienates, and retreats, an Integral Urbanism emphasizes connection, communication, and celebration. While integrating the functions that the modern city separated, this approach also seeks to integrate conventional notions of urban, suburban, and rural to produce a new model for the contemporary city. In doing so, it considers means of integrating design with nature, the center with the periphery, the process with the product, local character with global forces, and people of different ethnicities, incomes, ages, and physical abilities.

Integral Urbanism exemplifies five qualities: **hybridity, connectivity, porosity, authenticity,** and **vulnerability**. Together, these qualities describe an attitude that values context and multifunctional places over objects and the separation of functions. Rather than presume an opposition between people and nature, buildings and landscape, and architecture and landscape architecture, this attitude presumes more symbiotic relationships. It also prizes borders and edges, conceptual as well as actual. This approach emphasizes re-integration — functional, social, disciplinary and professional — porous membranes or permeable boundaries, rather than the modernist attempt to dismantle them or postmodernist fortification, and design with movement in mind, both movement through space, or circulation, and through time, access to the past as well as dynamism and flexibility. These interventions are arrived at intuitively as well as rationally. Bucking convention, they are not developed or represented primarily in plan and section, but through experience and imagery suggesting the latent experiential quality that the intervention would activate. This imagery may be representational or abstract.

An Integral Urbanism offers punctuation marks or reference points to inflect the landscape and our experience in it. This approach activates places by creating thresholds, or places of intensity, where diversity thrives. These interventions activate "dead" or neutral spaces; they acknowledge and care for abandoned and neglected spaces. By increasing density of activity and perhaps building mass, they weave connections between places, people, and experiences. These transformations can respond to current needs and desires while also allowing for change as people and activities converge. An Integral Urbanism allows greater self-determination and empowerment because it brings people together with more time and energy to develop visions and implement them. Instead of running just to stay still, it allows us to move towards greater conservation and less waste, more quality time and overall satisfaction, and less distrust, paranoia, and fear.

In sum, convergences (ecological, social, programmatic) in space and time generate new hybrids. These hybrids, in turn, allow for new convergences and the process continues. This is, in fact, the definition of development. While the modern paradigm discouraged convergences through its emphasis on separation and control, this new paradigm encourages them.

An Integral Urbanism emphasizes:

- Networks not boundaries,
- Relationships and connections not objects,
- Interdependence not independence or dependence,
- Natural and social communities not just individuals,
- Transparency or translucency not opacity,
- Flux or flow not stasis,
- Permeability not walls,
- Mobility not permanence,
- Connections with nature and relinquishing control, not controlling nature.
- Catalysts, armatures, frameworks, punctuation marks, not final products, master plans, or utopias.

You bring up new organizational structures and these are occurring, I believe, in response to the changes I've just described. Rotterdam is a particularly fertile ground for this: Rem Koolhaas's new office AMO was established to acknowledge and validate this process. Ben van Berkel and Caroline Vos as well as MVRDV have also been restructuring to accommodate these changes. I think that new organizational structures are also emerging in the US, though we are perhaps less deliberate and articulate about them

a b **In *Postmodern Urbanism*, you speak of "re-tribalizations". Does this trend tend to create or disintegrate boundary conditions, both physically speaking, as well as conceptually or socially?**

n e The act of re-tribalizing reflects a desire to satisfy something that is missing, generally a sense of community, sanctity, and rootedness. Developing social networks and sets of thoughts or behaviors that go along with them creates new boundaries and may disintegrate old ones, but is not inherently a good or bad thing. I think it depends on the nature of the boundaries. Retribalizations may span a spectrum with escapist (reactive) tendencies at one end and engaging (proactive) ones at the other. The escapist tendency has a clear sense of who is in and who is out, clearly defined and inflexible rules which invoke tradition (real or invented), a clear power hierarchy, and well-defined geographic boundaries or places specifically for its members. Its sense of superiority in relation to who is out promotes a sense of competition with others and therefore an attitude which does not wish others the best. The other end of the continuum engages the present condition with an eye towards preparing for the future, has permeable boundaries so that membership is dynamic, sees the welfare and success of all as related so wishes all well, and has a democratic and flexible power structure, as well as shifting geographic boundaries. The paradox is that whereas the reactive tendency is borne of insecurity, it breeds conflict. And while the proactive tendency thrives on change, it strives to create harmony. Whereas the reactive may be likened to a set compass with a clear center and boundaries, the proactive may be likened to a gyroscope: it has a center but this center is always in motion and it likes it that way.

a b **In *Architecture of Fear*, you discuss and present a number of examples of the gated community as an approach toward "safe" living – an idea of safety in "like" numbers. Why do gated communities draw criticism, when for instance, more "exclusive" apartment buildings do not, in essence the main objectives of security and controlled community are similar?**

n e You are correct. The exclusive apartment building is in many ways a vertical version of the gated community and precedes it by almost a century. There are several reasons that it does not draw the kind of criticism that gated communities do. One is that the apartment building generally accomplishes its goal of security.

Its single manned entry tends to be much more effective than the horizontal version which has many possibly points of entry and often no one at the gate. As studies have demonstrated, the gated community's security is generally more symbolic than real. The second reason has to do with the impact on the larger city. By privatizing streets and turning its back to the surrounding city, gated communities balkanize the city physically. Also, given their sheer size, they segregate the city socially. In contrast, the exclusive apartment building opens onto the street, abuts other buildings which may house a different income group or be non-residential, and only occupies a small footprint of the city.

ab **Fifty years ago, Henry S. Churchill wrote: "planning, which is only another name for social control over the use of land, arose from the need of maintaining social, political and economic order among large groups of people living in close proximity."[2] Has this opinion changed with regard to the development of urban boundaries, for instance, the gated development/community?**

ne Well, as he was saying that, the suburban boom was underway in the United States, leading to a vast dispersal of our population that has largely continued to produce our current sprawl. So while the need to maintain order is still a principle motive for planning, it is not necessarily related to "people living in close proximity" as the scale has shifted to the region, watershed, or even the globe. The scope has also grown to include environmental planning and perhaps communications planning. As the scale and scope of planning have enlarged, however, the power of planning agencies may have withered as neighborhood organizations and homeowners associations have grown exponentially in number and power over the last decade. This shift has definite pros since it is more inclusive and participatory, but also definite cons because the larger picture and consideration of the long-term can be neglected. The recent spate of ballot items concerning growth boundaries and environmental concerns suggests an increasingly progressive electorate with regards to these issues which is the key to truly "smart" growth.

N O T E S

1. Art critic Suzi Gablik, for instance, observed a "change in the general social mood toward a new pragmatic idealism and a more integrated value system that brings head and heart together in an ethic of care" (1993, p.11).

2. Churchill, Henry S. *The City is the People.* (New York: Reynal & Hitchcock 1945.)

Nan Ellin presented her research on urbanism to the School of Architecture and Planning on 7 October, 1998..

prints at left:

Untitled images at right completed by Joseph Sevene following first year graduate study at the University at Buffalo, State University of New York. The work shown is mixed media on cotton.

JOSÉ BUSCAGLIA

14 MAPAS DE PRECISIONES IMAGINATIVAS

José Buscaglia, M.Arch., Ph.D., es profesor auxiliar de la Facultad de Artes y Ciencias y director de los programas de la Universidad de Bufalo en Cuba y el Caribe. Su libro titulado *Naciones Imposibles: el cuerpo y el ideal en el mundo mulato del Caribe* [Editorial de la Universidad de Minesota] será publicado a finales de este año.

Tal vez no exista otro recurso del poder que haya gozado de una reputación tan intachable como el mapa en lo que a su alegada objetividad científica y neutralidad ideológica se refiere. El mapa es quizás el receptáculo que mejor cabida ofrece a lo que Timothy Mitchell denomina como las técnicas del orden y de la verdad que rigen en función de la lógica de la otredad.[1] Por esto la cartografía ha jugado un papel importante aunque poco estudiado en el desarrollo del protocolo espacial de la llamada modernidad y ha sido instrumento imprescindible en la invención y legitimización de las relaciones geográficas que han dividido al mundo entre un sujeto histórico e histriónico europeo o europeizante y uno que, de una u otra forma, nunca da el grado. En las Indias, la primera escisión establecida por la cartografía fue entre castellanos y caníbales, división esta que tuvo condiciones muy reales en términos espaciales en cuanto las islas fueron divididas por fuerza entre las que pertenecían al Rey de Castilla y las que los arauacos defendían con flechas ungidas en curare. La histeria que permeaba la ideología cartográfica en este caso era pura alucinación. Como bien ha demostrado Peter Hulme, respondió al miedo del indio caribe indomable y resultó en la invención de un otro absoluto cuya espantosa imágen acechó la imaginación del europeo como la antítesis misma del colonizador cristiano.[2] En este duo dinámico del bien y del mal la imágen del caníbal fue también un retrato del colonizador en su más extrema posibilidad del ser. A tal punto, podría decirse que fue un terrible cargo de conciencia el que bautizó a esta parte de la geografía indiana cuando en 1540 Alonso de Santa Cruz rotuló en su mapa a las Antillas Menores como las Islas de los Caníbales, término del cual se derivaría toda la nomenclatura de lo caribeño. En ese momento, en algún lugar entre las Antillas Mayores y Menores se trazó la línea que mantendría al europeo separado del caníbal —y de sí mismo como un caníbal— para enmarcar el orden y la verdad del mundo de la colonialidad hasta nuestros días.

He aquí, pues, los orígenes de lo que Raymond Craib llama "geografías imaginativas" que fueron generalmente usufructuarias del patronato imperial y que se caracterizaron por su carácter especulativo y por sus preocupaciones estéticas. Como parte de un mismo fenómeno Craib identifica también unas "geografías precisas" que respondieron a necesidades estratégicas y funcionales en el desarrollo del comercio y de la

JOSÉ BUSCAGLIA

14 MAPS OF IMAGINARY PRECISION

José Buscaglia, M.Arch., Ph.D., is an Assistant Professor in the College of Arts and Sciences of the University at Buffalo, State University of New York. He is also Director of Cuban and Caribbean Programs at the University. Currently Mr. Buscaglia is working on a book entitled *Impossible Nations: Body and Ideal in the Mulatto World of the Caribbean* [University of Minnesota Press].

Perhaps there is no other instrument of power which has enjoyed a more undeserving reputation than the map, at least as far as its alleged scientific objectivity and ideological neutrality is concerned. The map is perhaps the receptacle that best accommodates what Timothy Mitchell calls the techniques of order and truth which support the discourse of Otherness.[1] Because of this, cartography has played a very important although not sufficiently studied role in the invention and legitimization of the geographic relations that have divided the world of so called modernity between a historical and a histrionic subject of European or Europeanizing pedigree and one which, for some reason or another, is never a *quantum sufficit*. In this sense, the first major cartographic manipulation made in the New World was between Castillians and Cannibals, a division which came to have very concrete spatial delimitations in the West Indies where the islands were divided between those which belonged to the King of Castille and the ones which the native Arawaks defended with poisoned arrows. The hysteria which permeated cartographic ideology at the time was pure hallucination. As Peter Hulme has demonstrated, it responded to the fear of the irreducible Caribs and it resulted in the invention of an absolute Other whose fearful image stalked the European imagination as the antithesis of the Christian colonizer.[2] In this dynamic duo of good and evil the image of the Cannibal was also a portrait of the colonizer in its outmost potentiality for being. In fact, it could be said that this part of the geography of the Indies was baptized by a guilty conscience when, in 1540, Alonso de Santa Cruz labled the Lesser Antilles in his map as the Islands of the Cannibals, from whence the Caribbean nomenclature was eventually derived. Right then and there, somewhere between the Greater and the Lesser Antilles, the line that was to keep the European from the Cannibal—and from himself as the Cannibal—was drawn to frame the order and the truth of the world of coloniality to this day.

Here then are the origins of what Raymond Craib calls the "imaginative geographies" which were generally graced with imperial patronage and characterized by their speculative tendencies and their preoccupation with aesthetic concerns. As part of the same phenomenon Craib identifies "precise geographies" that responded

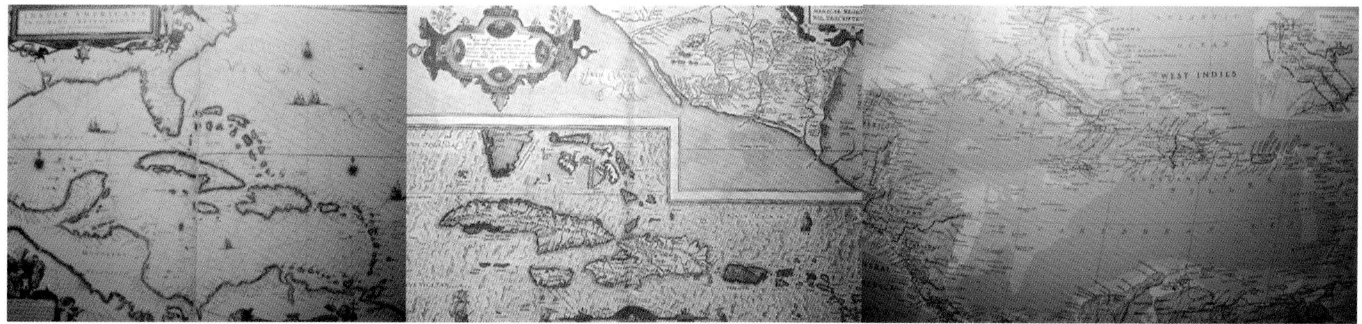

above, left to right:
Map of Abraham Ortelius, 1584;
Insulae Americanae, 1634;
The Caribbean, circa 1970.

sobre, ido a la derecha:
Mapa de Abraham Ortelius, 1584;
Insulae Americanae, 1634;
El Caribe, circa 1970.

colonización.[3] Ambas geografías—la imaginativa y la precisa—fueron inseparables, realidad ésta que ya era evidente en el mapa anónimo de la escuela de Dieppe fechado alrededor de 1540 hoy propiedad de la Biblioteca Koninklijke de La Haya. Basado en el padrón general de Carlos V, que en su tiempo recogió la información geográfica más fidedigna, lo preciso en este mapa comparte el escenario con la primera representación cartográfica del aborígen que trabaja felízmente para su encomendero castellano. Habrá quienes piensen que estas son cosas del pasado, producto de un mundo donde no se distinguía claramente entre la realidad y la fantasía. Hoy en día, mientras el transbordador espacial recorre las órbitas celestes en pos, se nos dice, de un mapa más científicamente detallado de la superficie terrestre, pareciera que la geografía precisa ha superado casi completamente las frivolidades estéticas y las manipulaciones ideológicas de la antigua geografía imaginativa. Nada pudiera ser más falso. Como bien apunta Craib, el mapa es por lo general una expresión del deseo más que la suma total de una realidad en particular.[4]

En cuanto a las Indias Occidentales, hoy conocidas como las islas del Mar Caribe, la agenda de la geografía precisa se había cumplido ya a finales del siglo XVI como se demuestra en el **mapa de Abraham Ortelius de 1584**.[5] Ya cuando Guillermo Blaeu publica su "**Insulae Americanae**"[6] en 1634 el Caribe ha sido cartográficamente reducido en cuanto a la ubicación precisa de sus tierras y la delineación detallada de las costas se refiere. Aún así, no podemos evitar percibir las maquinaciones estético-ideoleógicas que se nos presentan en este mundo ausente ahora de caníbales. Encima de la carta marina hay dibujos de navíos mercantes que surcan un mar calmado y de vientos favorables para el comercio. Tanta bienaventuranza nos podría hacer olvidar que mientras Blaeu trazaba sus mapas la importación de africanos a las Antillas se quintuplicaba en respuesta al desarrollo vertiginoso de la economía de plantación. En aquel entonces nada de esto era un secreto. Las conexiones eran más bien obvias. Además de poseer la casa impresora más grande del mundo, Blaeu era también cartógrafo oficial de la Compañía Holandesa de las Indias Orientales, la empresa mercantilista que armó el comercio Atlántico en torno a la trata negrera y al transporte del azúcar del Caribe y el Brasil a Europa. El negocio era redondo pues la Casa Blaeu no sólo manejaba el padrón holandés para la compañía mercantil sino que su Gran Atlas (o Atlas Major) llegó a ser el libro mejor cotizado de todo el siglo XVII. En otras palabras, la figura del cartógrafo reune en este momento histórico la piedra con la mano que la tira, las precisiones económicas con sus justificaciones imaginativas, y varios de los instrumentos más importantes de la época y del crímen más grande de la era: el látigo, el buque y la imprenta. Esta realidad nunca fue pasada por alto en la Casa Blaeu donde en 1635 se publicó el gran compendio cartográfico del mundo bajo el doble título de Novus Atlas o Theatrum, haciendo de esta forma alusión directa a la dualidad funcional de la geografía moderna. Y aunque la técnica de iluminación o coloración utilizada en "Insulae Americanae" es característica de la época, a mí siempre me ha parecido que es en este

to functional and strategic needs in the development of the commercial and colonial enterprises.[3] These two geographies—the imaginative and the precise—were inseparable, a fact that was already evident in an anonymous map of the school of Dieppe dated around 1540 which is today part of the collection of the Koninklijke Library in The Hague. Based on the "padrón general" of Charles V, the Spanish map which contained the most accurate information of the day, the precise geography in the Dieppe map shares the stage with the first graphic representation of an Indian who works happily for his Castillian master. Some may think that these are things of the past, the product of a world where no clear distinction was made between reality and illusion. It would seem that today, as the space shuttle orbits the Earth in order to obtain, we are told, a more detailed map of the planet's surface, the agenda of precise geographies has practically overshadowed the aesthetic frivolities and ideological manipulations of the old imaginative geographies. Nothing could be farther from the truth. As Craib points out, "a map is often an expression of desire rather than a summation of reality."[4]

As far as the West Indies is concerned, the agenda of precise geographies had been fulfilled by the end of the sixteenth century as evidenced in the **map of Abraham Ortelius of 1584**.[5] By the time Willem Blaeu published his "**Insulae Americanae**"[6] in 1634 the Caribbean had been cartographically reduced as far as the precise location of land masses and detailed delineation of its coasts was concerned. Nevertheless, we cannot hope to avoid the aesthetic and ideological machinations that are presented to us in this world now devoid of cannibals. On top of the chart there are drawings of merchant ships sailing effortlessly under the favorable trade winds. Such blessing could make us forget that while Blaeu composed his maps the importation of Africans to the West Indies was growing fivefold in response to the vertiginous development of the plantation economy. None of that was a secret then. The connections were rather obvious. Besides having the largest publishing house in the world, Blaeu was also the official cartographer of the Dutch East India Company, the mercantile enterprise that organized Atlantic commerce around the importation of African slaves to the Caribbean and Brazil and, in turn, the exportation of Caribbean and Brazilian sugar to Europe. Blaeu's business thrived for not only was he the keeper of the Dutch "padrón" but his Great Atlas or Atlas Major came to be the best selling book of the entire seventeenth century. In other words, the figure of the cartographer embodied the spirit of the age, linking the precision of the economic enterprise with its imaginative justifications and placing around his image all the evidence of the crime: the whip, the merchant vessel and the printing press. This much was never concealed by Blaeu and his associates who in 1635 published the great collection of the maps of the world under the double title of Novus Atlas or Theatrum, making a direct allusion to the functional duality of modern geography. And even when the coloration or illumination technique used in "Insulae Americanae" was characteristic of the time, I have always thought that it is in this image, more than in any other, where the essence of the mercantile world of coloniality is pictographically presented in the clearest of ways. These plum little islands that look like candy seem as if they could be picked off the map and placed in the mouth to be consumed one at a time. These are the sweet islands of the West Indies and this is the cartographic impression that has since sustained the geographic order of the insular subcontinent of the Americas.

There is, in fact, little difference between Ortelius' map and today's standard map of "**the Caribbean**."[7] Here the Pacific coast of New Spain, which appears in Ortelius' map in the upper right hand corner, was simply replaced by the map of the Panama Canal Zone. To emphasize the importance of the isthmian crossing the Canal Zone has been reproduced at a monstrous scale that seems to turn the US colony into the greatest of the Antilles. The placement of the Canal Zone along the eastern boundary of the Caribbean Sea may not be a coincidence altogether. In this Zonian tandem the United States controls the two entrance points to the inner sea in such a way

mapa, más que en ninguno otro, donde se resume pictográficamente de la forma más clara la esencia del mundo mercantilista de la colonialidad. Cualquiera diría que estas islas gorditas que hoy nos parecieran golosinas de diversos sabores pudieran recogerse con las manos para echárselas en la boca una a una. Estas son las islas dulces del Océano Septentrional y este es el cuño cartográfico que desde entonces ha dictado el órden geográfico del subcontinente insular americano.

Del mapa de Ortelius al mapa estándard actual de "**the Caribbean**"[7] solo hubo que dar un paso. Aquí simplemente se cambió la costa pacífica de la Nueva España, que aparece en el recuadro superior de la carta orteliana, por el mapa de la zona del canal de Panamá. Por supuesto, para enfatizar la importancia máxima del tajo ístmico, la zona del canal aparece en la esquina superior derecha, ampliada a una escala monstruosa que la convierte en la isla más grande de las Antillas. No por coincidencia debe haber sido situado el recuadro a la entrada o boca del mar Caribe, guardando la frontera superior que marca el arco de las Antillas. En este tándem zoniano los Estados Unidos controlan las dos entradas del Caribe de manera que la representación ampliada del canal cumple la función alegórica de ser una suerte de cinturón de castidad que convierte al Caribe en un mar cerrado, en el Mare Nostrum usoniano.[8] En este mapa la geografía precisa sigue compartiendo felizmente el escenario con la imaginativa. Pero todavía hay casos donde la última se impone sobre la primera, convirtiendo al Caribe en el objeto cartográfico que resume todo deseo.

Recuerdo que de pequeño siempre me parecía extraño encontrarme con el mantelito de papel que es tan común ver en los restuarantes turísticos o de comida criolla en mí país y que invariablemente muestra un mapa de las islas rodeado de una marginalia pictográfica que es todo un discurso de lo exótico y de su explotación. Desde entonces he viajado por casi todo el Caribe y he podido comprobar que mi país no es el único mundo que se coloca como aperitivo entre los dientes del tenedor y el filo del cuchillo. Lo mismo ocurre desde Cuba hasta Barbados, desde las Bahamas a Bahía.

Sometamos a escrutinio la geografía imaginaria en dos de estos mapas de comedor. En el primero, el **mapa amarillo de Puerto Rico**[9], la isla aparece protegida por seis recuadros cuya silueta imita la forma de la garita o caseta del centinela. En San Juan y en el resto de las ciudades muradas del Caribe todas las fortificaciones están coronadas por estas casetas de piedra. Pero ha sido en Puerto Rico donde, desde los años veinte, la propaganda del estado colonial ha promovido a la garita como símbolo iconográfico representativo de la ciudad de San Juan.[10] Esta es una alusión terrible a la historia de lo que por cuatrocientos años fuera un presidio o bastión militar y confirma la noción del puertorriqueño como centinela o guardián de las fronteras imperiales, rol este que, al menos oficialmente, los vecinos de la "Muy Noble y Muy Leal"[11] ciudad de San Juan parecen haber desempeñado fielmente, tanto bajo la corona española como bajo la águila imperial usoniana.

Para develar la transparencia ideológica del concepto valga prestar atención a las ilustraciones enmarcadas por las silueta de las garitas. Sobre el nombre de Puerto Rico hay una representación del monumento a Juan Ponce de León, adelantado en la conquista del Borikén y símbolo imperecedero del sometimiento y el exterminio del pueblo aborígen. Dando la vuelta hacia la izquierda, se encuentra la Capilla del Santo Cristo de la Salud, una ermita sanjuanera que en el mapa evoca el triunfo del cristianismo. Acto seguido hay una estampa del Castillo de San Felipe del Morro, símbolo máximo del régimen militarista y carcelario de la colonia, lugar que fuera una vez teatro de ejecuciones públicas y campo de acceso vedado para la población citadina. Podría decirse sin temor a equivocarse que quienes han controlado el Morro han regido a Puerto Rico y es por esto que el castillo, como toda la isla y sus

above, left to right:
Green Puerto Rico;
Yellow Map of Puerto Rico;
The New World, 1540

sobre, ido a la derecha:
Puerto Rico Verde;
Mapa Amarilla de Puerto Rico;
Mundo Nuevo, 1540

that the blown-up map of the Canal Zone serves the allegorical function of being a sort of chastity belt that turns the Caribbean into a closed sea, into the Usonian[8] Mare Nostrum. In this map the precise geographies continue to share the scene with the imaginative ones. But there are other cases where the imaginative geographies override and impose themselves over the precise ones, turning the Caribbean into the cartographic object that is the focus of all desire.

As a child growing up in Puerto Rico I remember always feeling a certain unease when looking at the paper place mats which are frequently featured in the restaurants that cater to tourists and to the lovers of "comida criolla" or Creole food, as they invariably showed a map of the main island surrounded by a pictographic marginalia which was a veritable discourse of the exotic and of its exploitation. Since then I have traveled throughout the West Indies and found that my country is not the only world that gets served as an aperitif between the points of the fork and the knife's jagged edge. The same phenomenon gets repeated from Cuba to Barbados, from the Bahamas to Bahia.

Let us scrutinize the imaginary geographies of two such dinning room maps. In the first one, a **yellow map of Puerto Rico**[9] is guarded by six picture windows in the shape of bartizans. In San Juan, as in the rest of the walled cities of the Caribbean, all the fortified walls are crowned with such guard posts. But it has been in San Juan where, since the 1920's, the propaganda apparatus of the colonial state has promoted the bartizan as the iconographic symbol most representative of the city. [10] This is a terrible reference to the history of what for four hundred years was a *presidio* or military outpost of the Spanish Empire and it promotes the notion that Puerto Ricans are the sentinels or guardians of the imperial frontier, a role which the residents of the "Very Noble and Very Loyal"[11] city of San Juan seem to have dutifully performed, at least officially, both under the Spanish Crown as under the Usonian imperial eagle.

In order to reveal the ideological transparency of this concept we need to consider the six images that are framed inside the silhouettes of the bartizans. Above the name Puerto Rico there is a drawing of the monument to Juan Ponce de Leon, conqueror of the land the natives called Boriken and symbol of the subjugation, and extermination of the aboriginal peoples. To the left is a picture of the Santo Cristo Chapel , a shrine whose image evokes the triumph of Christianity. Next is a view of the Castle of San Felipe del Morro, the strongest symbol of the military and penal colonial regime, a place that was the site of public executions and otherwise an area where residents of the city were kept from. It could be said that those who have held the high ground above the city from El Morro have ruled Puerto Rico and it is because of this that the castle, like the entire island and its peoples is, as we

gentes es, como decimos los puertorriqueños, propiedad federal. Justo debajo de Juan Ponce, se encuentra el Palacio de la Fortaleza de Santa Catalina dibujada de tal forma que se puedan observar ondeando sobre su planta superior las banderas puertorriqueña y usoniana. La Fortaleza ha sido residencia de los regidores coloniales de Puerto Rico en sucesión ininterrumpida, desde los primeros que reemplazaron a Juan Ponce hasta nuestros días. He aquí la colonia más estable y antigua de la historia moderna. Inmediatamente después encontramos la playa de Luquillo con sus palmeras y parasoles. Es importante mencionar que en la iconografía turística las palmeras son invariablemente la evidencia más directa de que se ha efectuado una agresión en el campo de la representación contra los naturales del país: las palmeras están ahí dando sombra al turista y haciendo las veces de centinelas mudos y ciegos que pueblan el paisaje en substitución de los temibles e inoportunos naturales. La sexta garita muestra a una pareja admirando la maravillosa naturaleza del bosque húmedo y tropical, de ese paisaje paradisíaco que igualmente ausente del elemento nativo recibe ahora al turista para que se suba a la cima del monte y, como diría Mary Louise Pratt, para que se sienta rey de todo aquello que divisa.[12] De alguna forma la historia de Puerto Rico que se resume en este mapa de comedor debió ser preparada para ayudar a la feliz y apacible digestión de todo comensal invitado a este banquete en homenaje a la más aparentemente exitosa y menos problemática empresa colonizadora. Sin duda esta cartografía imaginativa podría provocar la indigestión de otros tantos que pudieran ver el mantelito como una forma de propagar con impunidad el más descarado discurso colonialista. Pareciera imposible pero, en cuanto a mapas de comedor se trata, los hay todavía peores.

Podríamos llegar en avión a **un Puerto Rico verde**,[13] [véase ilustración en la paginación anterior] tierra de la más dulce piña, del maraquero mulato vestido a la usanza cubana de décadas pasadas y de la mulata medio mora que aguarda como flor misma de la frondosa selva tropical a que la recojan y se la lleven de recuerdo. Aquí nuevamente están las palmeras, ahora rodeadas de las imágenes del ocio y el placer. Ahí está la botella de ron como recuerdo de los malévolos pasatiempos de la plantación; la pesca de la aguja azul, que es una especie de safari caribeño; el buceador con todo su equipo, verdadero hombre de acción en la poco heróica categoría del turista como descubridor de mundos submarinos; y la gringa güera en paños menores cual Venus boticheliana haciendo su entrada triunfal en el mundo colonial sobre el cual viene a regir como representación viva de la belleza. Esta versión usoniana del "Jardín de las delicias" tropical fue impreso en Coatesville Pensilvania. Por esto no nos sorprende que, a diferencia de los personajes cuidadosamente armados por el Bosco, el autor de este mantelillo seleccionó imágenes de truchas y lobinas que, fuera de la lata, nunca se han visto nadar en agua salada. De algún modo, igual que el colonizador europeo ante el caníbal, este artista gráfico también estuvo viéndose a sí mismo dentro de esa otredad que fue en un momento el objeto de su deseo.

Visto de esta forma, todos los mapas del Caribe, tanto los mapas "oficiales" como "turísticos," parecen ser una invitación a la violencia. Todos presentan el lugar como uno de paso, de uso y de abuso, pero no como un lugar para crecer y multiplicarse. ¿Será posible que los pueblos caribeños carezcan aún de una cartografía propia que describa su mundo en su propio lenguaje y no cirniéndose a los protocolos que los cartógrafos del siglo XVII impusieron sobre su geografía? Creo que sí y es por esto que me he dado a la tarea de repensar de distintas formas el mundo que se recoge a orillas del seno caribeño, manteniendo en mente que tal proyecto debe ser por definición un discurso opuesto a las agendas colonialistas y a los designios de ciertas jerarquías socioraciales de la región cuyos miembros han favorecido generalmente los prejuicios europeos o europeizantes. Utilizando el método de la *charrette* de la antigua École des Beaux Arts como método de trabajo produje catorce mapas de precisones imaginativas en secuencia. En todos utilicé como plantilla el mapa estándard del Caribe de la compañía Rand McNally.[14] Demás está decir que estas son versiones personales, tentativas y muy preliminares de un

Puerto Ricans use to say, "propiedad federal" or U.S. government property. Right below Juan Ponce is the Palace of the Fortaleza de Santa Catalina drawn in such a way so as to highlight the Puerto Rican and the Usonian flags waving above. The Palace of the Fortaleza has been the residence of Puerto Rico's colonial governors in an unbroken succession, form the first ones who replaced Juan Ponce to this day. Here is then the most stable and the oldest colony of the modern world. Next we find a view of Luquillo Beach with its palm trees and umbrellas. It is important to point out that in tourist iconography the palm tree is invariably the clearest sign that an aggression in the representative order, directed against the natives of the land, has taken place: the palm trees are always there to provide shade for the tourist and acting as silent and blind guardians that populate the landscape in substitution of the native inhabitants who at times might seem a nuisance or pose a threat to the visitor. The sixth bartizan shows a couple admiring the marvelous vegetation of the rain forest, of that paradisaical landscape equally devoid of natives that now receives the tourist and invites him to climb to the top and to think himself the monarch of all that he surveys, as Mary Louise Pratt would put it.[12] In some way the history of Puerto Rico which is summarized in this dinning room map must have been prepared to aid the guests in the happy and most uneventful digestion as they sit at the table of the seemingly successful and less problematic of colonial enterprises. No doubt, this type of imaginative geography may cause the opposite effect on those who, witnessing such a colonialist discourse being propagated with impunity, may get a serious case of indigestion. Incredibly enough, as far as dinning room maps go, worst ones do exist.

We could arrive by plane to a **green Puerto Rico**[13] [see illustration on previous page], the land of the sweetest pineapple, of the Mulatto who plays the maracas dressed up in the fashion of the old Cuban musicians, and of the Moorish-looking Mulattress who waits, like a flower of the rain forest, to be picked and carried home as a souvenir. Here are the palm trees again. They are now surrounded by images of leisure and pleasure. There is the bottle of rum as a memento of the twisted pastimes of the plantation; deep-sea fishing which is a sort of Caribbean safari; the diver in full gear that is the image of the tourist as a man of action in the less-than-heroic category of discoverer of underwater worlds; and the blond Gringa in her bathing suit who, like a botichelian Venus is making her triumphal entrance into the colonial world she has come to rule over as the embodiment of Beauty. This Usonian version of a tropical "Garden of Delights" was printed in Coatesville Pennsylvania. Because of this it is not surprising that, contrary to the carefully assembled figures of Hieronymus Bosch, the author of this place mat chose to portray fish like bass and trout that have never been seen swimming in salt water. Somewhere along the line, like the early European colonizers before the Cannibals, this graphic artist was also projecting himself into that otherness that was at some point the object of his desire.

Seen in this light both the "official" and the "touristic" maps of the Caribbean are an invitation to violence. In every case they present the Caribbean as a good destination to visit, to use and to abuse, but not necessarily as a good place to call home. Could it be possible that the peoples of the Caribbean still do not possess a cartography of their own, one that describes their world in their own terms and not according to the conditions imposed upon their geography by the map makers of the 17th century? I think so and it is because of this that I have set myself to the task of creating an alternative cartography for the world of the Caribbean Basin. Such a project, I believe, would by definition need to think itself as a counter-discourse to the colonialist agendas and to the designs of certain socioracial hierarchies in the region whose members have generally favored the European or Europeanizing prejudices. Working in the tradition of the Beaux Arts' *charrette* I came up with a quick succession of fourteen maps of imaginative precission. In every case I used the standard Rand McNally map of the Caribbean as a template.[14] Suffice it to say, this is a very personal, tentative and preliminary iteration of a project that also by

above, left to right:
1. Colonial Cosmography;
2. The Fleet;
3. Genealogical Map.

sobre, ido a la derecha:
1. Cosmografia Colonial ;
2. La Flota;
3. Mapa Genealógico.

proyecto que, igualmente y por definición, necesita ser mucho más amplio. También de cierta forma he montado un juego de contrapunteo entre Cuba y Puerto Rico, por ser éstas las dos ínsulas americanas que mejor conozco.

Los orígenes de la cartografía caribeña son los orígenes de la colonialidad. Nada pudo ser más claro ya que, en un principio, el colonizador y el cartógrafo coincidieron en la misma persona. Ahí está Colón y, más importante aún, Juan de la Cosa quien vino en 1496 con Alonso de Ojeda acompañado de Américo Vespucio de tal forma que Vespucio le dió a América su nombre y de la Cosa le dió al mundo su primer mapa. En el mismo el pendón real está hincado firmemente sobre Cuba y La Española. Medio siglo más tarde, en 1540, Sebastián Munster colocó al "**Nuevo Mundo**"[15] en el centro del mundo y a las Antillas como el *axis mundi* de una cosmografía exógena, generada y reclamada desde fuera. El elemento más prominente del mapa son las armas de Castilla, colocadas sobre Puerto Rico en señal de posesión, gesto que está reforzado por la nomenclatura Hispania-Hispaniola que además efectivamente y por primera vez ilustra la relación inseparable entre la modernidad europea y la colonialidad caribeña. Medio milenio más tarde el Caribe sigue siendo un mar colonial y cerrado donde el orden se impone desde la América septentrional que en mi versión actualizada, titulada "**cosmografía colonial**" aparece señalada como la Usonia Imperium. Créanlo o no, aquí todavía rige prácticamente invicto el orden mercantil colonial clásico en cuanto Puerto Rico es el mercado cautivo por excelencia, puerto cerrado para todo buque mercante que no sea de bandera usoniana. Y ahí también está Cuba que, aunque insumisa, es igualmente cautiva en cuanto se mantiene cercada por la armada usoniana y forzosamente apartada del papel que le correspondería desempeñar en la economía regional.

Los antecedentes inmediatos de este teatro colonial se encuentran también en el siglo XVII, en aquel mundo de "**la flota**" que hizo de las islas verdaderas ciudadelas flotantes dentro de un orden mercantil que por primera vez le daba la vuelta al mundo. En esos años las riquezas de las naciones cruzaron a toda vela el Caribe mientras gentes de todas las naciones llegaron allí para echar raíces. Ahí están Veracruz, La Habana, Santo Domingo, San Juan y Cartagena, ancladas al servicio de intereses ajenos y relacionadas entre sí en un parentesco de presidios donde el convento y el prostíbulo compartían la cuadra bajo la sombra del castillo.

Cumpliendo tal vez con algún obscuro principio de la justicia geográfica decidí condenar a Francia, España e Inglaterra a ser arrancadas de la vera oriental atlántica y trasladadas a donde ellas un día deportaron a toda una humanidad. En este "**mapa genealógico**" las naciones imperiales están reunidas con sus antiguas colonias, fantasía esta que no queda muy lejana de la realidad, sobretodo en el caso de los departamentos ultramarinos franceses y en la nostálgia que se siente hoy en España por Cuba y que de alguna forma macabra se pone de

definition needs to be much broader. In addition, I have set up a certain game of counterpointing between Cuba and Puerto Rico as these are the two Caribbean islands that I personally know best.

The origins of Caribbean cartography are the origins of coloniality. It could not be otherwise for the colonizer was himself the first map maker. Such was the case with Columbus and, most notably, with Juan de la Cosa who accompanied Americo Vespucio in Alonso de Ojeda's expedition of 1496. Vespucio gave America its name and de la Cosa gave the world its first world map, one in which the arms of Castille were firmly planted over the islands of Cuba and Hispaniola. Half a century after de la Cosa, in 1540, Sebastian Münster placed "**the New World**"[15] in the center of the world and the Antilles, in turn, as the *axis mundi* of an exogenous cosmography that was generated and claimed from beyond itself. In it the flag of Castille flies above the island of Puerto Rico as the most prominent feature of the map, a claim that is reinforced by the labeling of both Hispania and Hispaniola (the Spanish island), effectively portraying for the first time the inseparable relation between European modernity and Caribbean coloniality. Half a millennium later the Caribbean continues to be a closed colonial sea ruled from North America which in my updated version of Münster's map, entitled "**colonial cosmography**", is labeled Usonia Imperium. Believe it or not, classic colonial mercantilism is still alive insofar as Puerto Rico is the captive market par excellence where no ship can trade lest it be under Usonian flag. Cuba is also there, always in a state of rebellion but equally captive to the degree that it is blockaded by the Usonian navy and is thereby forcibly kept from the role it should rightfully play in the regional economy.

The immediate antecedents of this colonial theater are also to be found in the seventeenth century, in the system of the Spanish galleon fleet, or simply "**the fleet**", which established the first truly global order and which turned these islands into floating citadels. In those years the wealth of nations sailed fast through the Caribbean while peoples from all the nations of the world came to call the place home. There is Veracruz, Havana, Santo Domingo, San Juan and Cartagena, hired to the service of foreign interests and related with each other in a system of military bastions where the house of God and the house of prostitution shared the same urban block under the shadow of the fortress.

Perhaps obeying some obscure principle of geographic justice, I decided to condemn Spain, France and England to be torn from the eastern shores of the Atlantic and cast off to where they once deported an entire sea of peoples. In this "**genealogical map**" the imperial nations are reunited with their former colonies, a fantasy that is not far from the truth, especially in the case of the French overseas departments and in the nostalgia that is felt today in Spain for Cuba which, in some deprived way, is evident in the obsession for the sadomasochist sex that a family reunion between the old master and his former slaves always generates. If the imperial nations stake their claims with their own colors, Africa enters into the Caribbean like a breast that has come to feed the islands with gray milk from the ashes of the burnt down plantations. On the other side of the isthmus the Pacific reminds us of the flames of Hell like a souvenir of sins that can never be forgiven.

By "**1800**" Saint Domingue blew over the Caribbean geography like a hurricane. Before the island was erased from the map and banished from the history of civilization, the Haitian Revolution spread through the region, penetrating deep into islands and continental territories with results that are to this day preliminary for, whereas the cause of political independence seems to have triumphed in some way or another over most of the region, freedom, which is the banner of the runaway peoples, remains unattained on account of imperial policies and, more importantly, on account of the racial dictatorship of the Creole classes that have invariably controled the

manifiesto en la obsesión por el sexo a golpes que implica siempre el reencuentro familiar entre el amo y su antigua dotación. Si las naciones imperiales europeas marcan el territorio con sus colores, Africa entra en el Caribe como un seno que amamanta las islas virtiendo sobre las aguas su leche cenicienta de ingenio quemado. Del otro lado del istmo, el Pacífico nos recuerda las brasas del infierno, *souvenir* imprescindible en este mundo de pecados difícilmente redimibles.

Allá para el **1800** Santo Domingo se impuso sobre la geografía caribeña como un huracán. Antes de que desapareciera la isla del mapa para ser borrada de la historia oficial de la civilización, la Revolución Haitiana se regó por el Caribe, penetrando todas las islas y tierras adyacentes con resultados que al día de hoy son todavía preliminares pues, mientras los proyectos de independencia política han triunfado de una forma u otra en casi toda la región, la libertad, que es el estandarte del pueblo cimarrón, sigue siendo víctima de la política imperial y de la dictadura racial de las clases criollas que invariablemente controlan el destino de todos estos pueblos en el nombre de la nación.

Fuera de la cuestión nacional y del problema que enfrentan en este sentido aquellas que yo denomino como naciones imposibles, no cabe duda que el mayor escollo en el camino de la felicidad de los pueblos caribeños es la hegemonía y el control que sobre éstos ejerce una Usonia que en esta parte del mundo asume proporciones geográficas gargantuescas. Aquí, en "**el charco**" la península de la Florida ha crecido desmedidamente para cerrar la boca de nuestro mar causando el empozamiento de las aguas. En la lista aparecen algunas de las intervenciones militares directas montadas por los Estados Unidos contra los países de la zona. En este sentido, el Caribe está geopolíticamente organizado en función de lo que los usonianos llaman su "seguridad nacional" y, en esto, nuevamente, la colonia y la plantación siguen vivas en cuanto, como dicen en mi tierra, los caribeños estamos todavía trabajando pal inglés.

A través de los años, versiones bastante imaginativas han tratado de esconder las precisiones de lo que podríamos llamar una economía de frontera militarizada. La isla de Puerto Rico, por ejemplo, ha sido pensada desde hace ochenta años como "**el puente**" entre la América Septentrional y la Meridional. Quienes conozcan mejor esta historia sabrán que el único puente que se montara de allí para otro lugar fue el puente del exilio forzoso en los Estados Unidos por donde cientos de miles de campesinos indigentes cruzaron para nunca regresar. En las tres primeras décadas de la postguerra el puente aéreo boricua — este fue el primer exilio masivo de un pueblo por avión — funcionó casi exclusivamente en una sola dirección y supuso el sacrificio de comunidades enteras en el nombre del progreso, la seguridad y la democracia, conceptos estos que resultan huecos en el contexto de la colonia, el militarismo y el racismo. Durante estos años más de la mitad de los jóvenes boricuas fueron expulsados de su país mientras casi la mitad de las jóvenes que se quedaron eran sometidas a la esterilización forzosa, cuidadosamente preparada por las autoridades estatales y federales. Aún así, el modelo económico puertorriqueño se exportó a las otras colonias usonianas: a las Islas Vírgenes y a Guam principalmente. En fechas más recientes y de forma muy alarmante, aspectos significativos de este modelo desbancado han sido adoptados por países vecinos. En mayor o menor escala, la industria de las maquiladoras mexicanas y el proceso de "disneyficación" del casco antiguo de La Habana presentan señales algo preocupantes de lo que se podría describir como una puertorriqueñización progresiva de estos dos países.

Claro que hubo un tiempo cuando Cuba fue el modelo a seguir, cuando el Caribe se pudo haber beneficiado de tener "**una, dos, mil Cubas**". De hecho, las dos revoluciones sociales más importantes del siglo pasado en el Caribe

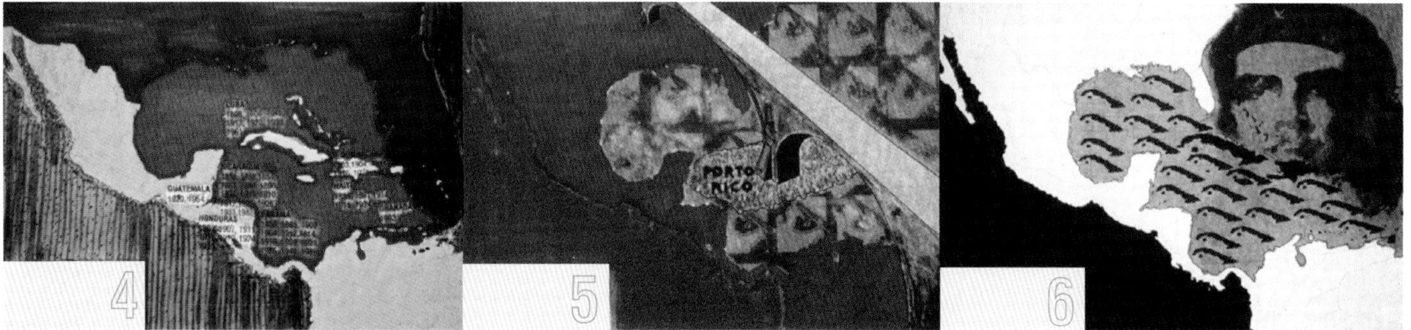

above, left to right:
4 The Puddle;
5 The Bridge;
6. A Thousand Cubas.

sobre, ido a la derecha:
4. El Charco;
5. El Puente;
6. Una, Dos, Mil Cubas.

destinies of all these peoples in the name of the nation.

Beyond the national question and of the problems faced by those countries which I see as impossible nations, there is no doubt that the biggest hurdle standing on the way of happiness for the peoples of the Caribbean is the hegemonic control exercised over them by a Usonia that in this part of the world assumes truly gargantuan proportions. In "**the puddle**" the Florida peninsula has grown out of proportion and closed-off the entrance to the Caribbean Sea effectively miring the waters. Included is a partial list of the major U.S. military interventions against the countries of the region. In this sense, the Caribbean is geopolitically organized in relation to what the Usonians call their "national security." As such, once again, the colony and the plantation are neither gone nor forgotten and the peoples of the Caribbean, like they say, are still "working for the Englishman."

Throughout the years very imaginative versions have attempted to hide what we could call the precisions of a militarized frontier economy. The island of Puerto Rico, for example, has been showcased as a "**the bridge**" between North and South America. A quick look at the historical record will show that the only bridge ever built from Puerto Rico to somewhere else was the span of the forced exile of hundreds of thousands of indigent peasants who went across never to return to their native land. In the first three decades following the end of World War II the Puerto Rican aerial bridge — this was the first massive exodus of a people by plane in history — worked almost exclusively in one direction only and resulted in the uprooting of entire communities in the name of progress, security and democracy, concepts that did not hold their own in the context of colonialism, militarism and racism. During these years more than half of the young men in the country were forced out while more than half of the young women who remained behind were forcibly sterilized in a program carefully prepared and jointly administered by the colonial government and Washington. Regardless of this the Puerto Rican economic model was exported to other Usonian colonies, mainly to the Virgin Islands and Guam. More recently it is worrisome to witness how significant aspects of that disastrous model are being adopted by neighboring countries. To a greater or lesser extent the industry of the *maquiladoras* in Mexico and the process of "disneyfication" of Old Havana are worrisome signals of what could be described as a deepening process of "puertoricanization" in these two countries.

Of course there was a time when Cuba was the model to follow, a time when the Caribbean should have had "**a thousand Cubas**". Without a doubt the two most important social revolutions of the twentieth century in the Caribbean were the Cuban and Puerto Rican ones. In the Cuban case the first class passengers were the ones sent packing. Both projects had great achievements. But the secondary effects of these experiments and the

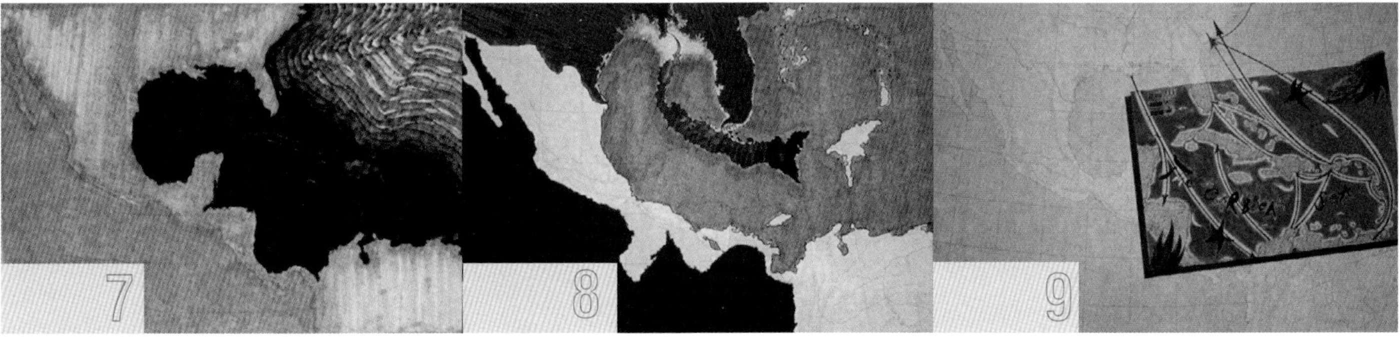

above, left to right:
7. Two Wings;
8. Cuba and the Night;
9. All Aboard?.

sobre, ido a la derecha:
7. Dos Alas;
8. Cuba y la Noche;
9. ¿Todos a bordo?.

fueron sin duda la cubana y la puertorriqueña. En el caso cubano, el exilio se reservó principalmente para los pasajeros de primera clase. En ambos casos fue mucho lo que se logró. Pero los efectos secundarios de los experimentos, y los accidentes de la historia, a la larga se han encargado de deshacer gran parte de lo que una vez fueron o quisieron ser estos proyectos que, en sus respectivas esquinas, de una forma u otra fueron verdaderamente importantes. Hoy, ambas revoluciones sociales se encuentran en la bancarrota política y las dos islas son nuevamente hermanas en una misma miseria de añoranzas extraviadas. Muy bien podría decirse que lo que a Cuba le falta a Puerto Rico le sobra, y viceversa, de forma tal que los versos de Lola Rodríguez de Tió, quien hace más de un siglo se refirió a las hermanas Antillas como "**dos alas**" de un mismo pájaro, pueden ser vistos hoy como una trágica profecía de mal agüero. [16] Lo cierto es que ambos pueblos van marchando por la misma vereda de una dominación neo-colonial que, como bien ha advertido Edouard Glissant, ya en estos tiempos no precisa de ideologías heróicas sino que más bien opera en función del control ejercido mediante el consumo pasivo y apoyándose en un discurso de la inevitabilidad.[17]

En retrospectiva, una de las debilidades principales de ambos proyectos, la cual intento expresar en "**Cuba y la noche**", fue el pensarse vanguardias o ejemplos, y acudir con prisa hacia una salvación individual que en ningún momento fue posible. El Caribe es una trampa geográfica. Por tanto, o salen a flote todas las tierras y pueblos a la vez, o zozobran cada una por su lado. Aquí ninguna se ha salvado de la trampa. Todas han caído: Cuba por creerse David con su honda martiana y Puerto Rico por confiar en la bondad y magnanimidad del amo triunfante. ¿Cómo puede predicarse el futuro en virtud de la práctica de la resistencia absoluta o de la lealtad incondicional al amo imperial? Seguramente tiene que haber otra forma de poder bregar con el atorrante de la vecindad...

Quizás este maniqueísmo sea precisamente lo que va quedando atrás en estos últimos años. Y es que, aunque en un plano imaginativo queda claro que Cuba no se rinde y que "**Puerto Rico, U.S.A.**" sigue defendiendo la frontera imperial, en un plano preciso, en Cuba se reconstruye apresuradamente la ciudad capitalista mientras en Puerto Rico el pueblo exige casi unánimemente la retirada inmediata de la armada usoniana de la isla de Vieques. Y resulta que son los cubanos fuera de Cuba quienes despliegan la bandera usoniana junto a la monoestrellada cual si fueran puertorriqueños colonialistas, mientras que los portavoces más coherentes de las demandas del pueblo boricua contra la marina de guerra son los hijos de la segunda o tercera generación del exilio en Chicago y Nueva York. El tema es complicado y no hay espacio aquí para discutirlo. Quede claro, sin embargo que, aunque ya nada es en blanco y negro, tampoco es color de rosa. En términos militares, Puerto Rico y las Islas Vírgenes usonianas conforman la base naval más importante de los Estados Unidos en el Atlántico. Es desde esta alegada "zona de maniobras" que se controla todo el océano y es a Roosevelt Roads, en Ceiba, Puerto Rico, donde regresarían los

accidents of history have in the long run conspired to undo a great deal of what the projects originally championed.

Today, both social revolutions are politically bankrupt and the two islands are again floating in a sea of broken dreams. It could easily be argued that Cuba has what Puerto Rico has not, and vice versa, in such a way that the verses of the nineteenth-century poet Lola Rodríguez de Tió, who once referred to the islands as "**two wings**" of one same bird, can retrospectively be read as a omen of bad luck.[16] Truth be said, both countries today are going down the path of a neo-colonial domination that, as Edouard Glissant has warned, "no longer needs the support of a heroic ideology. It is content to control through a passive consumerism and demonstrate its inevitability."[17]

In retrospect, I try to depict one of the principal weaknesses of both projects in "**Cuba and the night**" which was, I believe, falling into the temptation of thinking to think themselves as vanguards and of running fast towards an individual solution that was never possible. The Caribbean is a geographic trap. Accordingly, either all of the island and territories emerge at the same time or they shall all sink to the bottom of the sea one by one. No land has been spared here. All have fallen in the trap: Cuba on account of thinking of herself as David, wielding her Martian[18] slingshot, and Puerto Rico on account of believing in the kindness and benevolence of a triumphant master. How can the future be predicated around the exercise of unconditional loyalty or unyielding resistance to the empire? Surely there must be another way of dealing with the roughest kid in the neighborhood...

Maybe what is being left behind in recent years is precisely this manichaean discourse. While at an imaginative level it appears that Cuba will not surrender and that "**Puerto Rico, U.S.A.**" continues to defend the imperial frontier, on the level of the precise Cuba is fast rebuilding the capitalist city while the people of Puerto Rico are demanding almost unanimously the immediate withdrawal of all U.S. military forces from the island of Vieques. And it turns out that the Cubans outside of Cuba are the ones today displaying the Cuban flag next to the Usonian one like Puerto Rican colonialists while those speaking louder against the US Navy presence in Vieques are the sons and daughters of Puerto Rican immigrants in Chicago and New York City. There is no room here to go into details but it should be clear that, even when things are no longer black and white, they are not rosy either. In military terms, Puerto Rico and the U.S. Virgin Islands make up the most important naval military base of the United States in the Atlantic. It is from this alleged "zone of military maneuvers" from where the entire ocean is controlled and it is there, in the base of Roosevelt Roads, in Ceiba, Puerto Rico, where the latest generation nuclear submarines would come home after incinerating the planet.[19] Recently, the European parliament denounced that telephone, fax and e-mail communications from all over the world are intercepted in the Sabana Seca Army Base in Puerto Rico.[20] Meanwhile the most devastating mode of economic development continues to plow through the island destroying the physical and moral geography of the country. The leveling of the mountainous landscape and its revetment in reinforced concrete is primarily financed and directed by Cuban-exile interest in Florida.

Perhaps it is more urgent to discuss what is at stake. This map from the cruise ship company Princess entitled "**Caribbean Bound**" is the map of the region that everyone today can best recognize. Once again it is based on the standard seventeenth-century chart and, once again, we need to be weary at the presence of the nefarious palm trees. Ironically, while the Caribbean may not necessarily be a concrete reality for the insular and insularist peoples who inhabit its shores, it is definitely so for the thousands of tourist that each year chose it as a vacation destination. The Caribbean today is brought to you by your friendly cruise ship company which, as a mode of production and exploitation, is not such a distant relative of the galleon fleet.

submarinos nucleares de la última generación luego de incinerar al mundo.[18] Recientemente, el Parlamento Europeo denunció que en la Base de Sabana Seca en Puerto Rico se interceptan comunicaciones telefónicas, faxes y correos electrónicos de todo el mundo.[19] Mientras tanto el desarrollismo triunfalista en Puerto Rico marcha a todo vapor destrozando la geografía física y moral del país. El aplanamiento de nuestra escabrosa geografía y su recubrimiento en hormigón es financiado y dirigido principalmente por intereses cubanos en la Florida.

Quizás más urgente sería discutir lo que está en juego. Este mapa de la compañía de cruceros Princess titulado "**Caribbean Bound**" es el mapa del Caribe que el mundo conoce hoy. Nuevamente se basa en el modelo estandarizado ya en el siglo XVII y les aconsejo tener cuidado pues aquí otra vez nos encontramos con las malévolas palmas de coco. Si bien el Caribe no es necesariamente una realidad concreta para los pueblos insulares e insularistas que lo conforman, irónicamente sí lo es para los miles de turistas que lo eligen como destino vacacional año tras año. El Caribe actualmente es traído a ustedes cortesía de su compañía de cruceros favorita, esa modalidad de producción y explotación que poco tiene que envidiarle a su antecedente inmediato en el mundo de la flota.

Pero tras los incesantes flujos de turistas que llegan en busca de la playa desierta y el Hard Rock Café hay otras rutas que no caben en el mapa. "**¿Todos a bordo?**" Por cada visitante que desembarca en nuestros puertos en traje de baño hay varios paisanos bien vestidos que sueñan con cargarles las maletas tan sólo para regresar con ellos a su país de orígen. No es un secreto que en una vuelta extraña al mundo de la trata, la principal exportación del Caribe hoy en día — aparte de su música — es su propia gente. A su vez, las dos modalidades más puras y nefastas de la empresa privada, el narcotráfico y el mercado de las armas, utilizan al Caribe como corredor principal en sus transacciones hemisféricas. Las armas vienen del norte y las drogas del sur y justo en el medio de todo está Cuba. Cuesta decirlo pero Cuba es el gran premio de los narcos y tenemos que tener claro que si Cuba cae en manos de los principales intereses que rigen estos negocios mortíferos, el futuro bienestar de los pueblos caribeños quedaría irremediablemente comprometido. Baste tan sólo cotejar los altos índices de violencia en ciudades como Kingston o San Juan para ver de lo que estaríamos hablando. Se calcula que tanto en Jamaica como en Puerto Rico, más de una tercera parte de la economía está financiada por el narcotráfico. Sin duda alguna, en Cuba sería inclusive peor.

Mientras tanto, los cruceros siguen arribando a puerto, tomando por asalto regularmente nuestras ciudades para beneficio de corporaciones principalmetne ausentistas. ¡Que poco han cambiado las cosas! A este paso Disney podría acabar tomando el Caribe por la fuerza. ¿Qué sería peor, Disney o los narcos? Por lo que se observa en todo lugar, desde Cancún hasta Puerto España, el turismo cada vez con mayor fuerza se basa en la explotación sexual y racial de los caribeños. Me refiero a una economía de la nostalgia como imágen misma del deseo que no tiene nada de inofensivo y mucho menos de romántica. En todos los casos el turista viene buscando al Caribe la diversión de sentirse dueño de un mundo ya desaparecido en otras partes, de un mundo hediondo a plantación y a colonia, a casino y a burdelo. Todo esto ya se había confirmado con el éxito de las campañas publicitarias del gobierno de Edward Seaga en los años ochenta cuando se vendía la imágen de Jamaica con el lema: "Regrese a Jamaica. Regrese a la forma en que las cosas solían ser. Hága de Jamaica su destino y hágala suya."

Pero en este juego de las ilusiones perdidas el caribeño no es un agente pasivo. Las rutas del deseo entre vecinos son siempre caminos de doble vía. No en balde tantos caribeños sueñan con dejar sus tierras en pos de seguir sus ilusiones y no es ningún secreto que gran parte de ellos miren hacia los Estados Unidos y otros tantos hacia Europa con toda la fuerza que nutre a aquel que persigue un ideal aparentemente alcanzable como es el sueño que yo

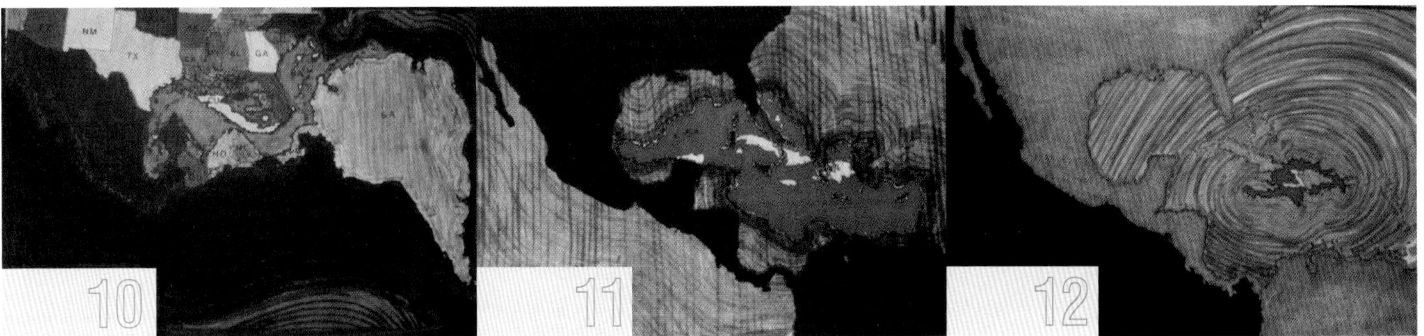

above, left to right:
10. U.S.A 2100;
11. Our Greece;
12. Closed Ranks.

sobre, ido a la derecha:
10. Dos Alas;
11. Nuestra Grecia;
12. Fila Cerrada.

But behind the unceasing flows of tourists who come searching for the deserted beach and the Hard Rock Cafe there are other routes that do not appear in this colorful map. "**All aboard?**" For every visitor who disembarks in our ports wearing a pair of shorts there are a couple of well-dressed natives who dream of carrying his or her bags so that they may return with them to their country of origin. It is no secret that in what must seem like a twisted return to the world of the slave trade, the principal export of the Caribbean today — besides its music — is its people. At the same time, the two most terrible and pure forms of free enterprise, the drug and arms cartels, use the Caribbean as the main hemispheric corridor for their transactions. The arms flow south and the drugs flow north and right in the center of it all is Cuba. It is difficult to say so but Cuba is the big price of the cartels and we must be clear that, if Cuba falls to them, the future welfare of the Caribbean peoples would be seriously compromised. Suffice it to consider the high indexes of violence in cities like Kingston or San Juan. It is estimated that in Jamaica as well as in Puerto Rico more than one third of the economy is financed by the drug cartels. Without a doubt it would be even worst in Cuba.

Meanwhile, cruise ships keep arriving at port, laying siege to our cities for the benefit of foreign corporations. How little have things changed! At this rate Disney could also end up taking over the Caribbean. What could be worst, Disney of the cartels? From what can be gathered, from all points south of Miami, the tourist economy is everyday more forcefully organized around the sexual and racial exploitation of the Caribbean peoples. I am referring to an economy of nostalgia as the image of desire that is not innocent and least of all romantic. In every case the tourist comes to the Caribbean in search of feeling what is is like to be the proprietor of a world long disappeared elsewhere, of a world that reeks of plantation and colony, of casino and brothel. This much had already been confirmed decades ago with the success of the advertising campaigns under the government of Edward Seaga which in the eighties invited people to "Come back to Jamaica. Come back to the way things used to be. Make it Jamaica, again, and make it your own."

In this game of lost illusions the Caribbean subject is not a passive agent. Among neighbors the routes of desire are always two way streets. Not surprisingly so many Caribbean people dream of abandoning their native land to follow their illusions and it is no secret that many of them look to the United States and others to Europe with the conviction that feeds the expectations of those who pursue an ideal that is seemingly attainable such as the

llamo "**U.S.A. 2100.**" Pocos son los que se tiran al mar oscuro en una balsa de fabricación casera acompañados de sus hijos pequeños y nadie se mete a mula ni se vende al matrimonio con un desconocido tan sólo porque se muera de hambre o porque viva del miedo. Estos desboques son casi siempre producto de un ideal que nos mueve a hacer locuras. En este caso el antiheróico pero muy claro ideal es tener acceso al consumo medioclasero y el poder encaminar a los hijos para que apunten más alto. En la cultura de la fuga, denominador común de todos los pueblos cimarrones caribeños, esta es la huida definitiva. En todos los casos, esta conducta invariablemente apunta hacia el fenómeno generalizado entre nosotros y que Alfonso Múnera define claramente, en el caso colombiano, como "el fracaso de la nación."[20] Ni corto ni perezoso el sur se desplaza hacia el norte y el continente va adquiriendo una nueva geografía. ¿Podrán ser estos los nuevos estados de la unión usoniana? Querrámoslo o no, esta es la utopía colectiva de Nuestra América—como llamó Martí al mundo americano más allá de Usonia—al arranque del tercer milenio. En este sentido también podría decirse que la fantasía está basada en un sueño puertorriqueñizante aunque no es ajena a realidades históricas en otros países como la República Dominicana o Cuba, donde el programa de la independencia y de la llamada anexión a los Estados Unidos han coincidido más de una vez a lo largo de la historia.

Y es que muchos caribeños tenemos la costumbre de vernos en otro lugar, respondiendo quizás a un dispositivo muy ancestral en nuestra cultura que nos predispone siempre para la fuga. Aquí en "**Nuestra Grecia**" he invertido esta tendencia trayendo el Mediterráneo al Caribe. Ambos están a la misma escala. Los teóricos hoy en día gustan pensar al Caribe como espacio acéntrico. Está de moda decir que nuestro mundo da para todo y que se puede tomar por donde se le agarre, que es un mundo de cuerpos inestables e ideas volátiles. Pero yo me pregunto, viendo como Grecia encaja sobre La Española, si no es aquella isla donde se inauguró el mundo de la colonialidad y se fundó su primera ciudad, el imán que recoge todos los males de la región. A la vez, vale reflexionar sobre el hecho de que fue allí también donde se dió la primera revolución en contra de la propiedad privada y del mercantilismo, y que aquel acontecimiento conocido como la Revolución Haitiana inauguró el camino de la agenda inconclusa de la modernidad anticolonial que es el proyecto mismo de la emancipación de la humanidad. Es también allí, donde de la forma más cruda se pone en evidencia la veleidad insularista que mantiene a los pueblos caribeños dándole la espalda al mar común que comparten con sus vecinos. Es allí donde haitianos y quisqueyanos compiten por demostrar quiénes en realidad abrigan el mayor desprecio por el otro. Aún así, parafraseando a Martí, nuestra Grecia sigue siendo preferible a la Grecia que no es nuestra.[21]

Pero el centro del Caribe no es el único punto perdido. Más importante aún, el Caribe es uno de los nódulos neurálgicos del comercio global y los pueblos que lo habitan apenas le sacan partido a esta estratégica ubicación. Pero es que es imposible sacarle partido a una posición geográfica ventajosa desde la postración cartográfica que hemos descrito. Enfrentarse a los órdenes geográficos del siglo XVII requiere montar una cartografía de "**fila cerrada**" donde el Caribe y sus rutas de tránsito y comercio sean administradas y defendidas por los pueblos de la cuenca. En un plano más concreto, el Caribe seguirá siendo un mar usoniano mientras no se repatríen las tropas y las fuerzas navales que hoy desde Puerto Rico y las Islas Vírgenes reclaman el control, no sólo del Caribe, sino de todo el Atlántico. No será esta tarea fácil.

Hace más de un siglo, en el poema antes citado, ya Lola Rodríguez había lanzado su llamado para hacer de Cuba y Puerto Rico "una patria sola."[22] Y antes que Lola, el cubano Manuel de Quesada en su proclama fechada en Santo Tomás el 16 de julio de 1874 invitaba a los borinqueños "a una sola sociedad para que nuestra divisa sea unidad en las Antillas."[23] A muchos hoy esta idea les parecerá un tanto descalabrada. Pero, hoy como ayer,

dream I call "**U.S.A. 2100**." Few are the ones who place their family in a rickety raft and go out into the darken seas, and nobody becomes a mule or sells his or herself off in marriage to a stranger just because they are starving or because they live in fear. Such feats are usually the result of an ideal which moves people to do the unthinkable. In this case the anti-heroic but very clear ideal being pursued is the possibility of having access to middle-class consumerism and to the opportunities for their children to aspire even higher. Within the culture of escape that is common to all the peoples of the Caribbean this is the most definite takeoff. In every case this behavior invariably responds to the generalization of the phenomenon that Alfonso Múnera, in the case of Colombia, has called "the failure of the nation."[21] Slowly but surely the entire south is drifting north and the continent is acquiring a new geography. Are these the future United States of the Americas? Whether we like it or not this is the collective utopia of Our America—as José Martí called the hemispheric world laying beyond the U.S.— at the start of the Third Millennium. In this sense it could be said that this fantasy is also based on a "puertoricanizing" dream although the dream is not altogether unrelated to similar traditions in countries such as Cuba or the Dominican Republic where the program of independence and of the so called annexation to the U.S. have coincided more than once in the course of the last one hundred and fifty years.

Truth be said many of us from the Caribbean have the habit of seeing ourselves somewhere else. This might be related to a certain cultural disposition which has always predisposed us to flee and escape. In "**Our Greece**" I have reversed this movement by bringing the Mediterranean to the Caribbean. They are overlapping at the same scale. Theorists today like to think of the Caribbean as an acentric place. It is fashionable to say that this world can be handled in an infinitude of ways and that it is a world of inconstant bodies and volatile ideas. But I ask myself, seeing the way in which Greece fits over Hispaniola if that island where the world of coloniality was inaugurated and where its first city was founded, is not the magnet that draws in all the evils of the surrounding lands and of the entire region. At the same time it is worth reflecting on the fact that it was there too where the first revolution against private property and mercantilism took place, being the Haitian Revolution as it was the event that opened up the road of the yet inconclusive agenda of anti-colonial modernity which is still nothing short of the emancipation of Humanity. It is there too where the most terrible form of insularist fickleness, the one that keeps the peoples of the Caribbean giving their backs to the sea and to the neighbors whom they share it with, manifests itself. It is there where Haitians and Dominicans compete with each other to see who among them has the greatest disdain for the other. All in all, to paraphrase Martí, our Greece is still preferable to the Greece that is not ours.[22]

The center of the Caribbean is not the only missing point. More to the fact, while the Caribbean is one of the nodal points of global commerce, the region hardly perceives any advantage from the strategic value of the geographic position it occupies. Then again, an advantageous geographic position cannot be taken advantage of in a situation of cartographic prostration such as the one we have described. Facing the geographic orders of the seventeenth century requires a cartography of "**closed ranks**" where the Caribbean and its trade routes would be administered and defended by the West Indians themselves. More concretely, the Caribbean will continue to be a Usonian sea until the troops and the naval forces stationed in Puerto Rico and the Virgin Islands are repatriated. This is no easy task since it is from that point where the United States claims control not only over the Caribbean but over the entire Atlantic Ocean.

More than a century ago, in the poem cited above, Lola Rodríguez de Tió had already championed the idea of making one nation out of Cuba and Puerto Rico.[23] And before Lola, the Cuban Manuel de Quesada, in his

quizás sea precisamente en tiempos difíciles cuando se pueda llamar a hacer un alto en el camino para tomarse el riesgo de explorar las posibilidades que, siendo pobres como son, son posibilidades aún. Lejos de pensarse como una utopía transnacional, la integración política de los pueblos caribeños es una necesidad económica directamente relacionada con las posibiliidades de obtener una mayor ingerencia en las decisiones que de otra forma se seguirán tomando por nosotros pero sin nosotros. Por supuesto la idea aquí es levantar el nivel y la calidad de la vida en nuestros pueblos y no necesariamente hizar ninguna bandera, y mucho menos de guerra. En términos cartográficos la resolución es sencilla: simplemente se trata de cambiar el mapa del siglo XVII por una nueva geografía para el Mar de las Antillas.

NOTAS

Este artículo fue originalmente presentado como conferencia en la Facultad de Artes y Letras de la Universidad de La Habana en junio del 2000. Una versión previa fue presentada en la Escuela de Arquitectura de la Universidad de Puerto Rico en marzo del mismo año. Este trabajo está dedicado a los alumnos de ambas universidades.

[1] Mitchell, Timothy. *Colonising Egypt*. (Berkeley: University of California Press, 1991.) p. 31-33.

[2] Hulme, Peter. *Colonial Encounters: Europe and the Native Caribbean, 1492-1797.* (New York: Routledge, 1986.) p. 13-43.

[3] Carib, Raymond B. "Cartography and Power in the Conquest and Creation of New Spain" in *Latin American Research Review* (35, 2000): 18.

[4] *ibid.*, 29.

[5] Ortelius, Abraham. "Hispaniolae, Cubae, Aliarumque Insurarum Circumiacentium," in Hans Wolff, ed. *America: Early Maps of the New World.* (Munich: Prestel, 1992.) p. 95.

[6] Blaeu, Willem. "Insulae Americanae," in *Blaeu's The Grand Atlas of the 17th Century*, John Goss, intro. (London: Studio Editions, 1990.) p. 160-161.

[7] "The Caribbean" in *The Edinburgh World Atlas,*1970 ed. This is a typical map from the Cold War.

[8] I prefer to use the Wrightian term Usonian instead of American when referring to the peoples and to the things pertaining to the United States of America, thereby reserving the term American exclusively for use in its original continental sense.

[9] © Smith-Lee Co., Inc.

[10] In *The Book of Porto Rico*, the official almanac of the insular government under the regime of Horace M. Towner, there is a photograph of a bartizan with the following caption: "Antiguo e incólume centinela de nuestra civilización.—A sentry box of olden times." (Old and unharmed guardian of our civilization).
E. Fernández García, ed. *El Libro de Puerto Rico/The Book of Porto Rico.* (San Juan: El Libro Azul Publishing, 1923.) p. 183.

[11] Titles given to the city by the King of Spain after the successful defeat of the English attack of 1797.

[12] Mary Louise Pratt. *Imperial Eyes: Travel Writing and Transculturation.* (New York: Routledge, 1992.) p. 205.

[13] © Royal, Coatesville Pa., 1978.

[14] Printed by Denoyer-Geppert and titled *(Mexico, Central America and) West Indies* (Desk activity map 25167).

[15] "The New World," in *America*, p. 91.

[16] See Lola Rodríguez de Tió. "A Cuba," in *Obras Completas*, vol. I. (San Juan: Instituto de Cultura Puertorriqueña, 1968.) p. 319-321.

[17] Edouard Glissant. "The Known, the Uncertain" in *Caribbean Discourse.* (Charlottesville: University Press of Virginia, 1989.) p. 88.

proclamation to the Puerto Ricans of July 16, 1874 had invited them to form "one single society so that our cause may be the struggle for Antillean unification."[24] To some today this idea might seem a long shot. But just like yesterday, the hard times we face may precisely be the ones that call on us to consider such possibilities, poor as they may be. Far from promoting a transnational utopia, the political integration of the Caribbean peoples is an urgent economic necessity related to the possibility of achieving greater control over decisions that are generally taken on our behalf but without our consent. Of course, the idea here is to raise the standard of living and the quality of life and not necessarily to raise the flag, least of all, the battle flag. In cartographic terms, the solution is simple: it is all about changing the map of the seventeenth century for a new geography for the West Indies.

NOTES

[18] A reference to Cuban poet and intellectual José Martí (1853-1895).

[19] The military importance of the Roosevelt Roads complex has been repeatedly emphasized. See, for example, "U.S. Naval Presence in Puerto Rico," in *Congressional Record.* (134:3, 1988): S2281-S2283.

[20] See "Red Echelon en P.R.: trae cola lo del espionaje" in *Primera Hora.* (10 March 00): 4A.

[21] See Alfonso Múnera. *El fracaso de la nación: religión, clase y raza en el Caribe colombiano (1717-1812).* (Bogota: El Áncora Editores, 1998.)

[22] See José Martí. "Nuestra América," in *Obras Completas*, vol. II. (Havana: Editorial Lex, 1946.) p. 108.

[23] Rodríguez de Tió, *op cit.* p. 321.

[24] Archivo Histórico Nacional, Madrid. Legajo 5113/33, nº 3.

This article was originally presented as a lecture in the Faculty of Arts and Letters of the University of Havana in June of 2000. A previous version was presented in the School of Architecture of the University of Puerto Rico in march of the same year. It is dedicated to the students of both institutions.

schneekloth

with

dreishpoon

kahn

steir

pfahl

essenhigh

LANDSCAPE

INTRODUCED BY LYNDA H. SCHNEEKLOTH

This section is a set of pieces and fragments that put in place some of the voices speaking to the idea and materiality of landscape at the opening of the twenty-first Century. The conversation raises questions about landscape, to include the history and evolution of the nature/culture dialogue; a presentation by artists of their work involving landscape; and the story of a landscape in the Ruhr Valley in Germany that has undergone an imaginal transformation. The pieces do not add up to a whole: so much escapes our attempts to bound landscape. But rather, this article is intended to provoke a dialogue about one of the most critical ideas and imaginations of the upcoming millennium — the relationship between humans and the rest of the world and the space we have named "landscape."

The impetus for this article was an exhibition and symposium sponsored by the Albright-Knox Art Gallery, Buffalo, New York, entitled "Landscape at the Millennium" curated by Douglas Dreishpoon. The exhibit ran from November 20, 1999 through January 2, 2000, spanning the entrance into the year 2000. The exhibit included nineteenth century works from the Parrish Art Museum and the Albright-Knox Art Gallery, with installations by Tobi Kahn and Pat Steir and work by John Pfahl and Inka Essenhigh.

opposite:

Industrial ruins and landscape design

Merge in Der Horstmarer Park in Lunen,

Emscher Park IBA.

LYNDA H. SCHNEEKLOTH

WHAT IS LANDSCAPE?

I continue to be perplexed by the question, "What is landscape?" because embedded in that one question are so many others, including "Who are we? Where are we? and How might we be?" Landscape tells us about the land, yes, but its main story is about human beings — as a culture and as a species. The query, *what is landscape,* reveals stories that do not seem to clarify our understanding of ourselves, but rather layer the question. At the end of this Christian millennium, we are no longer sure who humans are. We have even come to question the legacy of earlier religious cosmologies and the Enlightenment that had placed us as the apex of life on earth. In the short essay that follows, I would like to share some thoughts about the landscape and the questions embedded in our inquiry, focusing on three points: the invention of landscape, the colonization of the earth by landscape, and landscape as resistance.

Lynda H. Schneekloth is Professor of Architecture at the University at Buffalo, The State University of New York. She is author of *Placemaking: The Art and Practice of Building Communities* (1995) with Robert Shibley; *Ordering Space: Types in Architecture and Design* (1994) with Karen Franck; and *Changing Places: ReMaking Institutional Buildings* (1992) with Barbara Campagna and Marcia Feuerstein. Her current practice resides in the landscapes of Western New York and her scholarship is focused on the imagination of the relationship between people and the world.

It is probably important to remember that the word "landscape" is very recent in western human history. It came into the language at the beginning of modernity about the same time as the word "environment." Both of these words are related to the invention of perspectival space. It is hard for us today to realize what a radical shift in human perception occurred about 300-400 years ago. Until that time, the world and the earth certainly existed, but we were "in" it, and therefore didn't conceive of "it" as something necessarily outside of ourselves. As the anthropologist Edmund Carpenter said, "We don't know who discovered water but we can be sure it wasn't a fish." Yet we do know who invented landscape, and it was us.

opposite:
Landscape design in Mechtenberg, one of the projects of the Emscher Park IBA discussed in Part 3.
[Ganser, p. 52]

According to J.B. Jackson, the noted American landscape historian, landscape first meant a picture with a view and only later, the view itself. It is for that reason that landscape has always been closely associated with art and painting, and we continue that tradition in our discussion. Perspectival space was explored and reworked in landscape painting at the same time that our views of the content of the painting — cultivated and wild nature — were being transformed. The wildness of uninhabited portions of the earth were being tamed through our literal colonization and metaphoric gaze; wilderness was transformed from a place of demons and fear

right:
Landscape Installation in Mechtenberg, 1998. [Ganser, p. 7]

left:
Riding a bike through the landscape in Herten-Sud, Germany where working industry is juxaposed with abandoned lands. [Schwarze and Rodrian, p. 37]

into the revelation of God's hand and salvation of human kind. Wildness, the condition of being out of control, beyond the reach of the civilizing hand of God and humans, was no longer associated exclusively with "nature." Wildness now appeared in the emerging cities, where the teeming mass of humanity required to fuel the industrial revolution were believed to be beyond civilization.

By the 18th century, landscape had come to mean **the making** of the view on the earth; that is, the orderly arrangement of the land into a picturesque view resembling the style of painting. The word itself, landscape, grew out of a series of other words that referred to measurements of land or to an community or administrative unit that was responsible for land. It has always been a relational word, a **people/land word**, that is, a place manipulated by human hand and mind. This manipulation can be seen subtly in the enframement and modification of views painted, as well as in the actual remaking of the land as in LeNotre's grand vision for Versailles, Olmsted and Vaux's Central Park, or the vast stretches of agricultural fields.

The naming of "landscape" reflected a radical shift in human experience, a shift from being inside the world to being outside of it. Perspectival space moves the human out of the picture to a privileged position of seeing everything, of framing everything. The ability to see and draw oneself on the outside reflects the cultural move into modernity, a relocation strongly supported by science, with its objective eye, and technology, a practice bent on re-forming the earth. I am aware that when I speak in such generalities that I am on the verge of lying; nevertheless, the point is critical in understanding the evolution of the idea of landscape.

Metaphorically, we stepped out of the world and off the earth, and with our controlling gaze, have reformed it in our likeness. The earth and its nature have become an object to our cultural mind, and we have freely appropriated, used, misused and discarded it, concerned only with the well-being of human beings and not the welfare of the earth itself. The consequences to the earth of our modern belief that humans are separate and superior are becoming clearer everyday. We recognize increasing levels of pollution, the consequences of which we are only beginning to understand, and a changing global structure through habitat destruction, the result not only of the

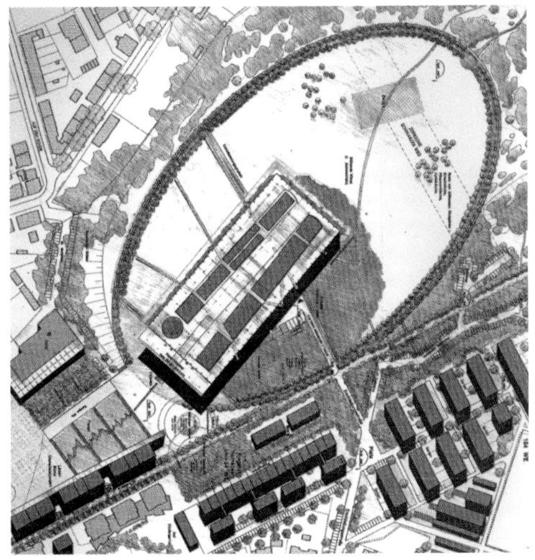

left:
The Local Town Center and Academy of Continuing Education, Mont-Cenis in Herne, where surrounding houses were renovated and new construction was built over the former mines in the town of Sodingen. The project uses state-of-the-art solar technologies, captures methane gas from the former mines, and has a rainwater collection system. Competition won by J+P, Lyon, France. [Mont-Cenis, p. 10]

right:
Garden in Meidericher Park, another project of the Emscher Park IBA. [Ganser, p. 57]

sheer numbers of the one species, *homo sapiens*, but of our apparently unlimited desire for material well-being.

It is perhaps more difficult to see the consequence of this modern perspectival story for ourselves. The location of humans as outside the world has made the earth the object of our inquiry and desire. In this consumptive relationship, we have lost our intimate relationship to the earth and the world as subject to subject. We are truly alone in the universe. In the desire to actually occupy the god space that is at the same time **nowhere and everywhere**, we find that there is no PLACE for humans — we have become placeless, rootless.

> Provided that human society does not lose its memory in the meantime, the last decades of the twentieth century will one day be remembered as among the most critical in history — a time when humanity as a whole was violently projected into a new, utterly divergent, millennium. The scale of the transformations we are witnessing today has no precedent either in natural or cultural history. The global uprooting of both nature and humanity makes each and everyone of us a refugee of sorts. How long we will remain refugees on earth no one can say, but the fact of homelessness has by now become obvious even to the most privileged or protected members of the human family. (Harrison, 1992, 238)

The perspectival shift transformed our imagination of who humans are in the cosmos. The fiction that humans somehow stand apart and are superior to all "others" in the world has evolved and dominated much of western thought, and has resulted in increasingly uninhabitable places and the destruction of the fragile ecologies of the earth. We have made a landscape that encircles the globe, remaking the earth in our likeness. The problem with making is that, with every making, we must unmake something else. In this sense, one might call "landscape" the great unmaking of the earth. One could argue that remaking the world in our likeness is a way of creating a place uniquely suited to us humans. But many suggest that the opposite has happened. Without the background, without the field against which we stand, without a subject, an equal, something like we have named "nature" for lack of a better understanding of that which is "not-us," we have displaced not only the earth but ourselves.

We are now a world of refugees, struggling to make a life in the new world we have constructed without the intimate knowledge of the everyday milieu and the myriad of our kin with whom we had evolved.

So, how does the idea of landscape reflect our newly constructed view of the human in the world? When we talk about landscape today, what do we mean? Where is it? What is it? And critically, what is not landscape? Interestingly, it is still a picture, still a picture with a view or an enframement of space. The view can re-present the world outside of us such as a photo of a grain elevator or a painting of the horizon, or it offers us a glimpse of the world within us. Painting, like all makings, always tells us more about ourselves than the subject of exploration. To a large extent, landscape painting is still a view in which we are outside the world, not inside of it; we are the subject and the makers, and even with the dissolution of perspectival space in twentieth century landscape painting, it is still that which surrounds.

Landscape also still means a place on the earth as in "let's go see the landscape of Niagara Falls," and even, "let's call the nursery and ask someone to come over and landscape our garden." A more recent manifestation of the word is its use as a metaphor as in "landscape of my mind" or the "landscape of the internet." Landscape includes the given world, the constructed world, and the imaginal world. In fact, landscape has come to mean everything – nothing seems to escape it.

The idea of landscape has so permeated the earth at the end of the twentieth century – literally and metaphorically – that McKibbens writes that we have reached *The End of Nature.* There is no place untouched by human beings, no context against which the text of land/earth resides. In its early manifestations, the opposite of landscape was wilderness – that which stood outside of human manipulation. Now even "wilderness" and "nature" have been subsumed under landscape as nature is conceived of as an idea that we have constructed and argue about, not as something that stands outside of humans, that preceded us. If there is no nature and no wilderness and only landscape, what is left? Jerry Mander in his book, *The Absence of the Sacred* writes that "Living constantly inside an environment of our own inventions reacting solely to things we ourselves have created, we are essentially living inside our own minds" (1992, p. 32). Where can humans stand if we are everything? One response suggests that it is time to move beyond nature/culture or landscape as a mirror and go back to the earth itself. Robert Sardello, for example, argues that although the landscape is our home for we have made it, it is the earth itself and not just the world that is our dwelling place.

Yet I would argue that landscape, a concept that emerged to describe our leaving of the earth, may actually be a way of returning, of reinventing place, of inhabiting the earth. Landscape has historically been about place, not space, and place is a grounded and rooted way of inhabiting the earth. Landscape ideas may be conceptual, but landscapes are particular and specific, differentiated and heterogeneous. If we attend to them carefully, they speak of discrete locales on the earth, and communities of biomes that are interdependent and related – and related to us. They place us not in universal homogeneous space, but in rooted and grounded spots with particular and stubborn communities. Further, we are, in truth, dependent on these landscapes and these places and in a sense, also responsible for them. Alexander Wilson in his book, *The Culture of Nature*, says it this way:

> My own sense is that the immediate work that lies ahead has to do with fixing landscape, repairing its ruptures, reconnecting its parts. Restoring landscape is not about preserving lands — "saving what's left" ... Restoration recognizes that once lands have been "disturbed" — worked, lived on, meddled with, developed (and I add, represented or appropriated) — they require human intervention and care. We must build landscapes that heal, connect and empower, that make intelligible our relations with each other and with the natural world: places that welcome and enclose, whose breaks and edges are never without meaning. (Wilson, 1991, p. 17)

Looked at in this way, landscapes are subversive, they work against the trend that would fling us out as autonomous units into an undifferentiated space — whether that space is our cities, outer space or virtual reality. They bring us back, they implace us as makers of the world and creatures of the earth. It is true that we can never return to an earlier way of thinking and being; we cannot be one with the earth for we have truly eaten of the fruit of the tree of knowledge. Even our explorations that deconstruct perspectival space through new forms of art are developed against the background of positionality, of being outside the frame of the picture.

But we are creatures that constantly make and remake the world. The invention of landscape, of perspective, of environment, and new forms of representation all manifest the creativity and adaptability of humans. It is in this sense that we have the potential to rethink and reconstruct our relationship to the earth — we have done this many times since we first conceived of ourselves as subjects. I believe that the current interest in landscape is based on its ambiguous position as being both about *us* and about the *not-us*. Landscape is a cultural phenomena, but it is also about the earth and its presence. The in-between condition of landscape gives us space as humans to explore our multiple positions as makers and dwellers. As Wilson says, landscapes can "make intelligible our relations with each other and with the natural world."

N O T E S

Sources Referenced:

Ganser, Karl. *Liebe auf den zweiten Blick: Internationale Bauausstellung Emscher Park*. (Dortmund: Harenberg Kommunikation Verlags- und Medien Gmbh & Co. KG, 1999).

Harrison, Robert. *Forests: The Shadow of Civilization*. (Chicago: University of Chicago Press, 1992).

Jackson, J.B. *Discovering the Vernacular Landscape*. (New Haven: Yale University Press, 1984).

Mander, Jerry. *In the Absence of the Sacred*. (San Francisco: Sierra Club Books, 1992).

McKibben, Bill. *The End of Nature*. (New York: Doubleday, 1990).

Mont-Cenis. (Herne: Entwicklungsgesellschaft Mont-Cenis, 1998).

Sardello, Robert. *Facing the World with Soul*. (Hudson, NY: Lindisfarne Press, 1992).

Schneekloth, Lynda and Robert Shibley. *Placemaking*. (NY: John Wiley and Sons, 1995).

Schwarze-Rodrian, Michael. *Parkbericht, Emscher Landschaftspark*. (Essen: Kommunalverband Ruhrgebeit, 1996).

Wilson, Alexander. *The Culture of Nature*. (Toronto: Between the Lines, 1991).

DOUGLAS **DREISHPOON**

LANDSCAPE ART

WITH:
TOBI KAHN
PAT STEIR
JOHN PFAHL
INKA ESSENHIGH

It could be said that the landscape has come to signify many things: an atavistic notion of an Edenic past; a foil for cultural forces in transition; and, in the visual arts, an archetypal motif with a thousand incarnations. *Landscape at the Millennium* offers a context, admittedly selective in its point of view, for addressing the representations of the landscape over the past one-hundred years. I set out to create a dialogue between the project's principal components that are internal as well as external — installations by two contemporary painters, a sampling of nineteenth-century landscapes, a manipulated photograph of historical picturesque sites, and a younger painter's abstract figuration project against a limitless space. They are internal insofar as the components generate their own issues and questions; external in their relevance to the permanent collection.

The landscape is envisioned as a philosophical tenet based on our physical and psychological rapport with the natural environment. It is so much a part of our cultural heritage, so ingrained in notions of who we are and what we have become, that it is easily taken for granted. And yet, over the course of one-hundred years, our relationship to and perception of this geographic body have undergone dramatic changes. During the nineteenth century, the landscape occupied a prominent place in the nation's collective consciousness, signifying on the one hand a boundless frontier whose awesome potential had vast consequences for a rapidly developing country, and on the other, a more manicured and domesticated terrain. Artists (painters, illustrators, photographers) were often in the forefront of discovery, accompanying surveyors and cartographers to document the landscape in transition. Their depictions, in most cases relying on established schema, ran the gamut from sublime to mundane, from transcendent to picturesque. With few exceptions, these works faithfully recorded the circumstances that led to their creation.

Not until the early years of the twentieth century did the landscape become the site for more subjective projections, as European and American artists, perceiving correspondence in natural phenomena, began to conceive abstract analogues.

Douglas Dreishpoon is curator of twentieth century art at the Albright-Knox Art Gallery, Buffalo NY. He has worked as curator of collections at the Weatherspoon Art Gallery, The University of North Carolina at Greensboro and as the curator of contemporary art at the Tampa Musuem of Art. His essays and reviews have been published in numerous catalogues, magazines and journals, including *Art Journal, Art News* and *Sculpture*. He is a frequent lecturer on art, and serves on the board of the American Chapter of the International Association of Art Critics.

opposite::
Wassily Kandinsky
Russian, 1866-1944.
Fragment 2 for Composition VII, 1913

Oil on Canvas,
34 ½ by 39 ¼ inches.
Albright-Knox Art Gallery,
Buffalo, NY, Room of Contemporary
Art Fund, 1947.

Wassily Kandinsky, for instance, saw the landscape as a symphony of lines, forms, and colors, like a musical composition endlessly varied. The group of vanguard painters gathered around the photographer-dealer Alfred Stieglitz — Arthur B. Dove, Marsden Hartley, Georgia O'Keeffe, and John Marin — and took liberties with the landscape. Inspired by the enigmatic canvases of Albert Pinkham Ryder — their paradigm for the homegrown, visionary American painter — they generated their own abstract equivalents. Consider each of these artists a trailblazer, who, in moving beyond traditional representations of the landscape, provided an alternative model for subsequent generations of painters projecting another kind of landscape.

Tobi Kahn and Pat Steir are part of this alternative. Kahn and Steir make a constructive pairing, given the stylistic range of these historical works. Distinguished by reductive designs, translucent color, and subtle modulations of surface texture, Kahn's interpretations of the landscape gravitate between representation and abstraction. While his subject matter is easily identified as landscape or seascape, the actual images are more suggestive. Transposing natural phenomena through memory, his images aspire to a universal condition through the most minimal of means. For this project, the artist conceived an installation of large-scale canvases whose varying horizons and colors evoke an environment in constant flux. Kahn's notion of abstraction shares a strong affinity with the nature-based abstractions of Dove and Hartley, as well as with Rothko's luminous field of transcendent color. Like them, he embraces painting's ability to renew itself through formal exploration and poetic distillation.

Steir's depiction of natural phenomena, like Kahn's, is based on equivalence. If Kahn's images suggest meditative serenity, hers explore more expressionistic dimensions. What Rothko is to Kahn, Frankenthaler and Still are to Steir: two sides of the same pictorial coin, each painting an abstraction with a different face. Since the mid-1980s, Steir has drawn inspiration from waves and waterfalls, creating monumental, undulating analogues for these chaotic forces in the form of works executed directly on the wall. Preparing for each encounter like an athlete, she enters the arena. Concentration and timing are essential. So is a positive state of mind.

John Pfahl uses the medium of photography to question representation — the camera's ability to expose the truth. With "Permutations on the Picturesque," a series of twenty prints based on picturesque views photographed in England and Italy between 1993 and 1996, his perceptual investigations take on a cybernetic dimension. From a distance, the results deceptively simulate traditional watercolor, only to dissolve, on closer inspection into pixilated fields. The notion of picturesque acquires a whole new meaning in this series.

In Inka Essenhigh's paintings, mutant figures devoid of limbs and heads tumble across vast expanses. Dramatic actors engulfed by radiant space, they writhe and spin, contort and extend, propelled by invisible forces and adorned by minimal props. These are strange worlds, where nothing seems familiar and yet a palpable pathos permeates the chaos — dystopian microcosms out of joint. Peering into these airless netherworlds, perplexed and baffled, we search for recognizable cues, all the while wondering what circumstances led to their creation. Against uninflected backgrounds, part human / part machine, bodies float in a time-warped world. The space of an Essenhigh painting is simultaneously finite and boundless, the equivalent of a cosmological void, a pictorial quagmire into which figures disappear or from which they emerge. These are helter-skelter, madcap worlds, where fragmentation and dissolution displace Euclidean order, and the only buffer to chaos is the arbitrary dimension of the canvas. *Landscapes* doesn't immediately spring to mind as a thematic handle befitting these works. And yet, on some level, apart from the obvious references to Midwestern cornfields and suburban malls, landscape seems appropriate as we ponder the future of advanced technology, especially its effect on our perception of ourselves and our environment.

The exhibition confirms that artists continue to be interested in the landscape as a vehicle for abstraction. At the same time, it raises philosophical questions regarding our relationship to the environment and the poignancy of place at this point in our millennial history.

NOTES

Albright-Knox Art Gallery. *American Landscapes: Recent Paintings by Inka Essenhigh*. (Buffalo, NY: The Buffalo Fine Arts Academy, 1999).

Albright-Knox Art Gallery. *Landscape at the Millennium*. (Buffalo, NY: The Buffalo Fine Arts Academy, 2000).

John Pfahl. *Permutations on the Picturesque*. (Robert B. Menschel Photography Gallery, Schine Student Center, Syracuse University: Syracuse, 1997).

Dreishpoon's text is based on the introduction to the catalogue, *Landscape at the Millennium*. The artists' comments are referenced from the same catalogue or from the transcription of a seminar held in conjunction with the exhibition on November 19, 1999.

Thanks to the artists, the Albright-Knox Art Gallery, and the Mary Boone Gallery for their assistance and cooperation in providing images.

left:

ORNAT [1995]

acrylic on canvas over wood,
40 x 50 x 2¼"
courtesy of the artist

My continuing interest in landscape has to do with its apparent timelessness and with the way that quality is filtered through my notions of memory . . . I use landscape as a reference point, a catalyst for association and distillation. In other words, the landscape will remind me of something else — a recollection, a body in repose, even a cell formation. Each landscape brings its own associations, depending on context and terrain.

(*Landscape at the Millennium*, p. 20)

above:

MADAI [1995]

acrylic on canvas over wood,
72 x 48 x 2¼"
from: Metamorphoses: *Tobi Kahn, A Traveling One-Man Show Curated by Peter Selz*
courtesy of the artist

above:

INSTALLATION VIEW [1999]

from: works from "Sky and Water" series
acrylic on canvas over wood
from the exhibition Landscape at the Millennium
11.20.1999 - 01.01.2000
Albright-Knox Art Gallery, Buffalo New York

I went to high school with a man who remains my closest friend and is now a renowned immunologist. Every summer we visit him at Woods Hole on the Cape. In the early 90s, he showed me microscopic photographs of cell formations, whose images were closely related to the paintings I was making. I became riveted by fractal geometry and its relationship to aerial views of landscape. Microscopic cell formations are surprisingly similar to land seen from the sky rather than from the line of the horizon. I sought images that related to both, so that the viewer could really see the interplay between cell formations and aerial views.

(*Symposium Transcription* 11.19.1999)

The horizon defines where you, as the viewer, are in relationship to the landscape. I want it to appear as it would in nature, not too artificial and not too straight. The horizon exists both as a spatial cue and a compositional element – as a means of orientation . . . Unlike other series I've done, the sky, land, and water images are indeed reductive. Yet they're complicated in the sense that as color varies with time of day, the possibilities become endless. At a certain point, in its most minimal form, the image becomes something else, more abstract, more suggestive.

(*Landscape at the Millennium*, p. 21)

above:
PAINTED RAIN [1994-1995]

oil on canvas,
108 x 108"
Albright-Knox Art Gallery, Buffalo NY
Charles Clifton, Edmund Hayes and
Sarah Norton Goodyear Funds, 1995

With this picture I can explore more fully my relationship to landscape and to nature. Since I was very young, I have been very interested in looking at Chinese landscape painting, especially the Southern Song Dynasty. Those painters didn't paint the landscape literally. They looked at the landscape, felt that landscape, and let the experience of the landscape pass through them. They did not interpret it, nor did they translate it; they portrayed nature by *becoming* it.

(Symposium Transcription 11.19.1999)

above:
INSTALLATION VIEW OF "MY GARDEN GHOST" [1999]

acrylic paint on wall,

from the exhibition Landscape at the Millennium
11.20.1999 - 01.01.2000
Albright-Knox Art Gallery, Buffalo New York

My notion of landscape painting is open to many possibilities and is, especially with the wallworks, influenced by the character of the space, how it's divided up and adapted to my work. Each wall offers a different scale and orientation. And I'm dependent on gravity. What I do on the surface of the wall can't be done on canvas.

(*Landscape at the Millennium*, p. 29)

opposite:
WIND AND WATER [1995]

oil on canvas,
108 x 108"
collection of Burt Aaron,
Detroit, Michigan
courtesy of artist

This is one of my favorite paintings. It's all thrown painting. I stand on the floor when I throw the paint. What you see is limited by my own size and rhythm, by what I can reach from the floor. I draw in the air what I want to see on the canvas and because of certain laws of physics I don't understand, the paint lands on the canvas in the same form as I drew it in the air.

(Symposium Transcription 11.19.1999)

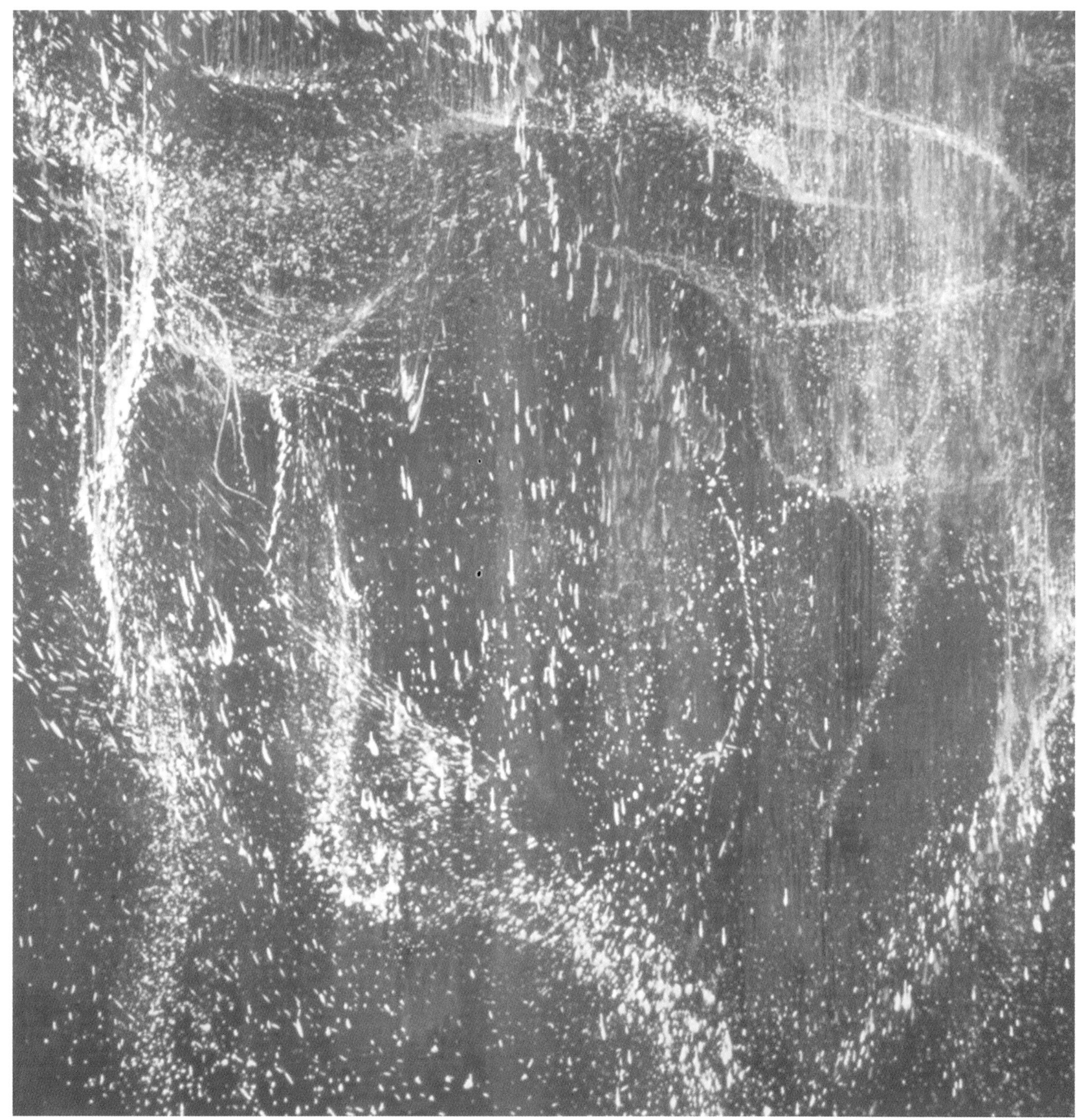

above:

GROTTO AT RYDAL FALLS, LAKE DISTRICT, ENGLAND [1995]

iris print,
13 x 16½"
courtesy of artist

above:

GARDENS OF THE VILLA MELZI, LAKE COMO, ITALY [1996]

iris print,
13 x 16½"
courtesy of artist

opposite:

HORSE AT RYDAL FALLS, LAKE DISTRICT, ENGLAND [1995]

iris print,
10 x 17"
courtesy of artist

This is a scene I photographed in England's Lake District very close to where William Wordsworth had his home. It was interesting to me because the little stone building there is one of the oldest extant grottoes in England, dating from the seventeenth-century. A grotto in this case means a place where one could go to contemplate a waterfall. The side of the building that you can't see had a huge window overlooking the falls. The idea was that someone would guide you into this building without your having seen the waterfall. You would sit down, they would open the curtain, and there, like a picture on the wall, was the actual scene in nature. It is a very clear example of the "picturesque" landscape, where nature is made to conform to pictorial conventions.

(*Symposium Transcription* 11.19.1999)

One of the favorite destinations of tourists of the picturesque was Italy. I photographed the Villa Melzi on Lake Como, in the Italian Alps, where William Henry Fox Talbot tried his hand at Picturesque drawing on his honeymoon in 1833. He was so disappointed with his amateurish results that he returned to England and promptly invented photography.

(*Landscape at the Millennium*, p. 33)

Technically speaking, my artworks were born in the camera, translated into lines and brushstrokes by an Apple computer and printed in watercolor inks on Wattman watercolor paper with an Iris ink-jet printer. In using the computer, I was able to modify each photograph: I removed distracting branches; exchanged dull skies for dramatic alternatives; and on one occasion, introduced a flock of sheep into an empty meadow. The digital watermark that runs through each image was intentionally created to remind viewers that these works were not a product of the last decade of the eighteenth-century, but rather, of the last decade of the twentieth.

(*Symposium Transcription* 11.19.1999)

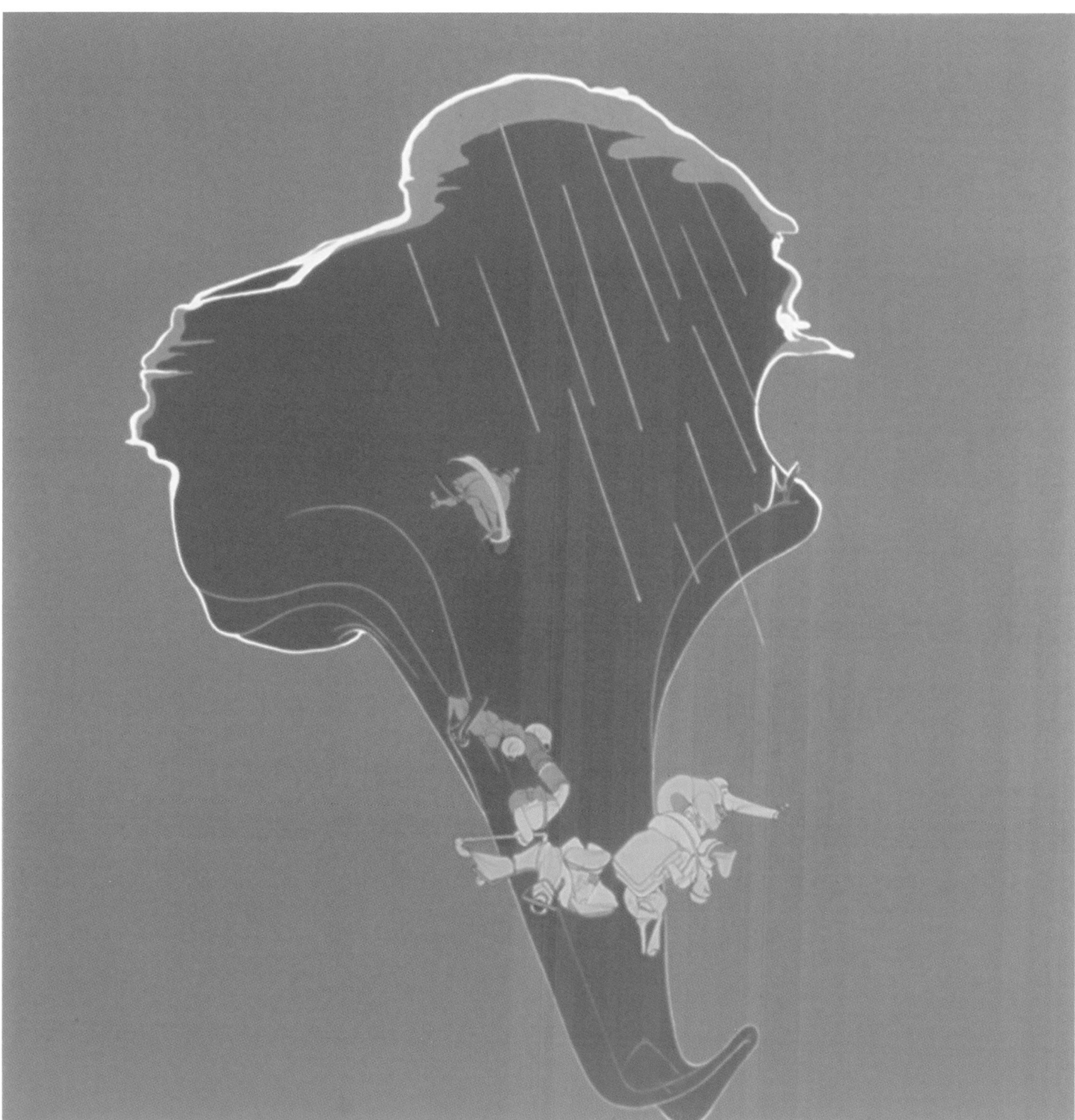

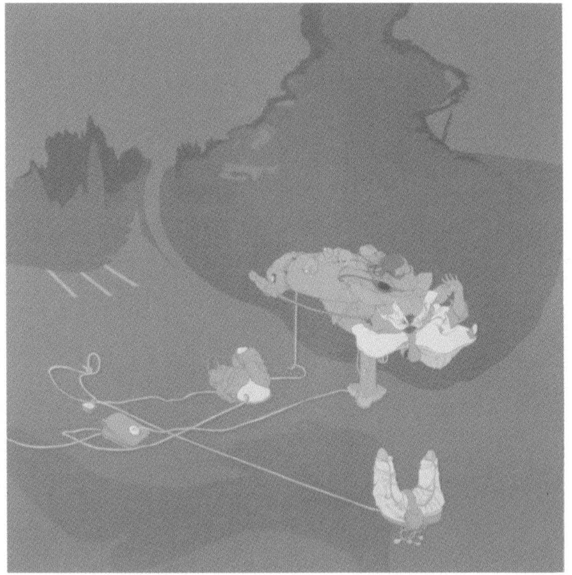

opposite:

DELUGE [1998]

oil enamel on canvas,
72 x 72"
Albright-Knox Art Gallery, Buffalo, New York.
Sarah Norton Goodyear Fund, 1998

above:

BLUE MOON [1999]

oil enamel on canvas,
72 x 72"
collection of Edward Boyer, New York, New York.
courtesy of Mary Boone Gallery, New York

above:

MALL PARKING LOT [1999]

oil enamel on canvas,
72 x 72"
collection of Vicki and Kent Logan, San Francisco, California.
courtesy of Mary Boone Gallery, New York

Jackson Pollock said, "I am nature." I go ahead and I do that, "I am nature." But you don't really need to know exactly what's going on in any work; they are meant to be loosely interpreted. I make my decisions based on abstract shape; I want something down here, and I go ahead and do it. I'm not trying to give you a straightforward narrative.

(Symposium Transcription 11.19.1999)

My work is landscape that combines nature and technology into one package . . . I'm not trying to say that technology is evil. I'm just trying to equate it with a force of nature.

(Symposium Transcription 11.19.1999)

I start out with one solid color. I sand down the canvass and I start drawing. Some images have come out of a doodle. Whatever happens, happens; anything can happen on the canvas. I can put a splot down here and it can turn into something. It is closely related to automatic drawing, but it is not automatic drawing because these are heavily edited. If I don't like something, I just sand it away. That's why I think of my work as very contrived and controlled. I edit and contrive a doodle into something, even if it's not something recognizable. I like to have it look three dimensional, as if it were an object you can buy in a store.

(Symposium Transcription 11.19.1999)

LYNDA H. SCHNEEKLOTH

REPAIRING THE RUPTURES
THE STORY OF EMSCHER PARK

> A landscape is a space deliberately created to speed up or slow down the process of nature. As Eliade expresses it, it represents man taking upon himself the role of time.
> — J.B. Jackson

One of the interesting aspects of landscape, especially large regional landscapes, is their sense of permanence. We find ourselves in landscapes made by our parents and their grandparents; we assume this is the way they have always been and always will be. And although we see changes to the land occurring during our lifetimes, they appear almost natural. But we know that most of them are not. With the exception of the ongoing subtle processes of weathering, too slow for our perception, and radical events such as floods, earthquakes and the like, the changes to the land are ours.

I want to tell the story of a region that has deliberately taken upon itself the transformation of its landscape, and in this case, to speed up time. The former industrial region of the Ruhr Valley has responded to the spirit of Wilson's words when he said, "the immediate work that lies ahead has to do with fixing landscapes, repairing its ruptures, reconnecting its parts" (Wilson p. 17). What is critical about the story of Emscher Park in Ruhrgebiet, Germany, is the breadth of the intervention, and its attention to both the transformation of the physical landscape and of the imagination of the place. The creative use of institutional structures such as the IBA (International Building Exposition) combined federal power and its access to the European Union with the immediacy and knowledge of local initiatives. The blend of art, of ecological restoration, and of economic development is a story of hope and regeneration, of mending a landscape and its people.

opposite::
Industrial buildings at Duisburg-Nord are experienced as light sculpture and are open at night for adventuresome walks up, around, and through the old industrial ruins.
Landscape architect, Peter Latz.
(Ganser, p. 172)

Germany didn't enter the industrial revolution until the later part of the nineteenth century, but then rapidly transformed areas like the Emscher River in the Ruhr Valley. Coal mining, steel, chemical and other industries radically remolded agricultural and forested landscapes into factories and open pits; villages and towns sprang up to provide workers and services. By the 1950's, this mode production "turned the Emscher area into the most densely built-up industrial landscape in central Europe with the highest levels of environmental pollution and the most intensively carved up open spaces" (Internationale Bauausstellung Emscher Park, 1989, p. 10).

above, left to right:

New and renovated housing in Gelsenkirchen sit adjacent to the old mines and the slag "mountains" created while the mine was operating. Architects: Zeche, Halde und Zechenbahn. [Ganser, p. 65]

The former blast furnace at Duisburg-Nord is now a theater for outdoor productions. [Ganser, p. 174]

Landscaped gardens at Duisburg-Nord remake the spaces of industry into places of contemplation and play. Landscape Architect, Peter Latz. [Kessler, cover]

By the mid 1980's, the outmoded methods of production and intensity of extraction took their toll on the landscape, its people and their work. Mines and factories were closed and unemployment grew, an unintentional consequence of the formation of the European Union and reunification of Germany.

As the region fell into a state of distress, there were a number of actions by the government that set a context for change. Early in the process there were, for example, monies available for brownfield reclamation and site recycling. In the 1970s, a group under the visionary leadership of individuals such as Professor Karl Ganser, Gerd Seltmann and Michael Swarze-Rodrian, worked to create a strategy for renewal that enabled local town and cities to re-make themselves through the creation of an IBA (International Building Exposition). This program was administered at the local level by the Kommunalverband, an organization that initiated many local projects that were particular and relevant to the place of Emscher Park. The purpose of the IBA was the redevelopment of the region, but not from a purely economic perspective. The basis for all economic change in the old industrial region would rest on social, cultural and ecological measures, and would only work if the regional and local entities collaborated and worked together to transform the region.

The Emscher Park IBA , a program of North Rhine-Westphalia, Germany, was created in 1989 and ended in 1999. During its peak it employed 30 people. Seventeen towns in the region voted to join, representing a population of about 1 million, and covering 784 square kilometers. Structurally, it was governed by a cooperative board that included local government authorities, industry, trade unions, conservation and other associations and NGO'S. A Steering Committee approved projects proposed by local entities, making them eligible for funding. Responsibility for implementation of approved projects rested with established contracting bodies, usually local governments but also businesses. Financing was done through the collecting of funds for existing aid programs to the region (thirty-six in all), and structural development support from the national government of Germany and the European Community. Over ten years, DM 5 billion[1] (2/3 public funds; 1/3 private) were spent on one hundred twenty projects in the six central working areas. To be certified as an IBA project meant that the project proposal demonstrated the integration of ecology, social and cultural objectives, and economic feasibility.

There were five central tenets of the IBA: The Green Framework, Urban Development and Renewal, Preservation of Industrial Monuments, Housing Construction, and Social Initiatives. Each focus built on the other with the recognition that a restored ecology without jobs and job training did not build community, that jobs without adequate

housing did not improve the quality of life, and a landscape without respect for its history, does not tie a people to place.

> In this economically weakened region with its ravaged landscape, it is important to identify new perspectives for the future. For this reason, one of the universally applied principles is that a widespread ecological renewal must precede any lasting economic perspective in their lives.
>
> (Internationale Bauausstellung Emscher Park, 1995, p .4)

The transformation begins with the restoration of the Emscher River, 350 km of waterways that has been used as an open industrial sewer. The project is opening up adjacent lands that now hold 230 km of bicycle paths, and 130 km of walking area. In a region of fragmented and carved up spaces, the spine of a greenway called Emscher Park and its accompanying network radically shifts the conditions and imagination of the region from pieces to a whole, from isolation to connection. There is still much work to be done on the Emscher River, the channelized fragment of a historic stream, to restore it to an ecological and sustainable body of water. But the work has begun, the people are coming, and bringing with them a new sense of the Emscher's place in their lives.

The closing of industry, deleterious to the economic well-being of the area, nevertheless greatly reduced the pollution load on the region. However, the area is laced with hazardous waste sites and brownfields. Because ecological restoration was one of the tenets of the IBA, there has been an intensive expenditure of funds for environmental cleanup. New projects and new development have been focused on former industrial lands so that each new intervention improved the quality of the landscape twice — first by removing or containing environmental hazards, and second, by offering a new economic opportunity.

Within this green framework, IBM has built nineteen areas of modern commerce, service and science facilities, always on former industrial sites, and always close to urban centers. The most up-to-date ecological features were used in the buildings, conserving water and energy. All the new fabric was designed to be as sustainable as possible, countering the former heavy pollution load and industrial image of the region. Each new intervention was thoughtfully and beautifully designed, using architecture and landscape architecture competitions to bring in the best design talent.

above, left to right

The Thyssen Steelworks at Duisburg-Nord before they were transformed into the Duisburg-Nord Park with an exhibition hall, scuba diving, rock climbing and restaurants.
[*Emscher Landschaftspark Regionaler Grünzug A*, p. 20]

This aerial view shows the fragmented landscape of the Gelsenkirchen region. The Rhein-Herne Canal is on the right, the Emscher "River" to the left.
[Schwarze-Rodrian, p. 7]

last two images:

The Emscher River was channelized during the industrial period and used as a sewer for industrial wastes. The process of cleaning it and restoring it as an ecologically intact stream is underway.
[Schwarze-Rodrian, p. 22-23]

above, left to right:

A new housing project in Gelsenkirchen-Feldmark uses an innovative rainwater collection system as an architectural and landscape element. [Ganser, p. 83]

The industrial buildings as light sculpture are open at night. [Ganser]

On top of a huge pile of mining remains in Bottrop, the Tetrahedron stands as a symbol of the new landscape. Architects Christ, Statiker Bollinger and Light Artist, Fischer. [Ganser, p. 154]

The renovation of existing worker housing and the construction of new housing followed the same guidelines as commercial development. Areas were environmentally cleaned-up, and new housing incorporated the latest technologies of conservation with high quality design. There were approximately twenty-six housing projects as a part of IBA, with at least 2,500 new flats and about 3,000 renovations of existing units, of which 75% are public sector and affordable.

One of the most challenging and exciting parts of the IBA was the attention to old industrial ruins and landscapes of the region. Instead of destroying the old factories and erasing the landscape, IBA asked and received the most innovative proposals for the reuse of these facilities and redesign of the landscapes, including the gigantic coal heaps. They used the old ruins as new art, cultural and recreational centers. For example, at the Nordsternpark, a federal flower show was used as the generator of the clean-up (1997); the Gasometer is now an exhibition hall and observation tower to view across the region. Two of these projects are particularly interesting. One is Duisburg Nord Landscape Park, where the former Thyssen steelworks plant was transformed into a regional park, lit by a magical show of lights at night. It now houses an exhibition hall, a diving center, rock climbing walls, an interpretation center, a theater, and endless gardens. The Zollverein Colliery built in 1930 in Essen as a show case coal mine is a new center for art and culture called "a Cathedral of the Ruhr."

The landscape itself, constructed through the years of industry, was given as a pallette for artists. The crafted hills are celebrated and on top of a few strategically located slag heaps, art was commissioned to stand as a beacon of the transformation. Along the bike trails within the greenway, other installations dot the landscape, making use of abandoned artifacts, celebrating rather than erasing the story of human intervention on the land, that is, *the landscape.*

After ten years, the confederation known as IBA was dismantled as agreed. Other institutional structures have emerged to continue the transformation and economic/ecological redevelopment. This short story of the Emscher Park IBA reminds us that our landscapes are made by us either through our neglect or our care. The work of the IBA was very difficult and many struggles for ideas, projects, processes and strategies are embedded in the account above. But the lessons are also there. We can and do make our landscapes, and if appropriate institutional structures are created and maintained, local innovative ideas and ideals accompanied by sustainable and quality design, can repair ruptures and heal landscapes. What the ten year work in Emscher Park has done is to give the region a new sense of hope and energy that this area is no longer the most polluted region in Central Europe with a fragmented landscape. It is a place-becoming through the conscious manipulation of the landscape, rested on a foundation of social, cultural, ecological and economic concerns.

NOTES

[billion is used here in its "American" case, meaning 1,000 million] *ed.*

Sources Referenced:

Emscher Landschaftspark Regionaler Grünzug A. (Duisburg: Arbeitsgemeinschaft Regionaler Grünzug A, 1994-5).

Ganser, Karl. *Liebe auf den zweiten Blick: Internationale Bauausstellung Emscher Park.* (Dortmund: Harenberg Kommunikation Verlags- und Medien Gmbh & Co. KG, 1999).

Internationale Bauausstellung Emscher Park: Memorandum on Content and Organization. (Gelsenkirchen: Gesellschaft Internationale Bauausstellung, 1989).

Internationale Bauausstellung Emscher Park: The Emscher Park International Building Exhibition. (Gelsenkirchen: IBA Emscher Park, 1995).

Internationale Bauausstellung Emscher Park: Short Information. ([Gelsenkirchen]: IBA Emscher Park, 1999).

J. B. Jackson. *Discovering the Vernacular Landscape.* (New Haven: Yale University Press, 1984).

Kessler & Co. GmbH. *Ausstellung zum Emscher Landschaftspark.* (Essen: Kommunalverband Ruhrgebiet, 1999).

Schwarze-Rodrian, Michael. *Parkbericht, Emscher Landschaftspark.* (Essen: Kommunalverband Ruhrgebiet, 1996).

TOPOS: European Landscape Magazine. [Special issue on the Ruhr Valley IBA.] (1999, March 26).

Wilson, Alexander. *The Culture of Nature.* (Toronto: Between the Lines, 1991).

The author wishes to thank the Waterfront Regeneration Trust for organizing the International Brownfields Exchange to permit scholars and politicians from the United States and Canada to visit projects such as Emscher Park in Germany and vice versa. The Exchange has been supported by Environment Canada, the German Marshall Fund of the United States, US Environmental Protection Agency, and the Heinrich Boll Foundation.

C O L O P H O N

intersight was set in Pagemaker version 6.5(2) on a Gateway G6-200 running Windows NT. Final prints were made on a Komori Lithrone 40 press in Buffalo, NY and perfect bound by machine. This edition was printed in a run of 1200 copies.

The body text is set in Univers (originally designed by Adrian Frutiger); notes and captions in Univers Condensed. Other fonts used include: Futurist, Swis721 Bold Condensed Outline Black, and Helvetica.

opposite:

Joseph's Back

completed by Joseph Sevene.
Graphite on white board.